REFINING THE WATERFRONT

Refining the Waterfront

Alternative Energy Facility Siting Policies for Urban Coastal Areas

Edited by

David Morell
Grace Singer

Princeton University

 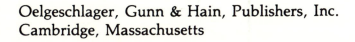

Oelgeschlager, Gunn & Hain, Publishers, Inc.
Cambridge, Massachusetts

International Standard Book Number: 0-89946-035-6

Library of Congress Catalog Card Number: 80-12839

Printed in the United States of America

Library of Congress Cataloging in Publication Data

Main entry under title:

Refining the waterfront.

Bibliography: p.
Includes index.
1. Energy facilities—United States—Location—Addresses, essays, lectures. 2. Energy policy—Environmental aspects—United States—Addresses, essays, lectures. I. Morell, David. II. Singer, Grace.
HD9502.U52R42   338.6'042   80-12839
ISBN 0-89946-035-6

Contents

List of Figures

List of Tables

Acknowledgments

The research for this book was sponsored at Princeton University's Center for Energy and Environmental Studies by the U.S. Department of Energy, Office of Environment, Office of Technology Impacts, Division of Policy Analysis. We particularly wish to thank our DOE Project Officer, Ms. Suzanne Wellborn, for her continuing support, assistance, and advice throughout this endeavor.

Many people contributed to this effort. The authors of individual chapters, of course, deserve special note, and brief biographical sketches of each contributor are included at the end of this volume. Additional supporting research was conducted by Dr. Joenathan Dean, Ms. Virginia Farrell, Ms. Mildred Goldberger, Dr. Mitchell Moss, and Ms. Hannah Shostack. Important editorial assistance was provided by Dr. Frank Sinden; Mrs. Robin Austin was supremely patient in typing and retyping the manuscript.

The conclusions are the responsibility of the editors of this volume and do not necessarily reflect the policies of the U.S. Department of Energy or Princeton University.

Princeton, N.J.

David Morell
Grace Singer
March 1980

REFINING THE WATERFRONT

Chapter 1

Coastal Zone Conflicts and
Urban Opportunities

David Morell and Grace Singer

Energy and environmental policies constantly confront conflicting goals in pursuit of an amorphous national interest. Urgent policy decisions must be made in the face of incomplete data and competitive demands from powerful interest groups. Nowhere are these dilemmas more apparent than at the confluence of energy siting, coastal zone management, and urban development. Alone, each of these three policy areas poses difficult choices between growth, equity, and environmental preservation. When an energy facility is proposed for an urban waterfront that is the scene of revitalization, the pressures become intense.

Along the coast, rural and urban interests often are in conflict. The Coastal Zone Management Act of 1972 and most state coastal laws have been framed with an emphasis on preservation of rural and recreational areas. Their principal objective is to protect fragile wetlands, unspoiled beaches, and sand dunes from the effects of further residential and commercial development and from the impacts of new energy and industrial facilities.[1] Although some mention of the urban coast can be found in most of these statutes, their main impact has been to shift siting of new facilities with major environmental impacts away from the rural coast, and thus presumably into urban areas. Urban revitalization groups, on the

1

other hand, have resisted introduction of such facilities along city waterfronts, where they are seen as incompatible with the human uses these groups envision for the future. Those seeking sites for energy facilities thus find themselves whipsawed from one area to the other.

The research for this book was focused on the problems of siting energy facilities on city waterfronts or in alternative locations. Past trends and existing programs of coastal zone management, energy facility siting, and urban waterfront revitalization across the country were examined to isolate general principles, identify critical policy issues, and devise new siting policies. Specifically, the researchers tried to determine mechanisms for finding sites for necessary new energy facilities that are compatible with the conflicting mandates of rural coastline preservation and the changing uses of urban waterfronts.

TRANSITION IN THE USE OF
URBAN WATERFRONTS

Most of the world's large cities are located on navigable bodies of water. Indeed, "of the 20 largest cities in this nation, 17 are situated at the intersection of a navigable body of water with land."[2] With cities serving as the nation's primary manufacturing, commercial, and distribution centers, urban ports and waterfronts prospered. The waterfronts became the center of shipping, railroad transportation, and the location of industrial facilities and produce and other markets that desired to be adjacent to the water. With the urban waterfront serving these variegated but related functions, the city's noncommercial life developed inland, its social and cultural functions now isolated from the coastal edge that had been the city's original raison d'etre.

Urban development patterns were different in Europe, where waterfront areas were incorporated into the fabric of city life before industrialization; the use of the water's edge as an amenity was never entirely displaced by industry.[3] In contrast, industrial development in American cities focused on the urban waterfront from the beginning because of the relatively low cost of water transportation for bulk commodities and the proximity of metropolitan markets. Most urban waterfront areas were occupied by railroad tracks, piers, warehouses, multistory industrial buildings, and similar facilities. As a result, the American public's access to waterfront amenities has been quite limited.

Exclusion of less intensive, nonshipping or manufacturing uses from the waterfront led to the neglect of this area by planners and government officials. Almost from the start, municipal governments were reluctant to propose alternative or complementary uses for the waterfront. The concentration of highly productive uses already in these areas, in their view, constrained the ability of waterfronts to accommodate different new uses.

Institutional arrangements also served to remove the urban planner and policymaker from waterfront concerns. Autonomous or semi-autonomous port commissions and authorities saw waterfront management as a business outside the realm of the municipal government. And where the city did retain control of its waterfront, management was most frequently under the auspices of a municipal port authority or real estate department, agencies that regarded the waterfront "almost exclusively in terms of its revenue generating capabilities."[4] Rarely was the waterfront considered by planners in a coordinated manner, as a distinctive element in the character of the city. Land development on and near city waterfronts often served to segregate these areas even further from the remainder of the city; arterial highways in Manhattan, Seattle, and Boston and railroads in Jersey City and Hoboken, New Jersey, are typical examples.

In the years after World War II, several new factors combined to accelerate the deterioration of many once-valuable U.S. urban coastal areas.[5] The truck replaced the train as the principal form of transportation, thus influencing the siting of new industrial facilities. New plants were located along interstate highways, especially metropolitan area beltways, rather than on the waterfront with its railroad lines. Sprawl suburbanization based on the automobile shifted consumer demand centers to outlying areas. Single-story industrial facilities became the preferred mode, requiring access to cheaper suburban land. Air transport replaced the ocean liner as the principal means of long distance travel. Shipping practices altered from use of traditional piers to new container ports on the fringe of old harbor areas. Security in older waterfront areas became unreliable, enhancing companies' preference to locate in suburban industrial parks.

These conditions on the waterfront—disjointed administration and a narrow management philosophy—saw most places ill-equipped to deal with the challenges posed by changing technology and larger changes in the economic role of cities. Containerization as the preferred means of handling general cargo was particularly significant as a technological innovation affecting the waterfront. In the past cargo had been loaded and unloaded from crates, but now containerization allowed direct movement of goods to a destination without the costly, time-consuming, and theft-prone break-bulk process. Almost all bulk cargo movements shifted to containerized technology, requiring new ports in outlying areas.[6] In one stroke, this change made the compact urban ports obsolete, owing to the substantial space needed for container ports (an estimated 30 to 50 acres "are needed for each container berth for the storage and handling of containers").[7] In the New York region, for example, the focus of dock activity was moved from Manhattan, Brooklyn, and older New Jersey ports to the Port Elizabeth and Port Newark facilities.

Another innovation that changed the character of the urban port was construction of offshore deepwater ports for the largest and newest class of oil tankers, whose contents can then move directly to mainland storage areas through underwater pipelines.[8] Several such facilities exist abroad; and one is under construction off the coast of Louisiana. The need for storage facilities remains, of course; policies are required to guide the siting of storage tank terminals into inland or coastal locations, either in rural or urban areas.

Among the most significant technological changes affecting the means of distribution of goods has been the emergence of the interstate highway system and truck transport as the preferred means of moving goods to and from the harbor and hinterland. Highways and trucks have been major contributory factors in the general decline of the nationwide rail industry. Alone, this need not necessarily have a deleterious effect on the competitiveness of the urban waterfront. However, insofar as railroads have traditionally been major holders of urban waterfront property, and roads to the area are congested, the question of the disposition of much vacant, abandoned, or under-utilized property is a real problem—and an opportunity—for urban waterfront communities.

The changing economic character of older metropolitan areas also points to changes in the placement and utilization of port facilities. The intimate functional link between the port and manufacturing centers makes many older ports no longer economically or strategically sound. Removal of much manufacturing to suburban locations and the decentralization of metropolitan populations suggest the possible liability of the urban port, "given the congestion of city streets and lack of interstate highway roads"[9] and the segregation of ports from their newer consumer markets.

As a result, the older port areas were left behind, with unused railroad yards, rotting piers, abandoned industrial buildings, and vacant land. Although this land still had great intrinsic value, by the late 1960s much of it was underutilized, pending new decisions by American society as to desired land use patterns in the urban coastal zone.[10]

CONFLICTS IN DEVELOPMENT
OF NEW WATERFRONT USES

All of these port-related factors—changes in management, transportation technology, and urban economics—point to a shift in port activities away from older centers, making large portions of the urban waterfront potentially available for new uses, especially people-oriented activities. Here the conflict has arisen between energy facility siting and other uses of the vacant urban waterfront, however. Energy companies have proposed to locate many of their new facilities on urban waterfronts: onshore service bases, pipeline terminals, and similar facilities required for offshore oil and gas development; refineries; oil storage depots; petrochemical plants; and so on.[11]

Economic pressures for coastal energy development are intensified by the belief of many federal planners and corporate executives that such development is in the national interest. The necessity to reduce American dependence on imported oil accelerates demands to increase domestic exploration and production. Despite the discouraging results to date in the Baltimore Canyon off the shores of the mid-Atlantic states, especially for crude oil, further drilling on the Outer Continental Shelf seems certain. The U.S. Department of Energy's expressed concern for the national interest was an important factor in two recent cases: the Sohio Terminal in Long Beach, California, designed to bring Alaskan oil ashore; and an oil refinery in Portsmouth, Virginia. Overall, in the 1970s siting of energy facilities became one of the most contested land use and coastal planning issues.

Unfortunately for planners, decisionmakers, and the overall political system, urban siting of such facilities was not to be accomplished easily, whatever the wishes of energy company managers. Instead, new agendas began to compete. Indeed, rural coastline preservation strategies posed the overall siting dilemma with increasing clarity. For while major industrial and energy facilities were compatible with existing land uses in many urban coastal areas, and jobs and tax payments made them attractive to urban politicians, air quality constraints, citizen opposition, and emergence of local urban waterfront revitalization movements made the siting process ever more difficult.

Government policies now give priority to cities in the creation of jobs and larger tax bases. The Carter Administration's national urban policy calls for federal funds to be diverted from urban-fringe development to rehabilitation of facilities within the cities. Federal jobs are to be located in cities where feasible; and the policy gives government procurement priority to goods and services produced in urban areas.[12]

On the other side, various citizens' groups are opposing industrial development on the urban coast. As can be seen in Appendix A, different kinds of energy facilities emit widely varying kinds of pollutants. In some cases, such as nuclear power plants or liquiefied natural gas (LNG) facilities, the main concern is not with continuous emissions, but with the possibility of an accident.[a] Although urban leaders are under intense pressure to improve employment and tax revenues in their districts, research for this book shows that many are becoming increasingly discriminating about energy facilities as their relative job and tax potentials become clear. Facilities such as storage tank farms that provide very few jobs per acre of land, especially in prime areas like the waterfront, are no longer automatically accepted as net economic assets.[b]

Citizens' concerns about land use are related primarily to urban revitalization and the emerging realization that waterfronts can provide beauty and breathing space not otherwise available in the old cities. A park on the water is effectively larger than its land acreage alone because the water itself adds space by opening the vista and allowing the breeze to flow freely. Efforts in Baltimore, Boston, Chicago, Detroit, New Haven, Philadelphia, San Francisco, and Seattle are especially noteworthy. In many of these areas, the perceptible move away from waterfront use for industrial production and toward diversified consumer amenity use, including housing and commerce, conflicts with the pressures for urban siting of major new energy facilities.

---

[a]The events at the Three Mile Island nuclear power plant in Pennsylvania, which began on March 28, 1979, seem certain to reinforce this element of citizen concern.

[b]Appendix A also shows employment associated with various energy facilities, as well as their land requirements and degree of coastal dependence.

STRUCTURE OF THE STUDY

This book emphasizes deepening understanding of the growing policy conflicts between coastal zone management, urban waterfront revitalization, and energy facility siting. Part I is focused on the older urban coast, simultaneously the scene of both decline and opportunity, despair for the present but with hope for the future. Chapter 2 presents a case study of conflict over siting of energy facilities in Hudson County, New Jersey, only 2,000 yards across the Hudson River from New York City. Faced with strong citizen opposition, five oil-related facilities proposed by energy companies were rejected here between 1972 and 1976.

This area is ideal for observing the dynamics of urban coastal energy facility siting. All of the pressures for and against development occur here: access to large metropolitan markets, proximity to labor concentrations, good road and rail transportation, well-dredged harbors, exploration for offshore oil and gas, on the one hand, and heavily polluted air and water and a strong revitalization movement, on the other. The in-depth study of the ensuing conflicts paid special attention to emergence of the citizens' movement that finally blocked the five energy projects.

The principal issues are best illustrated in the 1974 proposal to locate a $20-million deepwater terminal with 242 six-story tanks to accommodate storage and shipment of 4 million barrels of fuel oil and chemicals, some of them toxic, carcinogenic, and volatile. This facility, to have been the largest such terminal on the East Coast, was to have been located on the end of a man-made peninsula protruding into the Hudson River on the Jersey City waterfront. In spite of strong initial support from the city's mayor and advocacy by the New Jersey Department of Environmental Protection (NJDEP), the proposal was rejected in 1976 after vigorous opposition by citizens.

In an area with heavy industrialization and a severe shortage of open space, many citizens wanted new uses of their waterfront to be primarily for amenity and recreational activities. Physical access to the waterfront had been blocked for many years by a complex of railroad lines. Now that these railroads were no longer operating, the citizen activists saw an opportunity to change their area. An important first step was taken in the early 1970s with the proposal for the 800-acre Liberty State Park in Jersey City, the first section of which actually opened on the waterfront directly behind the Statue of Liberty and Ellis Island in June 1976. Citizens feared that the proposed new petrochemical operation would give the industry a "foot in door" toward eventual domination of the waterfront, undoing the impetus provided by Liberty State Park.

A second concern was the terminal's pollution and safety hazard. The facility would have contained a number of dangerous chemicals and emitted 100 tons of hydrocarbons annually. NJDEP backed the urban siting proposal primarily as a means of keeping such facilities away from the cleaner (i.e., rural coastal) areas of the state and worked with the company on an emission offset scheme almost a year before this policy was officially enunciated by the U.S. Environmental Protection Agency (EPA). The company planned to add pollution abatement equipment to facilities it rented some 10 miles from the new terminal site, thereby achieving a theoretical 2-percent net reduction in hydrocarbon emissions. Opponents contrasted this offset approach with the federal government's mandate that hydrocarbon emissions in their area be reduced by 68 percent.

The third major area of citizen opposition was based on economic concerns. Like most petrochemical facilities, this one had a low employment rate, providing a maximum of 80 jobs on 40 prime waterfront acres. In view of the area's 1976 unemployment rate (14 percent), this ratio of two jobs per acre conflicted with the goals of Hudson County planners to make employment generation a major criterion in siting new industrial facilities. Planners were using 25 to 30 jobs per acre as a minimum in their densely populated county. Moreover, the opponents felt that the facility's pollution and safety hazards would scare away other more labor-intensive commerce. Thus in Jersey City, whose official motto is "Everything for Industry," and in Hudson County generally, by the 1970s perceptions of what is good for the public were beginning to diverge from the old, fiscal planning approach.

The Hudson County case study presented in Chapter 2 helps explain the broader phenomenon of citizen opposition to petro-chemical facilities in other parts of the country, especially in New England where oil refineries have been unable to receive a single approval. Several New England states mandate local referenda prior to further consideration of proposed oil refineries. In 1978-1979, Portsmouth, Virginia, was the scene of a controversy over siting an oil refinery. In California in 1977, the Dow Chemical Company was denied a large proposed installation; the company then chose to expand existing facilities in Illinois, Louisiana, and Texas. In 1978, Dow applied for permits for a $30-million chemical transshipment terminal on the Delaware River in Bordentown, New Jersey. This terminal would have generated 50 permanent jobs on 50 acres of prime waterfront land, a ratio of only one job per acre. Public concern about the toxic chemicals to be stored and shipped on the Delaware and possible contamination of several municipalities' water supplies, as well as a series of petrochemical facility accidents, caused Bordentown officials—originally strong supporters of the terminal—to pass an ordinance banning tank farms from their community.

Eleven selected examples of the changing situation elsewhere along the older urban coast are examined in Chapter 3, especially in relation to possible impacts of offshore oil and gas development on the mid-Atlantic Outer Continental Shelf (OCS). The emergence of energy self-sufficiency as national policy and exploration in the Baltimore Canyon, Georges Bank, and other new OCS areas require new onshore support activities. Critical issues of economic, social, and aesthetic impact challenge coastal cities like Camden, New Jersey, Chester, Pennsylvania, and New Bedford, Massachusetts, to determine the highest and best use of their waterfronts.[13] Notably absent from the cities' considerations has been a recognition of the possible benefits from regional cooperation in waterfront planning and development. With few exceptions, and despite the emergence of state coastal zone management plans, each city is making its own decisions on whether—and how—to integrate energy facilities into the overall waterfront setting.

Air quality is the principal environmental constraint to locating energy and other heavy industrial facilities on most existing urban waterfronts. This was certainly the case with the terminal proposed by the Sohio Company in Long Beach, California, to receive and transship oil from Alaska.[14] Yet it is very difficult to relate air quality planning to land use decisions, especially at municipal and county levels where most siting decisions are still made. This issue is analyzed in Chapter 4, with a focus again on the situation in Hudson County, New Jersey. Research in this waterfront area found federal and state programs of air quality improvement essentially unrelated to the siting perceptions and decisions of local officials. Citizen commitment to urban waterfront revitalization in Hudson County, at least, seems sufficient to ensure that few if any large new stationary sources of air pollution would be located in the area. Air pollution associated with automobiles and other vehicles is a different matter, however. Since transportation issues are not as dramatic nor as obvious as the problems resulting from a petroleum storage depot on the waterfront, it is unlikely that citizens will act as they did in opposing the proposed energy facilities. They will continue to rely on federal or state actions and the technology of cleaner automobiles to improve their air quality with respect to air pollutants from mobile sources.

The discussion of air quality is continued in Chapter 5, with a special focus on EPA's "emission offset" policy, a key mechanism for siting energy or industrial facilities in many urban areas that do not meet federal air quality standards (so-called nonattainment areas). This policy was a principal issue in conflict over Sohio's proposed terminal in Long Beach, California; and the key to resolving air quality issues associated with siting the proposed new oil refinery on Chesapeake Bay, near Portsmouth, Virginia. Examination of several cases in which emission offset was actually used (or proposed) suggests that although this kind of policy will contribute to maintaining air quality once national standards are achieved, the availability of offsets—and thus the siting of major new energy facilities—remains in doubt in many nonattainment urban coastal areas.

A contrast to the older urban coast is examined in Part II. Here the focus is on energy facility siting along the Texas-Louisiana coast of the Gulf of Mexico. This region's vast open spaces and traditional citizen acceptance provide an environment in which new energy facilities are still welcome. The Louisiana case study in Chapter 6 explores the siting of the largest oil refinery ever built in a single phase within the United States. Although the East Coast was the company's preferred location for this facility since markets for its products were primarily there and in the Midwest, company executives felt that "time was of the essence." The delays they anticipated before receiving the necessary permits and approvals for the refinery discouraged them from seeking an eastern site. In addition to the usual physical siting criteria, company planners explicitly considered local and state economic and political climates: tax policies, labor availability and receptivity of local government officials, for example. After considering 30 different sites in South Carolina, Mississippi, and Louisiana, they selected one on the Mississippi River between New Orleans and Baton Rouge. Little opposition was encountered to this energy siting proposal, and construction was completed quickly.

Another example of Gulf Coast energy facility siting, this one for a petrochemical facility near Corpus Christi, Texas, is explored in Chapter 7. Here, again, the contrast with the older urban coast is striking. Like many other petrochemical plants, siting near sources of raw materials was crucial. In this case, the new facility's liquid feedstocks were to come from an existing refinery owned by the company on the Corpus Christi waterfront, five miles from the new plant's inland location. One innovative siting feature was the use of pipelines to move products to and from the waterfront. Other factors explicitly identified in the siting decision were the ease of obtaining necessary permits and the generally favorable business climate in Texas. This case, then, reinforces the general assessment that siting of major energy facilities, including refineries and petrochemical plants, is far easier along the Gulf Coast than in most other areas.

These regional distinctions and their policy implications are explored more broadly in Chapter 8. Virtually every characteristic that makes a coastal site attractive to industry—particularly to industries engaged in large, energy-related activities—can be found in Texas and Louisiana. Their long coastlines contain many physically and geographically suitable sites for major energy facilities. The states' booming economies, available energy resources, favorable public opinion, and the tone of government regulations all favor further industrial growth. Thus these coastal areas are as attractive today for new energy facilities as they have been in the past, when they attracted massive energy investments. All of this stands in sharp contrast to the East and the older urban coast generally, as typified by the situation seen in New Jersey. Such areas are attractive for new energy sites because of their proximity to ready markets for refined products, thereby eliminating the need for expensive transportation. However, announcement of a company's plans to locate even a modestly sized energy facility in many older urban coastal areas has generated sharp public opposition. The political climates in Texas and Louisiana strongly support further energy development. The public at large and government officials at all levels do not see new energy facilities as incompatible with their waterfronts or their quality of life. For the foreseeable future such attitudes seem likely to distinguish the Gulf Coast from the East, drawing corporate attention to this area and lessening conflicts over energy siting in areas concentrating on urban waterfront revitalization.

The next section, Part III, delves directly into the economics of energy facility siting, adopting the perspective of the companies that make the huge investments needed to finance modern energy plants. The goal of the analysis is to identify the specific economic relationships between different locations and alternative site approval (permitting) processes in order to determine if the additional costs to the firm of an alternative site—away from the urban waterfront, for example—could be offset by an easier permit approval process at that location, where conflicts with environmental fragility and urban revitalization might be much less severe.

The process of obtaining the federal, state, and local permits needed to build a typical new oil refinery is studied in Chapter 9. Key parameters for a company facing an investment decision are the cost of the process, its length, the probability of failing to receive any of the required permits, and the impact of possible mid-construction delays resulting from challenges to permits already obtained. The site chosen will have a direct impact on the length and probability of successful completion of the permitting process. Examination of case studies of 16 refineries proposed in recent years for East Coast sites, and then rejected in the approval process, illustrated several trends. Local approval was the biggest siting obstacle; while federal laws have not directly resulted in refinery rejections, federal requirements have caused substantial delays.

In Chapter 10, economic analysis is used to determine the effects of permitting delays on a proposed refinery investment. Three baseline cases were used, assuming marginal, medium, and high returns on a capital investment of $641 million and projected annual operating costs of $85 million (1978 dollars). The impacts were then calculated for three permitting delay scenarios: 3 years, 5 years, and 10 years. The researchers found that permitting delays can have a large impact on an investment's net present value, such that a refinery investor using this criterion might well be willing to choose a different site with higher capital or operating costs in exchange for a lessened permitting delay. In contrast, delays would have only minor impacts on the refinery investment's internal rate of return. Thus companies using this decision-making criterion would have less reason to select an alternate site. Delays that halt construction after it has begun can be particularly damaging to an investment's profitability (since much more capital is already committed to the facility at that point). Obviously, alternative siting strategies that lessen the risk of midconstruction delays would be very attractive from the corporate perspective.

This analysis of investment economics is extended in Chapter 11 to encompass specific locational dimensions: coastal versus inland and urban versus rural. Advantages and disadvantages were identified for each kind of site, with special attention to the possibility that inland sites could lessen competition for scarce (and environmentally sensitive) coastal locations. Calculations indicate that the additional crude oil and refined product transportation costs associated with inland locations would have only a moderate impact on the desirability of the refinery investment. Thus a refinery sponsor might well consider an inland site if it appeared that such a location could reduce the length of the permitting process or increase the probability of a successful result. Chapter 11 showed further that use of a deepwater port rather than a coastal facility for crude oil delivery, combined with an inland refinery location, could produce very desirable impacts on the overall investment picture when probable permitting delays were taken into account.

In general, this analysis demonstrated the importance of viewing energy facility investments in a broad perspective that includes the positive or negative impacts on the permitting process of various alternative siting patterns: inland as well as coastal, and also offshore. Selection by the energy companies of somewhat more expensive but environmentally or socially preferable locations, in exchange for more rapid and predictable (and thus less expensive) permit approval processes, can benefit both industry and the general public. Such innovative siting concepts can contribute greatly to lessening the pressures to site major new energy facilities in coastal areas in general, and on urban waterfronts in particular. These are themes that the proposed Federal Energy Mobilization Board might usefully take into account.

In Part IV, the last section of the book, the future of energy facility siting on the urban coast is explored from two different perspectives: technology, on the one hand, and public policy, on the other. The analysis in Chapter 12 examines the possible contributions that five alternative energy technologies might make to alleviating siting and political tensions created when new, large-scale energy facilities are proposed for urban areas. These five technologies—cogeneration, modular integrated utility systems (MIUS), integrated community energy systems (ICES), fuel cells, and low Btu gasification—all have selective advantages and disadvantages from the perspective of the urban coast. In general, most were found to be appropriate for urban siting, with their implementation over time reducing the number of new energy facility sites that would otherwise be needed. Most use fossil fuels efficiently, providing the opportunity for smaller scale and energy conservation. None is free from constraints, however, and none would be easily implemented. Moreover, each of these alternative energy technologies needs to be considered as part of a larger strategy that is compatible with both the national energy situation and the urban environment.

Finally, the overall public policy recommendations emerging from this research are summarized in Chapter 13. Policies toward energy facility siting, urban waterfront revitalization, alternate energy technologies, permit processing, and coastal zone management are all addressed. The overall approach in proposing these 40 specific policy recommendations is to alter the existing situation wherein proposed new energy facilities often directly contradict urban coastal revitalization. In essence, three critical national priorities need to be made compatible in a siting strategy: greater energy self-sufficiency, urban revitalization, and protection of fragile rural coastlines.

NOTES

1. See Robert Warren, "The Role of Cities in Managing the Urban Coast," *Coastal Zone Management Journal* 6, no. 2-3 (1979): 126.
2. Mitchell L. Moss, "The Urban Port: A Hidden Resource for the City and the Coastal Zone," *Coastal Zone Management Journal* 2, no. 3 (1976): 223.
3. A study of the London situation is presented in Nicholas Falk, "Conservation and Redevelopment Policy for British Urban Dock Areas," *Coastal Zone Management Journal* 6, no. 2-3 (1979): 187-213.
4. Mitchell L. Moss, "The Redevelopment of the Urban Waterfront," transcript of remarks presented before the 57th Annual Convention of the American Institute of Planners, San Antonio, Texas, 1975, p. 1.
5. For a discussion and statistics on socioeconomic factors in the urban coastal zone in New Jersey, see Mildred Goldberger, *Socio-Economic Factors in the Urban Coastal Zone: New Jersey as a Case Study* (Princeton: Princeton University, Center for Environmental Studies, Working Paper no. 44), February 1979. Also see Mitchell L. Moss, "The Lost Waterfront of New York," *Coastal Zone Management Journal* 6, no. 2-3 (1979): 167-185.
6. William W. Seifert and Kathryn N. Corones, eds., *Project Bosporus—Boston Port Utilization Study* (Cambridge, Mass.: Massachusetts Institute of Technology, 1970), p. 174.
7. Moss, "The Redevelopment. . . ," op. cit.
8. See U.S. Department of Commerce, Maritime Administration, *The Economics of Deepwater Terminals* (Washington, D.C.: U.S. Government Printing Office, 1972).
9. Moss, "The Redevelopment. . . ," op. cit.
10. See David Morell and Grace Singer, "The Urban Coastal Zone: Challenge of Redevelopment," *Coastal Zone '78*, vol. 1, published proceedings of conference in San Francisco, March 1978 (New York: American Society of Civil Engineers, 1978), pp. 66-80.
11. Many power plants have also been proposed for coastal locations in order to gain access to cooling water. It is estimated that about 100 new fossil fuel and nuclear power plants will be built in U.S. coastal areas by 1990. (Interview with Daniel Hoydysh, Program Analysis Officer, Coastal Energy Impact Program, NOAA, April 3, 1979.) Most of these new coastal power plants, however, have been proposed for rural rather than urban locations.
12. Community impact is to be analyzed by federal agencies before seeking new funding or proposing new legislation. Federal agencies will be required to conduct "an analysis of the impact of their major policies and programs on urban and regional areas" (*Land Use Planning Report*, Silver Springs, MD.; Business Publishers, Inc., July 17, 1978, p. 225).

13. An interesting discussion of several waterfront renewal plans during the early 1970s as well as obstacles encountered in their implementation can be found in Bess Balcher and Jack Linville, "The City Waterfront: Ending an Era of Neglect?" *Nation's Cities*, 9, no. 4 (April 1971): 8-19. Ambitious multiuse redevelopment plans for the Portsmouth, Virginia, waterfront are summarized in Robin Chapman, "Portsmouth: On the Waterfront," *New Norfolk* 14, no. 22 (October 1976): 20 ff. Other notable waterfront projects are considered in "Urban Waterfronts: Design and Planning," *Progressive Architecture*, 6:75 (June 1975): 41-65. Also see Virginia Farrell, *Development and Regulation of the Urban Waterfront: Boston, San Francisco and Seattle* (Princeton: Princeton University, Center for Energy and Environmental Studies, Report no. 95), February 1980.
14. See Louis Weschler, "Environmental Quality Within an Interorganizational Matrix: A Case Study of the SOHIO Project," *Coastal Zone Management Journal* 6, no. 2-3 (1979): 233-252.

PART I

The Older Urban Coast: A New Jersey Perspective

Chapter 2

People and Petrochemicals: Siting Controversies on the Urban Waterfront

Grace Singer

With the ever-increasing momentum of change in American society, especially in industrial technology, concerned citizens have been forced to respond with increasingly sophisticated measures. These actions are often based on an acquired knowledge of complex issues and technologies with great impacts on people's lives. Most important, citizens have had to gain a keener understanding of how to employ the political process. The advent of a new awareness of environmental problems manifested in the first Earth Day celebration in 1970, along with passage of far-reaching federal and state environmental laws,[a] brought a renewed focus to quality of life issues. Citizen groups emerged dedicated to specific environmental objectives.

[a]The National Environmental Policy Act (NEPA) of 1969 fostering citizen involvement by its mandate for publicly available information in Environmental Impact Statements; establishment in 1970 of the Environmental Protection Agency; enactment of the Clean Air Act of 1970, Federal Water Pollution Control Act of 1972, and the Coastal Zone Management Act of 1972. In addition to these and other federal environmental statutes, states established for the first time specific agencies and laws for environmental protection. (In New Jersey, for example, the Department of Environmental Protection, NJDEP, was organized in 1970 followed by enactment of a host of environmental protection laws.)

Although the goal of most environmental laws is clearly preservation of unspoiled areas, we have in recent times witnessed environmental activism in urban areas as well. Included in this category are objections to nuclear facility siting (e.g., the Clamshell Alliance in New Hampshire); opposition to oil refinery siting throughout New England and elsewhere; and urban citizen opposition to the supersonic transport (SST) landings and the Westway superhighway on the Hudson River, both in New York City. These citizen activities have met with varying degrees of success.

HUDSON COUNTY, NEW JERSEY:
AN URBAN CASE STUDY

Hudson County, New Jersey, on the Hudson River in New York Harbor (see Figure 2-1), is of particular interest because of the high degree of success that citizen groups in this urban area have had in causing the rejection of five energy facilities in as many years: 1972 to 1976 (see Figure 2-2 and Table 2-1). Like other urban areas in the United States in the last quarter century, Hudson County has suffered from socioeconomic decline. Its unemployment rates are among the highest in the state and nation (an average of 14 percent in 1976).[1]

In addition, environmental degradation has been a serious problem in this densely populated (611,000 people in 31.5 square miles),[2] highly industrial area that has approximately 96 percent of its land already developed, 44 percent of which is devoted to industrial use. Such degradation is epitomized by the 1977 *Annual Report* of the New Jersey Department of Environmental Protection (NJDEP), which indicates that Jersey City, the largest of the 12 municipalities in Hudson County (260,000 people in 15.1 square miles),[3] had the dirtiest air among 20 New Jersey cities. On 113 days of the year ended June 30, 1976, Jersey City's air was found to be "unhealthy," with possible deleterious effects on humans, animals, and property. The city's air quality was considered "unsatisfactory" on 172 other days and "satisfactory" on only 48 days of the year. Furthermore, Jersey City was among 6 of the 20 cities monitored that had no "good" days. Statistics also indicate that white males in Hudson County have had the highest cancer mortality rates in the state, which in turn has had among the highest cancer mortality rates in the nation.[4]

In response to these conditions, citizen groups have emerged in Hudson County dedicated to opposing further environmental

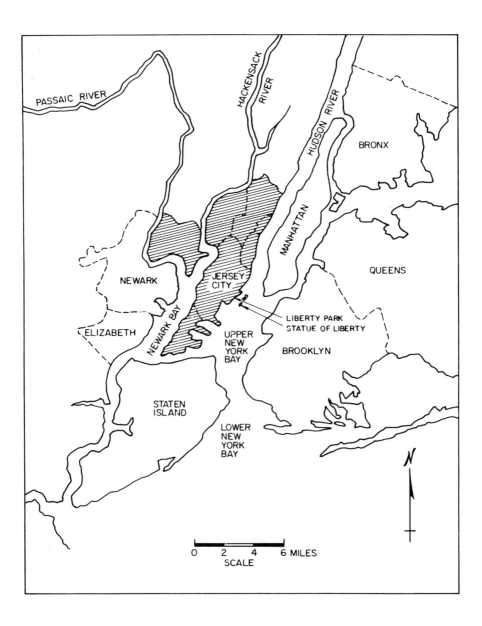

Figure 2-1. Hudson County location.

Table 2-1. Rejected Energy Facilities in Hudson County

Company	Type	Location	Acres	Number of Tanks	Storage Capacity	Date of Final Rejection
Steuber Company, Inc.	Deepwater terminal for storage of bulk fuel oil and chemicals	Jersey City and Bayonne	40	242	4 million barrels	1976
Metropolitan Petroleum Company	Terminal for storage of bulk fuel oil	Jersey City	30	18	3 million barrels	1976
Cosmopolitan Terminal	Deepwater terminal for storage of bulk fuel oil	Hoboken and Weehawken	55	16	3.8 million barrels	1975
JOC Oil, Inc.	Oil refinery and facility for storage of bulk petroleum products	Jersey City	80	20	100,000 barrels	1974
Super Marine, Inc.	Desulfurization facility and storage terminal	Hoboken and Weekawken	55	Uncertain	Uncertain	1972

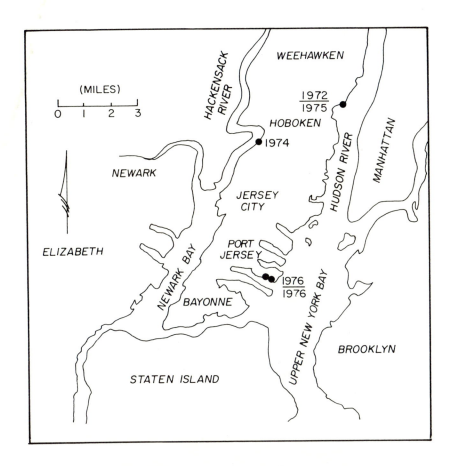

Figure 2-2. Location of rejected oil facilities.

deterioration. Instead, they want an upgrading of their community. This attitude is particularly prevalent with regard to the valuable Hudson County waterfront. This area has a spectacular view of New York's harbor and skyline (2,000 yards across the Hudson River) and the Statue of Liberty directly in front of the 800-acre Liberty State Park in Jersey City opened in June 1976 (see Figure 2-3).

Currently much of this waterfront is characterized by decay and vacancy; 2,000 out of 3,000 acres in Jersey City alone are available for redevelopment. This area has become the focal point of citizen groups who see Liberty State Park as a catalyst for the eventual

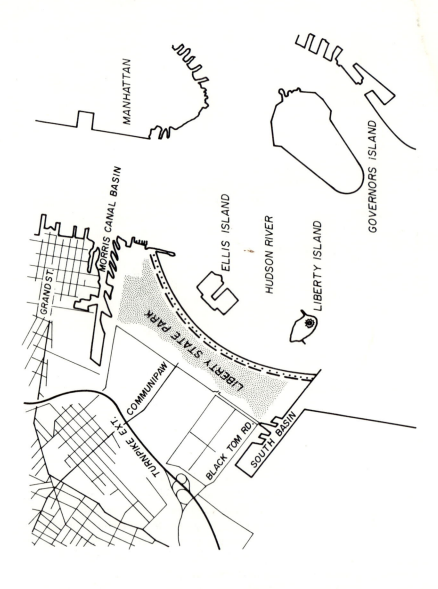

Figure 2-3. Liberty State Park, Jersey City, New Jersey

24

improvement of their community. Who are these groups, and why have they been so extraordinarily successful? What are their concerns, interests, and motivations? What roles have they played in rejection of the five energy facilities proposed in this area in recent years?

Since citizen activists played the leading role in defeat of the various proposed energy facilities in Hudson County, sometimes against great odds,[b] leaders of nine of the groups were interviewed to gain an understanding of their viewpoints, hopes, and concerns.[5] Twenty-three individual groups formed the Waterfront Coalition of Hudson and Bergen Counties in February 1977.[6] Its purpose is to bring together citizen groups and individuals to create a regional planning and implementation mechanism along the Hudson and Hackensack River waterfronts. The coalition's principal focus is the 18-mile Hudson River waterfront from the George Washington Bridge (connecting New York and New Jersey) in Bergen County to the southern tip of the Hudson County peninsula at Bayonne (see Figure 2-4). Formation of this coalition was a direct response to the piecemeal, uncoordinated planning approach embodied in the energy siting episodes.

THE CITIZEN GROUPS

Bayonne Against Tanks

At one time, Bayonne (1975 population: 73,638) was referred to as "Oil City" because of its large number of oil-related facilities, including storage, processing, and research (see Figure 2-5 for the location of Bayonne and other municipalities in Hudson County). In the late 1950s, however, the Tidewater Oil Company, the largest oil company in the area, moved from Bayonne to Delaware, greatly diminishing this industry's importance in the city.[7] Even with this decrease, 17 percent of Bayonne's tax base is derived from oil company facilities, with Exxon, Hess, and Texaco having the largest facilities of the five companies remaining.[8] [c]

The Steuber Company's proposal to locate a large petrochemical terminal at Port Jersey, on the border of Jersey City and Bayonne, was the direct stimulus for formation in October 1976 of Bayonne

[b]In at least one case (Steuber Company, Inc.), both Jersey City's mayor and NJDEP were in support of the petrochemical facility, which was opposed by citizens.

[c]Approximately 5 percent of Hudson County's total land is devoted to oil-related facilities, and about 2 percent to chemical facilities.[9]

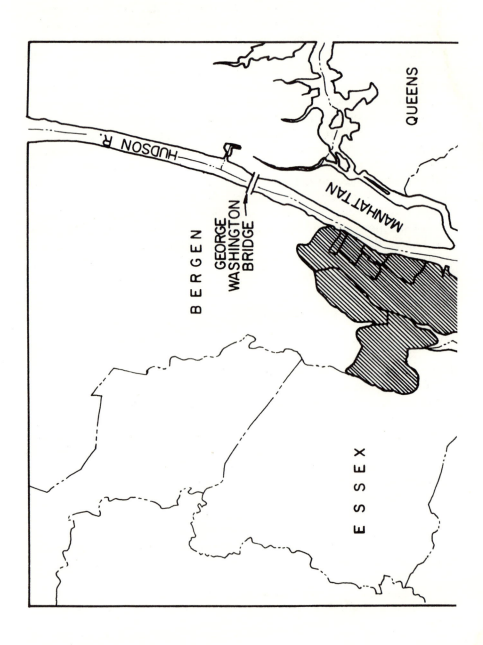

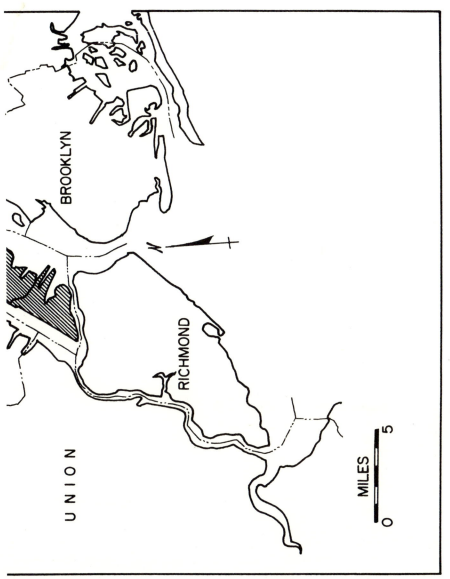

Figure 2-4. Hudson and surrounding counties.

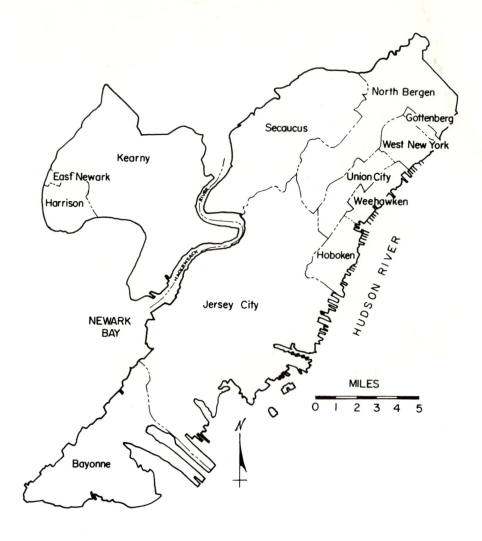

Figure 2-5. Hudson County, political boundaries (*Source:* Hudson County, Office of Planning, June 1, 1977).

Against Tanks (BAT), a citizen group opposed to the 242-tank terminal. Before forming their own organization, some BAT members had worked to oppose the Steuber facility as members of Jersey City groups.

BAT has a flexible structure. Under a steering group of 12 to 15 people, it has divided the city into geographic areas. A nucleus of people represent each section. Some BAT members had worked individually in their own neighborhoods on specific issues; when BAT was formed, however, they joined forces. As is true of most citizen groups, active membership in BAT ebbs and flows according to the needs and issues that arise. Most members have lived in Bayonne all of their lives; but some newcomers to the area are involved, including a few black and Puerto Rican residents.[d] Many of the people active in BAT are professionals, although blue-collar workers are also well represented. Because most of these families have two incomes, they are relatively comfortable economically. In addition to its members, BAT has several "consultants": doctors, lawyers, and even oil company employees who help on technical issues.

A large percentage of residents own their own homes and have lived in the same location for generations. The city has a reputation for its high percentage of families, generally with ethnic (European) backgrounds, who remain together either in two-family homes or in the same neighborhood. It is not uncommon for a daughter to marry and take the upstairs apartment in her parents' home. These residents are members of the white middle class who chose not to flee the area when it was common to do so during the 1950s and 1960s (indeed, a slow trickle of those who left have been returning to Bayonne in the 1970s). The small-town atmosphere, fostered by home ownership, strong family ties, and Bayonne's geographic location at the southern tip of the Hudson County peninsula, has perhaps given it a more insular flavor and kept its population more stable than that of other municipalities in Hudson County. Bayonne has been designated the second safest city in the state (after Clifton). It is a city where one- and two-family homes prevail, rather than high-rise apartments, fostering middle-class values and concerns associated with property ownership. According to Mrs. Rachel Budd, President of BAT and a teacher in Hudson County, the city has a good educational system with a large percentage of its youth going on to college. The city's high-quality educational system is seen as one of the key factors keeping middle-class residents there. A substantial percentage of Bayonne's residents work in New York City whose proximity is seen as another important advantage of Bayonne and indeed of the whole Hudson County area. Clearly,

[d]As is true with most urban areas, Hudson County has a diverse ethnic population. In the county as a whole, black residents represent approximately 10 percent of the population, and Hispanics (including Puerto Ricans and Cuban refugees) approximately 15 percent. The county is predominantly Catholic with a large Italian community.[10]

Bayonne differs socioeconomically from Jersey City (the largest municipality in Hudson County), and from Newark and Trenton, which have experienced the worst urban decline.

The Steuber storage terminal and facilities like it, with a pollution and safety hazard, are seen as an enormous threat to the fragile hold that these citizens have as urban dwellers. This is particularly so in Bayonne because of its history as an energy (oil) center and because companies like Exxon own vacant land on the eastern shore of the city bordering the Hudson River. Citizens fear what these companies might do with this land. In addition, unlike Jersey City where "tank farms" have been zoned out in recent years, Bayonne is zoned for petrochemical storage facilities (although citizens have been trying to have this changed).

In its short history BAT has been involved in other issues beyond the Steuber case. However, all were related to the waterfront, an indication of Bayonne's peninsular geography and citizens' changing perception of this area as a special entity. These organizational activities have included cleanup of the waterways and opposition to a highway extension that would cut off citizen access to the city's western shore; currently the eastern shore is inaccessible to residents. As its name indicates, Bayonne Against Tanks is primarily opposed to any more petrochemical storage tanks and related facilities that this group of citizens see as a deteriorating influence in their delicately balanced urban community.

Citizens Committee of Hudson County

Since its inception as a formal organization in 1966, the Citizen's Committee of Hudson County (CCHC), based in Jersey City, has had a battle-scarred history including a large number of victories. An organization of roughly 500 citizens, its board of directors has 12 members. CCHC's president, Theodore Conrad, is an architectural model maker and one of the earliest supporters (in the early 1960s) of the formation of Liberty State Park. According to Conrad, on an important issue his organization can stimulate 1,000 people to attend a public meeting.

While Hudson County has a large blue-collar work force (almost 55 percent in 1970 compared to 41 percent in New York, 49 percent in Newark, and 48 percent for the nation),[11] CCHC includes several professionals (lawyers, engineers, teachers, doctors, and businessmen) as well as homemakers and many nonprofessionals. Most members are long-time community residents (Conrad's family arrived in 1849). Many active CCHC members are retired or semi-retired, thus freeing them for civic involvement. These older residents are often motivated by their memory of the area's better days. They hope to induce revitalization or at least prevent further deterioration. Property ownership appears to be one common denominator among these activist citizens, although this is by no means absolute. According to Conrad, Jersey City, in spite of all its changes and decline, has historic landmarks worth preserving. He sees historic preservation as especially important in rapidly changing urban areas. Property ownership, family ties, and proximity to New York City (15 minutes by train) are some of the major factors that keep middle-class residents in this community, in spite of some very difficult urban facts of life (socioeconomic decline, pollution, and high taxes).

The first president of CCHC, Dr. Ethel Lawner, a physician, joined with a group of Jersey City residents to form the organization after they had successfully opposed removal of the stately trees for a proposed expansion of Kennedy Boulevard through the center of Hudson County. Dubbing themselves the "Save the Boulevard Committee," the irate residents banded together to fight the $1,675,000 project. Their main objection was that they believed the road widening to be totally unnecessary. As they researched the project they became convinced that the sole reason was to enrich local politicians with contract kickbacks. The citizens, though novices in political affairs, nevertheless plotted their successful antihighway strategy at kitchen table meetings. They scheduled demonstrations, petition drives, and confrontations with public officials. While then-Hudson County political boss John V. Kenny vowed he would "have that group down on their knees to me,"[12] the citizens went to court to prevent construction of the highway. Hudson County has a long history of tainted politics and strong political "bosses," including the notorious Frank "I am the Law" Hague, whose more than 30-year rule ended in the late 1940s. Federal officials who later examined Jersey City records discovered that virtually every city contract was inflated 5 to 15 percent to cover kickbacks to city officials.[13] In 1966 a state Supreme Court justice abolished the Hudson County Boulevard Commission, which was responsible for building the new road. Shortly thereafter the entire project was killed. After this controversy, aroused citizens determined to be more watchful of local government.

Since its original battle, CCHC has been embroiled in many others, including preservation of the 65-year-old Hudson County Court House, with its tall Corinthian pillars, classic facade, and marble interior. The county had planned to demolish this building to make way for construction of a new jail, along with multimillion dollar contracts to friends of the political machine. CCHC enlisted the aid of well-known architectural critic Ada Huxtable, and mustered several hundred residents to appear at a public hearing on the proposal. As a result, the plan was dropped and in 1970 the courthouse was declared a national landmark. It is now being considered for various other uses including a museum. Other issues of concern to CCHC are development of Liberty State Park and planning for the larger waterfront area; tax abatement practices used by government to attract industry, but seen by citizens as an unnecessary giveaway which places a heavier tax burden on homeowners; rehabilitation of railroad tracks for mass transit and freight use; and preserving parkland threatened by proposed use for high-rise apartments that would cut off an exceptional view of the New York City skyline and the Statue of Liberty.

These and several other prominent controversies—and victories—have been the training ground and stimulus preparing CCHC members for their opposition to the various oil-related energy facilities proposed for Hudson County. As one of the largest and oldest of the Hudson County citizen organizations, CCHC members played a prominent role in all of the energy siting proposals from 1972 through 1976. Their dedication, flexibility of operation, and ability to muster large numbers of people (and news coverage) at public meetings have been key factors in this group's extraordinary success.

Historic Paulus Hook Association

Paulus Hook is a residential neighborhood in Jersey City adjacent to the waterfront. The area has had permanent residents since 1640, and the American Revolution Battle of Paulus Hook took place there in 1779.

The calling card of the president of the Historic Paulus Hook Association (HPHA), Joseph Duffy, states the purpose of the organization as "neighborhood preservation, safety, and development." Duffy, retired, lives a few blocks from the Hudson River waterfront. He is steeped in the history of his neighborhood, which has been declared an historical district by Jersey City. Nevertheless, over the years industry has come into the area, and railroad tracks have dominated the waterfront, although currently most tracks and attendant facilities are in disuse.

In response to problems of deterioration of the area, Duffy and several neighbors formed HPHA in September 1974. The group has 40 members, with a dozen forming the leadership core. Many are "old-timers" who do not have the economic choice of mobility. Although one or two black residents attend HPHA's meetings, black and Puerto Rican members of the community generally have formed their own groups and have not been very active in HPHA.

Although Duffy feels that development of light industry might be acceptable for the waterfront, he and his group were heavily involved in opposition to the Steuber terminal, seeing it as a "foot in the door" for petrochemical domination of the waterfront. Jersey City's mayor since May 1977, Thomas F. X. Smith, during his election campaign had expressed strong opposition to this and similar facilities. Smith's position was in sharp contrast to that of his predecessor, Mayor Paul T. Jordan, a strong Steuber supporter. Aside from appealing to those voters opposed to the energy facility, Mayor Smith's origins as a resident of Paulus Hook, so close to the waterfront, might have sharpened his sensitivities to land use in the area, thus making him more sympathetic to a different community destiny.

Duffy attributes the success of his and other citizen groups in the energy siting controversies to the extraordinary letter writing campaign they directed at the media, thereby alerting a large number of county citizens to the negative implications of the siting proposals. In addition, at least two priests were active in opposition to the Steuber facility. The political impact of this was not lost on the city council in a community with a large percentage of Catholic voters. Aside from preservation of its neighborhood and historical monuments, HPHA is involved in other issues, including development of Liberty State Park nearby.

Hoboken Environment Committee

In its 1966 report, *The Lower Hudson*, the Regional Plan Association described Hoboken in this manner:

> Hoboken is a special place on the Lower Hudson and therefore in the Region. The only town built right up to the River's edge, Hoboken has retained its authentic character from the railroad and steamship era and still has a waterfront flavor. Its small scale gives it an intimate community feeling—even with 50,000 people. The many blocks of fine townhouses with aligned cornices and uniform styles endow sections of the Town with a charm that is rare in the Region. It has several elegant individual buildings and squares. With a successful, growing engineering university (Stevens Institute) and a transit connection to Manhattan (PATH), Hoboken has great potential as a place for more people to live and for others to visit and enjoy.[14]

Some of this exciting potential has seen slow realization in Hoboken over the last few years in the "brownstone renaissance" bringing a trickle of middle-class residents back to the formerly fine homes in this square-mile city with a population (1975) of 46,545. Its valuable location, approximately one mile across the Hudson River from Manhattan to which Hoboken has excellent transportation, and the city's acknowledged charm are some of the key factors in the current revival. Against this hope lies the reality of a city that has shared the general decline that has been the fate of most urban areas, including much of Hudson County.

The Hoboken Environment Committee (HEC) was founded in November 1971, based on an initial concern about air pollution and other environmental quality issues. Since that time, HEC has broadened its definition of environment to include land use, socio-economic development, and similar urban concerns. The group has more than 300 members. Its original and current chairman is Helen Manogue, previously employed at Stevens Institute's Center for Municipal Studies on a waterfront redevelopment project in Hoboken. Manogue is also a cofounder of the Waterfront Coalition of Hudson and Bergen Counties. HEC has an executive committee of 9, and 15 to 20 active people who attend meetings and "can be counted on" when the need arises. This core group is augmented by members and nonmembers with specific talents in the professions, writing, graphics, and so on. A substantial number of these members are long-time residents of Hoboken, primarily white-collar employees with income and educational levels above the city's low averages.[15] In a seeming paradox, Hoboken, with a strong ethnic flavor and one of the highest population densities in the nation (285 people per acre),[16] has a large number of people who have remained there over the years because of the comforts of its "small-town atmosphere"; many others, of course, have stayed because of the lack of economic mobility.

Two of the five controversial energy facilities—Super Marine and Cosmopolitan—were both proposed for a site at Weehawken Cove on the Hoboken–Weehawken waterfront. HEC became deeply embroiled in the Super Marine proposal, which began in 1971 and culminated in March 1972. The group was also involved in the Cosmopolitan siting conflict, which began in 1972 (just after the Super Marine affair) and lasted until 1975.

In a departure from the informal procedures of most of the Hudson County citizen groups involved in the energy siting battles, HEC follows a highly formalized procedure in confronting questionable development proposals affecting Hoboken. These steps have been employed to gain factual information and, perhaps as importantly, to earn credibility for the fledging citizen group. HEC's successful format includes the following:

1. An invitation is extended to the president of the applicant company to attend a meeting with HEC. The president is encouraged to bring anyone else and to send site plans and specifications to HEC in advance of the meeting. These plans are then evaluated by professionals (civil engineers, architects, lawyers, and others) who are either HEC members or work with the group. At the meeting, company representatives are given uninterrupted time to present their plans, followed by a question and answer period. Subsequently, a newsletter summarizing the meeting is sent to HEC members for their reaction.

2. HEC then speaks to officials of key local government agencies to learn what benefits the facility will bring to the city. State and federal agencies are also contacted to learn the status of the application and to obtain as much other information as possible.

3. If the group concludes that the proposed facility would be detrimental, HEC communicates this view to the relevant government agencies. In opposing a facility, HEC works with other citizens groups within the county, coordinating press releases, letters to the editor, leaflet distribution, attendance at public meetings, and so on. (In the Cosmopolitan case, HEC worked very closely with people in Weehawken since the facility was to be on the boundary of both municipalities. HEC also helped establish the Weehawken Environment Committee, offering them the experience it had gained in the Super Marine controversy.)

In the Cosmopolitan battle, HEC relied on its 90-page land use study of northern Hoboken, which listed existing conditions and made recommendations. This information was compiled after HEC conducted interviews with experts to solicit their recommendations as to types of facilities that should be located in the area. This approach was successfully emulated by the Jersey City citizen groups in their later fight against the Steuber facility.

In addition to its stance of opposition, HEC has initiated a wide variety of civic projects. Hoboken's compact geography renders some of these programs more feasible than is the case, for example, in Jersey City, which is 15 times Hoboken's size. A partial motivation for these activities is a desire to establish credibility, thereby combating the negative image a group like HEC often receives when it opposes proposed developments. Some of HEC's projects have included obtaining state and national historic site designation for the Erie-Lackawanna Terminal; newspaper recycling in a cooperative effort with the city's public works department (profits are turned over to HEC for beautification programs); installing 250 shrubs on housing stoops in a "tub and shrub" program to ameliorate the city's lack of trees; making up and delivering 300 window flower boxes; and operating annual tours of the interesting, renovated houses so vital to Hoboken's revival. This latter event is a major effort requiring the work of 120 volunteers.

In employing politically sensitive, sophisticated methods—and a great deal of effort—the Hoboken Environment Committee has gained the credibility and success it has sought. Most important, perhaps, through its activities the group has raised the consciousness of Hobokenites to the fact that their city is well worth preserving.

Jersey City Environmental Protection Committee

Because it is a nominal agency of municipal government, the Jersey City Environmental Protection Committee (JCEPC) differs structurally from other Hudson County citizen groups. This organization, however, has much in common with these groups: its activist approach, apparent independence from government influence, and close working relationship with citizens involved in the energy siting episodes.

JCEPC was an outgrowth of a citizens advisory council created in the mid-1960s when the U.S. Department of Health, Education and Welfare (HEW) mandated citizen participation as a prerequisite for funding of various urban programs. In 1973 the current committee was formed with 12 to 15 members appointed by then-Mayor Paul Jordan. JCEPC's powers are more limited than that of the 300 municipal environmental commissions established in New Jersey under state enabling legislation. Jersey City chose not to create such a commission, apparently because of City Hall's reluctance to relinquish political authority. The committee was handicapped by lack of staff. It has not established a clear relationship with the new Smith Administration after having been ignored by former Mayor Jordan, who was displeased with JCEPC for—among other reasons—its very strong opposition to two of the three energy siting proposals in Jersey City: JOC Oil and Steuber.[e]

JCEPC's chairman, Dr. Joseph Weisberg, is chairman of the Geoscience Department of Jersey City State College and chairman of the Environmental Committee of the New Jersey Education Association. Weisberg testified at public hearings and generally spoke out against the energy facility proposals. One of JCEPC's most serious concerns about the Steuber facility was the lack of disclosure by the company or the New Jersey Department of Environmental Protection (NJDEP) about the "worst possible case" accident or the margins of error in calculations on chemical compounds to be stored. Weisberg was also disturbed that comments by the U.S. Bureau of Mines and the U.S. Occupational Safety and Health Administration were couched in general terms, not specific to Steuber's plans for storage of 4 million barrels of oil and various chemicals. Against this risk, the committee saw no substantial benefits accruing to the city in either jobs or taxes. Another concern was the company's recitation of benefits to the city based on full tax payments, followed by its application for tax abatement status whereby the city would receive very little or no financial benefits for a number of years. In JCEPC's view, this distortion considerably clouded the proposal.

The expertise, professionalism, and activism employed by Weisberg as head of his environmental committee offered some semblance of official disapproval of the proposed facilities. Such defiance by appointees of an administration position was unheard of in past days of iron-fisted political rule in Hudson County and many other urban areas. This departure is symbolic of a new urban citizen attitude, especially toward the important waterfront area.

Save the Palisades Association

The skyscrapers of New York City are matched by the majestic Palisade cliffs to the west in Hudson and Bergen counties. The panorama of the Hudson River and New York skyline are quite spectacular from various vantage points along the Palisades. Likewise, the view from New York of this dramatic natural phenomenon serves as relief to those who live and work in glass towers. The Save the Palisades Association (SPA) was organized in 1929 to

[e]The committee did not oppose the Metropolitan facility, seeing it as quite a different proposal from the others. Metropolitan has existing oil storage tanks on the waterfront and the shift to a new site was seen as an improvement, whereas JOC and Steuber were entirely new entities.

counter development threats to accessibility and an unfettered view from the Palisades. It was dormant for many years thereafter because of a lack of construction activity, a symptom of the Great Depression of the 1930s. In 1968 the organization became active in court battles over construction of high-rise apartment buildings from Fort Lee, near the George Washington Bridge, to Weehawken in Hudson County.

According to James Drago, president of SPA and a resident of Union City, which is not directly on the waterfront (Drago's home is three miles west of the Palisades and a "stone's throw" from the Cosmopolitan-Super Marine proposed site in Hoboken and Weehawken), membership in his loosely structured group numbers about 100 with a board of directors of 15. Drago has lived in this area most of his life, and a majority of the active citizens with whom he works have lived there for 15 years or more. Most have remained in this urban area because they have ties with family and friends and because of home ownership; another instance of lack of economic mobility.[f] In addition, Hudson County's strategic location and mass transportation make it accessible to several areas of job opportunity, including New York City. Generally, the level of education and income of members of SPA is higher than that of the community, a feature most of the groups have in common. Drago is self-employed as a design engineer. Although Union City's 1975 population of 57,840 is roughly one-half Hispanic (Cuban refugees or Puerto Rican), neither these nor black residents have been active with SPA.

The group was involved in all five siting controversies, initially because it was called upon for help by other organizations. Ultimately, Drago became one of the most evocative spokesmen for the citizen groups. Following is a sample from his testimony at the Steuber-Metropolitan public hearing in December 1975:

New Jersey, especially the Northeastern corner, is already drowning in oil. We are carrying far, far more than our share of this polluting industry. The amount of storing and refining that our small state is presently doing is comparable in volume to what the huge states of California, Texas and Louisiana are doing. . . . Are we second or third class people here condemned to have, see, smell, breathe and slosh through nothing but oil and its products?

[f]The lack of moderate priced housing elsewhere has kept many urban home-owners in the city.

Generally reacting to crisis situations, SPA has engaged in at least one far-ranging episode involving siting of LNG storage tanks outside Hudson County in the town of Carlstadt. This issue involved the Hackensack Meadowlands Development Commission (HMDC), which lost in a court case with Transcontinental Gas Company. This involvement in a case in another county about six miles from SPA's immediate area illustrates this group's broader concerns.

Union City Citizens League

The Union City Citizens League (UCCL) was formed as a political action group in 1969-1970 with the express purpose of unseating an entrenched local administration. The group's original leader was Father Graziano, a priest, and its current president is Leo Pia, proprietor of a dry cleaning establishment. Membership in UCCL remains at about 70, with roughly 25 of these members comprising the organization's active core. Many UCCL members are retired, long-time residents who are concerned about their homes and feel threatened by the many changes in their community. Environmental quality is a serious problem in Union City, as in Hudson County. Union City's air pollution problems are largely caused by the New York-New Jersey Lincoln Tunnel approach roads, which run through the area. Because the city is nearly fully developed, there have been suggestions that development take place in the air rights over these roads even though this would exacerbate the area's air pollution.

Although Union City is not directly on the waterfront, UCCL has worked closely with SPA's James Drago to oppose the various county energy siting proposals. Many UCCL members see the waterfront as a regional resource to which they want access. In addition, Pia put it succinctly when he said of the energy proposals: "our noses are right over their emissions." This is a literal testament to the geographic elevation of Union City and other northern Hudson County municipalities on the ridge leading to the Palisades. Supermarine's 300-foot-high smoke stack for its desulfurization plant proposed for adjacent Hoboken and Weehawken is an example of the kind of air pollution and visual intrusion these citizens so strongly oppose.

Weehawken Environment Committee

As a direct response to the Supermarine and Cosmopolitan siting proposals for Weehawken Cove on the Weehawken-Hoboken border, the Weehawken Environment Committee (WEC) was formed in the early 1970s. The 50-member organization has an active core of about 15 people and is concerned with issues of environmental quality, recreation, and open space preservation in its community of 13,300 people. In contrast to the other Hudson County citizen groups in this study, WEC is composed primarily of new residents, many of whom could afford to live elsewhere. For example, James Dette, Chairman of WEC (and an engineer and partner in a firm that does geotechnical and environmental engineering and safety analysis for energy facility sites), returned to this country after living abroad and chose to live in Weehawken. He and others active in WEC have moved here because they see the possibilities of a fine residential community that could rival some of the coastal cities of Europe. To realize their hope of improving their chosen community, these citizens have "become fighters" and have opposed the energy facilities that they saw as incompatible with these hopes.

Weehawken shares with Hoboken and other Hudson County communities excellent vistas of the Hudson River and New York skyline. It has some fine, tree-shaded residential streets, although it also shares in the socioeconomic strain prevalent in the area. An indication of WEC's broader concerns is seen in its involvement with other citizen groups in a lawsuit against the Hackensack Meadowlands sports complex for the lack of transportation planning, inadequate provision of mass transit in particular. This was primarily an air pollution issue and one that the citizen groups lost. WEC also has been involved in a high-rise housing controversy in its community, one of the smallest of Hudson County's 12 municipalities. Citizens opposing the development claimed that its 798 units on 7.7 acres far exceeded the site's zoning allowance for a maximum density of 40 units per acre.[17]

An important element in the decline of the cities has been the loss of middle-class residents. A small number of these people, epitomized by WEC's members, have started to return. They are a new breed of urban dwellers who have a measure of economic mobility and have chosen urban life more for the hope it offers than for the current reality of its problems. Members of WEC have chosen to live in urban Hudson County because of its proximity to New York City—many work there—and for other amenities not available in the suburbs, including mass transit. These citizens are prepared to fight to bring a better quality of life back to the cities.

Help Our Polluted Environment

An interesting parallel to the Hudson County citizen group activity in opposing energy facilities is seen in Bordentown, New Jersey.

This community is in Burlington County on the Delaware River in the central part of the state, about five miles south of Trenton, the state capital. Here in July 1977 a group called Help Our Polluted Environment, known by its acronym HOPE, was formed in direct response to the Dow Chemical Company's proposal to build a $30-million "tank farm" for storing and transferring some 50 chemicals, many of them hazardous and carcinogenic. This proposal, similar in many ways to the Steuber plan for Jersey City,[g] elicited the same kind of negative citizen response and local government acceptance. Government officials were primarily influenced by the facility's estimated annual tax payments of about $1 million. They told citizens that the Dow facility would enable them to reduce homeowners' property taxes by $200 per family.

Some members of HOPE had first become involved in public issues in the peace movement of the 1960s; most had not previously been active in environmental causes. A 60-member group, HOPE has no organizational officers but assigns areas of responsibility. Its 15-person steering committee consists of several professionals, including a doctor, lawyer, planner, several teachers, and a corporate public relations person. Most of them are relatively new residents of the area. For example, one steering committee member, James Parker, a cofounder of HOPE and a professional photographer, has lived in Bordentown for three years.

Bordentown Township has a population of 7,800. It completely surrounds Bordentown City, which is only one-square mile and has a population of 4,600. Dow's proposed site was in the township, on the Delaware River. In December 1976 the township responded to Dow's proposal by changing the zoning law to allow petrochemical storage tanks.[h] Opponents of the proposal claimed that the wording used in the zoning change was patterned after that in a Dow environmental statement, suggesting close cooperation between local officials and the company.[i]

---

[g]Steuber, with 242 tanks on 39 acres, was to be much larger than the Dow proposal of 65 tanks on 52 acres, although subsequent expansion of the Dow facility was a possibility.

[h]This action, just one year after the Steuber and Metropolitan facilities were rejected, would seem to indicate that Bordentown's officials were not aware of or did not relate the citizen opposition warning signals from Hudson County to their own situation. Nor apparently did the well-publicized rejection of a Dow Chemical facility in California sway Bordentown officials from their support of the proposal for their community.

[i]The change in zoning resulted from a private meeting between township officials—then in the process of revising the zoning ordinance—and Dow on October 6, 1976.[18]

Bordentown's waterfront is used for recreation: boating, swimming, water skiing, and fishing. The only heavy industry in the immediate area is a Public Service Electric and Gas Company (PSE&G) fuel shipment facility. The other closest heavy industry is Fairless Steel, across the river in Pennsylvania, from which Bordentown and other New Jersey localities receive substantial air pollution. Bordentown is in a nonattainment air quality area, a condition that citizens feared would be exacerbated by Dow's additional emissions. Another parallel to the opposition in the Steuber case was seen in the low jobs-to-acres ratio. Dow proposed to generate 40 to 50 jobs on a 52-acre waterfront site, less than one job per acre (even less than Steuber's two jobs per acre).

Bordentown was the site of an earlier energy facility siting controversy, PSE&G's defeated proposal to build two nuclear power plants on Newbold Island, in the river offshore from the proposed Dow site. (PSE&G had earlier proposed to locate two reactors in Burlington Township, within 10 miles of Bordentown; this proposal too was defeated.) In addition, the Rollins hazardous waste disposal facility in Gloucester County, about 35 miles from Bordentown, had a serious explosion in December 1977 in which five people were killed. These threats were vivid in the minds of HOPE members (none of whom had been involved personally in the nuclear siting controversies). The Dow proposal was examined by NJDEP, which had supported the Steuber petrochemical terminal for Hudson County. Dow threatened to take its facility elsewhere, citing local citizen concerns as a factor causing approval delays.[19] In early 1978 the company withdrew its proposal.

ATTITUDES OF THE CITIZEN ACTIVISTS

The Bordentown and Hudson County areas differ in many respects. Hudson County is far more densely populated and industrialized, while Bordentown has a more suburban flavor, although it is within 15 miles of metropolitan Philadelphia. Attitudes of the citizen groups in both areas, however, are remarkably similar. In both locations these citizen activists are saying essentially two things: (1) we are not willing to accept the risk to health and safety presented by certain polluting facilities, and (2) we see our coastal (or riverfront) location as a unique feature, to which citizens should have access and amenity use. These yearnings for a better quality of life are in sharp contrast with the views of some local officials whose strong sense of fiscal planning precludes consideration of the waterfront in terms other than the taxes new development there could generate.

Although differences in structure, procedures, and activity exist among the citizen groups involved in the five energy siting controversies in Hudson County, most of their leaders agree on the major issues. A summary of their responses to questions posed in the interviews follows.

What were your principal reasons for actively opposing these facilities? While pollution and safety were seen as serious, immediate concerns, several respondents felt that appropriate land use was a prime consideration, especially for the waterfront. They did not want the petrochemical industry to get a "foot in the door," perhaps ultimately coming to dominate the area. This concern was heightened by imminent offshore oil and gas exploration on New Jersey's coast, an effort causing several of the respondents to be suspicious. In addition, it was strongly felt that the community would reap very few benefits in comparison to the burdens placed upon it by having these facilities in its midst.

Did you perceive these facilities to be primarily pollution or safety hazards, or both? Do you differentiate between the two where energy or industrial facilities are concerned? Although pollution and safety were seen as equally dangerous by most of those interviewed, some felt that the public is more responsive to the immediacy of safety hazards, perhaps because accidents receive more dramatic media coverage than does pollution. With the recent disclosure of high cancer mortality statistics in Hudson County and in the state as a whole, citizens have perceived the long-term effects of pollution on health, and this has affected public opinion.[j] "It can get you either way" seemed to characterize the response to this question.

Are visibility and proximity of energy or industrial facilities a major factor? That is, "out of sight, out of mind"? As evidenced by the fact that the citizen groups based in different municipalities

[j]In a 1977 survey of New Jersey residents, city dwellers said pollution, urban blight, and crime were their prime concerns.[20] These findings supported those in a 1973 survey taken in Jersey City, where people interviewed said environmental problems were the second most important local issue after crime and the third most important national problem after crime and inflation.[21]

of Hudson County worked closely with each other in their opposition to unwanted facilities, the answer to this query was a resounding "No!" Because the county is compact, with 12 municipalities crowded into its confines, a threat to one community is seen as a threat to all. In addition, many of these citizens feel that the state as a whole already has more than its "fair share" of polluting facilities, particularly those connected with petrochemicals, and it should not accept any more. "Out of sight, out of mind" is not descriptive of the attitude here. With the knowledge that air and water pollution do not respect political boundaries, any site in the county is seen as the backyard of all.

Do you see certain kinds of energy or other heavy industrial facilities as acceptable and some as objectionable? What makes the difference? All of those interviewed object to any facility that is a pollution or safety hazard and that is aesthetically incompatible with the new Liberty State Park, views of the river, Statue of Liberty, and the New York skyline. Some felt that light industry and shipping activities might be satisfactory (e.g., tugboat repairs). Two people felt that a service base for the Outer Continental Shelf exploration effort could be considered for the area, but that such plans would have to be closely scrutinized for suitability. However, fears were expressed that such a facility could lead to eventual tank farm siting, which the citizens have vigorously rejected. Labor intensity was given as an important factor in any siting decisions for urban areas.

Where do you think polluting energy or industrial facilities should go, if not in Hudson County? Several respondents felt that New Jersey as a whole should restrict further development of such industry. Some felt that any areas with high population densities and existing pollution were totally unsuited for these facilities. Others added that recreational areas were unsuitable and that communities downwind of proposed "dirty" facilities will have to be carefully checked. It was pointed out that polluting energy industries are often not labor-intensive, for example, "refineries practically run themselves now," thus not serving the employment needs of urban areas.

While almost all of those interviewed knew where the facilities should *not* be located, only one respondent suggested an alternate site; colocation of new energy facilities at the Bayway refinery area in Linden, New Jersey. Even this person expressed some misgivings about the transport of air pollutants to populated areas. Clearly, this issue of alternate siting is the most difficult dilemma facing citizens as well as government decision makers. The interviewees were certain that their severely impacted communities, and others suffering from pollution, could not allow further degradation without seriously affecting the health of large numbers of people; but they had little to offer as to preferred sites.

How important are employment and tax incentives in siting decisions? Because the energy facilities offered so few jobs, substantial employment was not at stake in rejection of any of the proposals. Respondents recognized that had the facilities been labor-intensive, it would have been much more difficult to refuse them in the face of the county's high unemployment rates.[k] Hudson County's Economic Development Program recommends labor intensity and high productivity as major industrial siting criteria:

> Those industries that have adapted to core conditions rank high in land use intensity and productivity. With few exceptions the obverse is true. In a county of this size and degree of urban density these two variables are exceedingly important. Enterprises which do not have a moderate-to-high degree of intensity along these dimensions cannot be encouraged to locate in Hudson County.[22][l]

With recent county unemployment rates as high as 14 percent, capital-intensive facilities such as the Steuber terminal, with its two jobs per acre, are seen as not meeting the needs of this urban community. In addition, it is felt that many technologically sophisticated energy facilities would not draw employees from the local unskilled labor pool.

The tax issue is a complex one in some Hudson County municipalities, including Jersey City, which attract new industries by offering tax abatement for a period of 5 or even 10 years. Many of the citizens interviewed bitterly opposed this mechanism, as they see their individual property taxes skyrocketing. Many view polluting facilities as an economic disincentive to urban areas because they might discourage potential new "clean," labor-intensive industries from locating there, and because they believe such facilities would

---

[k]One interesting confrontation took place at the public hearing on the Steuber proposal in December 1975. A very large contingent of union members, perhaps 500, showed up at the behest of their leaders. When they learned that very few construction or operating jobs would be generated by the project, the union attendance rapidly dissipated.

[l]The county recommends a minimum of about 30 jobs per acre.

further stimulate the flight of middle-class residents from the city.[23] Residents of Hudson County have stated their concerns:

> Members of the middle class, so necessary for the survival of any city, are fleeing to the suburbs. . . . Will the tanks prove an inducement to remain for those contemplating a move to the suburbs? Will the presence of tanks encourage people from other communities to move here? Will the tanks add to the beauty of Jersey City's waterfront?[24]

> Urban living is a real challenge. We are constantly fighting for survival. The problems of crime, pollution, rising taxes, lack of services plague us. . . . Let's make the Jersey City waterfront attractive to all, industry, residents and visitors. The construction of a tank farm will result in more unhealthy air and perhaps a mass exodus of residents who will flee this city fearing for their health and their lives.[25]

What is your opinion of the "emission offset" approach to air pollution control, the mechanism employed in the Steuber proposal? Steuber's projected annual emissions of 100 tons of hydrocarbons in Jersey City were to be offset by installation of new pollution control technology at a storage terminal the company rented in Carteret, some 10 miles away, achieving thereby an estimated 2-percent reduction in emissions in the airshed both cities share. This concept elicited very strong objections from citizens during the siting controversy.

With this memory still vivid, citizens reacted strongly against EPA's "emission offset" policy.[m] To them, any additional air pollution was unacceptable in their area, already under federal mandate to reduce hydrocarbon emissions by 68 percent. Existing pollution and population density were the principal concerns of these citizens, who felt that the theoretical 2-percent improvement in air quality was a bad bargain. They admitted that the offset policy might be viable in cleaner areas, but not in nonattainment areas like their's. Citizens were suspicious of the calculations used to formulate the tradeoff for the Steuber facility, and they vowed to challenge the figures with their own experts should a similar situation arise in the future.

Jersey City's motto is "Everything for Industry." Does this still describe the prevalent attitude in Hudson County, or do you sense a change? If so, how does this manifest itself? This broad topic elicited varied responses from group leaders:

[m]See Chapter 5.

Politicians need taxes to run services, but they are not willing to be imaginative. They continue to think in the same old ways about attracting ratables at any cost. Instead, our political leaders must pressure state and federal agencies for the cities' fair share of the pie. State programs are still too heavily oriented toward the suburbs (e.g., Green Acres). People will no longer accept ratables at any cost.

In the late 1960s, Hoboken, at very great expense, erected a sign on the waterfront advertising 'Hoboken Welcomes Industry'. People here now have pride in their city and know they have something worthwhile to preserve. They will no longer accept any and all comers.

The best industry in Jersey City is the individual homeowner who pays full tax rates [an allusion to tax abatement for new industry].

Citizens are aware that industry does not have the public interest in mind. Some of our local industries do not make an effort to hire local people. No large labor-intensive industries have come to the area in the last 30 years. Only the oil companies, which do not offer many jobs, have shown an interest. Even now there is a new proposal for an oil storage facility under the Pulaski Skyway [an elevated, heavily trafficked highway in Jersey City]. Large industries have a moral commitment to help prevent the decline of the cities. Investments of multinationals overseas rather than in America's urban areas are a harmful policy.

New industry which has come in under tax abatement has stayed as long as it was convenient. People now travel and have seen other coastal cities, e.g., Boston and San Francisco; they know the potential of their waterfront location and are not willing to trade it away for minimal benefits.

As evidenced by the "brownstone movement" in Hoboken and to a smaller extent in Jersey City, a small number of middle-class residents have moved back to this area. They see it as a place to live and are not going to want additional pollution generated by some industries.

Why do you think citizen groups were so effective in rejecting the five energy facilities proposed for Hudson County? The groups have an extraordinary "batting average" of successful action in all five siting controversies, sometimes against great odds. Group leader responses indicated the multiplicity of strategies employed in their complex urban setting.

Because six of the nine groups were organized prior to the siting battles,[n] and most were seasoned in dealing with difficult urban controversies, when siting proposals surfaced they were not hampered by the need to recruit members and launch new organizations.

[n]Only Bayonne Against Tanks, Help Our Polluted Environment (Bordentown), and the Weehawken Environment Committee were formed in direct response to the energy siting controversies.

Strongly motivated by a lack of trust in government's ability or willingness to serve them—especially in the Machiavellian political arena of Hudson County, where patronage jobs had been a traditional means of keeping the populace subservient to the will of a strong political organization—these citizens were imbued with a commitment to protect themselves. In addition, they felt that even well-intentioned, albeit misguided (from their viewpoint) political leaders, responding to the severe socioeconomic problems of their area, might grasp at any proposal without properly judging all of its ramifications.

In general, citizens made their views and themselves known and heard where it counted, convincing public officials that there was broad, concerted citizen opposition. No countervailing citizen constituency came forth in support of the facilities, primarily a testament to their lack of labor intensity. Even the local chambers of commerce did not wage a strong campaign to counteract citizen opposition.

Some specific citizen activity seemed particularly effective. For example, in cooperation with residents of areas closest to the site, including some racial and other minorities, the groups formed a "Ban the Tanks" coalition of nearly 20 organizations from Hudson County and beyond. Adopting the slogan "Thanks, but no tanks," citizens collected thousands of signatures on a petition supporting their stand. This communicated to local politicians broad support that could manifest itself in election day voting patterns. Public education via letters to the editors of influential newspapers[o] and network television eventually led to local and outside editorial support. For example, WNBC-TV in New York City stated in an editorial:

> Let us assume that despite the fact that many of the chemicals to be handled are toxic and some highly flammable, that the Department (NJDEP) is right about safety. It is clear neither the Department nor the Jersey City administration are much concerned about beauty. New York's harbor was once a thing of rare beauty. . . . This project would make the Jersey side of the harbor a visual horror with wall to wall chemical and oil

[o]One newspaper in particular, *The Newark Star Ledger*, with statewide influence, was especially hard-hitting in its coverage of the Steuber siting controversy in its environmental column written by Gordon Bishop. It became a prominent voice in opposition to the proposal and is credited by some state officials as one of the principal causes of the facility's defeat. Citizens were, however, the catalyst in obtaining and continuing prominent focus on their viewpoints.

storage tanks from Bayonne to Liberty State Park. . . . Jersey City's own Environmental Commission has opposed the tank farm. So has this station. If you are concerned, we suggest you make your feelings known to Jersey City's Mayor Paul Jordan who is trying to push the project through.[26]

The *Jersey Journal* in Jersey City wrote in an editorial:

We would be stuck for our lifetime with a landscape not only unattractive but depressing. The deed would be irrevocable. . . . we would regret what we had done with it. And it would then be too late. There is no secret about what makes some cities inviting and others unpleasant. . . . We are not desperate enough to destroy our future potential for $1,300,000.[p, 27]

Large turnouts of citizens from all parts of the county at public meetings, achieved by extensive telephone contact and leaflet handouts, were also very important. For example, in spite of inclement weather 800 people showed up at the Cosmopolitan public hearing in January 1974, indicating strong public displeasure with the proposal.

Although these were the major citizen actions that ultimately led to their success, other smaller factors also played a part. For example, the proposal encountered strong active opposition by at least two or three priests who are accorded special respect by local politicians in this county. In addition, citizens successfully solicited the assistance of professionals, often academicians, who acted as their expert consultants on some of the complex technical issues. This is of increasing importance as technologies become more complicated. Lack of such expert assistance has been particularly evident in nuclear siting issues.[28] An element of timing was also inadvertently on the side of citizens when a series of oil facility accidents[q]

---

[p]This figure is the estimated total tax from the Steuber and Metropolitan storage terminals, although the numbers appear to have changed several times during the long course of the siting controversy.

[q]At least four of these incidents took place in Philadelphia and New York. In April 1974 an oil tanker exploded at the Atlantic Richfield Company's Fort Mifflin Marine Terminal in Delaware County, Pennsylvania, as crude oil was being pumped from it. The terminal, on the Delaware River, is just across the county line from Philadelphia. Twelve people died in the explosion and at least 14 more were injured.[29] Another incident occurred in August 1975 at a Gulf Oil Company refinery on the Schuylkill River in Philadelphia when eight firemen were killed fighting a blaze. This was followed in October 1975 by an episode at another Atlantic Richfield facility when fuel oil storage tanks exploded at the company's 800-acre oil refinery also on the Schuylkill River in Philadelphia.[30] Still another fire and explosion took place in January 1976 in Brooklyn, New York, at the Patchogue Oil Terminal Corporation storage area. The smoke from this blaze was visible throughout Hudson and Bergen Counties in New Jersey.[31]

took place during the course of the Cosmopolitan, Metropolitan, and Steuber episodes. These incidents received extensive media coverage.

As noted, county residents considered environmental problems in their area second only to crime; thus Hudson County activists apparently tapped a vein of broad citizen dissatisfaction. Their success was not merely the result of a good public relations campaign but was based on issues with broad public appeal. Without this, it is questionable whether even the extraordinary efforts of the citizen groups would have resulted in success in all five siting cases.

Which siting controversy presented the most difficulty for citizen opponents? Some citizens feel that the two-year Steuber case presented the toughest battle because of strong support for the facility from Jersey City's mayor and NJDEP in addition to some influential local banking interests. Others feel that Cosmopolitan was the most difficult case because it lasted the longest—three years. These perceptions depend on which citizens assumed the lead responsibility in each case and thus felt the burden most heavily. JOC Oil and Super Marine were relatively short-lived episodes—less than a year—and did not require the same kind of sustained effort. Metropolitan was inextricably tied to the Steuber proposal because the two facilities were to share the same general site. Metropolitan's defeat is felt to be a result of this tie.

In general, how do you assess citizen input to local decisions? Overall, there is dissatisfaction with the receptivity of local officials to citizen input in decision making. Some examples follow:

> Citizen input could be sought and accepted in a positive manner but it is not. Politicians seem to be fearful of diminishing their power, but they forget their power is derived from the people. The state "Sunshine Law," mandating that all meetings be open to the public, has not really helped except in Board of Education meetings. Although the bit political "machines" have been shaken, the tendency on the part of local politicians is still to consolidate their power.
> The political atmosphere is about the same throughout Hudson County municipalities. There is a divergence between political aspirations and the needs of the people. In the past the attitude on the part of politicians has been that the citizenry is ignorant and thus does not have to be included in local decisions. Two things have helped to change this attitude: the federal government edict that funds be withheld for urban programs if public participation is not included in the decision-

making process, and the first siting controversy in 1972 (Super Marine), which acted as a signal that citizens would no longer blindly accept official decisions. The attitude of "you can't fight City Hall" is crumbling.

The modus operandi of local government has been to withhold information from the public, thus frustrating its participation in decisions. Very little independent thinking exists; many local politicos still accept "the party line." Under the "Sunshine Law," they may listen to citizen input but give very little weight to it.

One positive note was struck by a citizen leader who felt that local government was receptive and improving. Part of this improvement is a result of moves by church groups to become involved in local affairs. This has elicited a favorable response both because of the groups' numbers and the religious establishment that they represent.

Which level of government should have primacy in energy or industrial facility siting? In calling for a regional mechanism for waterfront planning, the Waterfront Coalition of Hudson and Bergen Counties is seeking to eliminate the conflicting, piecemeal municipal siting approach that its members consider destructive of a regional resource. While there is some disagreement about the form and extent of authority of this mechanism or agency, most of the citizen groups agree that a regional approach—with strong municipal input— would represent an improvement over the existing framework.

Reflecting on their experience with the energy proposals, varied views were held by citizen leaders on this complex issue. The following comments are representative of these views:

Theoretically the county level should prevail, but not in Hudson County. Here we need state control with overall monitoring by the federal level. Municipal government is so bad in the county that I would be willing to give up home rule. This is one of the reasons for a regional approach to waterfront planning.

County planning authority would have to be beefed up to handle this responsibility. Municipalities are too small to deal with high impact facilities. That leaves the state to do the job.

A regional structure is best because local planning boards in this area consist of political appointees who do not operate with much independence of the political structure.

In the Steuber case citizens thought they could depend on the state DEP to protect environmental interests, but instead citizens found they had to fight the state *and* local government. I no longer know which would be best.

The local level of government should prevail. Even if they make the wrong decisions, at least citizens will have input and can hold politicians accountable for their decisions. This is not the case with state bureaucrats who have not been sympathetic to urban areas.

The ideal situation would be local decision by citizen vote on important facilities. Barring this, all levels of government should have input.

Overall state planning with local decisions on specific facilities would be best. The waterfront should not be controlled by any one municipality. It belongs to the people of the United States and should be treated differently than other land areas.

On this issue, the citizen leaders struggled with their inclinations toward home rule and the realization that continued opposition is no longer enough; they would need a mechanism to coordinate waterfront planning across municipal boundaries. In addition, while some of the citizens agree with the theory of home rule, they do not have sufficient faith in their own local government's ability to plan effectively for the vital waterfront resource. This is a reaction to the divergence of opinion (evident in the siting controversies) between the citizens and some municipal officials on the kind of development that should and should not be allowed at the water's edge.

What would you prefer to see in terms of waterfront land use? Access, diversity, and amenity use to balance the heavily industrial nature of the area are the major goals of these citizens. The Hudson River waterfront from the George Washington Bridge to Liberty State Park has poor access, a barrier to enjoyment of the water's edge. Most citizens mentioned the shortage of recreational areas in the county. They pointed out that according to national standards relating population to recreational needs, Hudson County is deficient by approximately 5,000 acres. The waterfront area is seen as an ideal place to serve these needs, for example, bike paths. Although Liberty State Park will serve some of the county's recreational needs, this is a state facility that will draw millions of visitors from throughout the state and region.

Most of the citizens feel that appropriate light industry and commercial use of the waterfront could be satisfactory, but they want the predominant feeling to be that of green space and amenity be-fiting the vistas of New York Harbor and some unique landmarks: the Statue of Liberty, Ellis Island, the New York skyline, and the new state park.

What are your greatest concerns and hopes for your community? Quality of life goals were apparent in responses from these citizens, who have been willing to expend a great deal of effort to improve their communities. Most want a safe and comfortable environment free from the fear of pollution and catastrophic accidents. Beyond these basic yearnings, they expressed the hope that citizens would continue to work together to affect positive change and that fiscal planning would be eliminated as destructive to the area. The desire to continue upgrading their community is the overriding theme of these citizen activists. Anything that is perceived as contrary to this principal goal will be vigorously opposed.

SUMMARY AND CONCLUSIONS

With nearly every major city in the United States located on navigable water and almost half of the U.S. population living within 50 miles of a coast, urban coastal areas play a key role in national affairs. Because many of the waterfront areas of these cities are part of an aging industrial era, they are often characterized by decay and vacancy. These prime waterfront locations in many cities are thus ripe for redevelopment. In response to this condition and in recognition of this valuable coastal resource for amenity use, many cities have been undergoing waterfront revitalization programs.

The Hudson County energy siting controversies raise some important challenges to traditional assumptions. With federal government mandates for public participation as a prerequisite to program funding (for example, 701 and 208 planning), which is an important factor in urban areas, increased citizen involvement can be expected. The rural preservationist focus of the federal Coastal Zone Management Act of 1972 and many state laws encourage urban siting for those energy and other facilities not wanted in unspoiled areas. However, the citizen groups in Hudson County are saying that they have a different urban agenda, particularly for their valued waterfront area.

Socioeconomic Characteristics of the Groups

These groups have emerged from a socioeconomic milieu atypical of those usually associated with environmental activism, thereby challenging certain assumptions. For example, in writing about the rise in public concern for the environment, Charles Jones noted:

> Suburban dwellers seem to be more aroused over the environment than big city residents, perhaps because of higher average education, and because many of the suburbanites are commuters or refugees from smog.[32]

Hudson County is characterized by recent high unemployment rates and a median family income about $2,000 below the state average. The area is 55 percent blue collar, high by comparison to the national average of 48 percent. Given these socioeconomic factors, one must look closer at the makeup of the groups to realize that their active members apparently have higher educational levels, professional status, and, by implication, incomes than the typical residents of their community. Yet their leaders certainly have been sensitive to the political currents of their predominantly blue-collar community, and they are able to mobilize large numbers of citizens and gain the attention of local elected politicians. The groups bear out observations that levels of education, social position, and length of residence create an awareness of environmental problems and a commitment to do something about them.[33] With a few notable exceptions, these organizations are composed of white, middle-class, long-time residents. The county is largely Catholic and ethnically diverse, with black residents comprising approximately 10 percent of the population, slightly lower than the national average (this figure is much higher for Jersey City, perhaps double the county average).[r] The Hispanic community, composed primarily of Puerto Ricans and Cuban refugees, is large and growing, and it was approximately 15 percent in 1970.[s] Although representation of minorities was evident

---

[r]This rate is low compared to that in New Jersey's other large cities—Newark and Trenton—where the black population is close to or over 50 percent.

[s]Residents of Jersey City's Greenville area, a predominantly Italian and Irish working-class neighborhood just west of the Steuber site, strongly supported the "Ban the Tanks" Coalition, as did the black population in areas to the north of the site. The JOC site was near the solidly Italian Marion section of Jersey City. Residents there joined the citizen groups in opposing the proposal. These instances were the first where the civic and environmental groups joined forces with ethnic and black residents in Hudson County, adding political strength to their actions.

in the later siting controversies, when they joined the ad hoc "Ban the Tanks" Coalition, generally they are not permanent or active members of the civic and environmental groups involved in the siting episodes. This bears out another observation by Jones:

> Most important is the probability that political action is more likely among high SES [socio-economic status] groups, a reasonable inference given that those lower on SES scales have more immediate needs than cleaner air.[34]

Stages of Development and Structure of the Groups

Theorists who have studied the genesis of social movements have formalized models of the stages through which group development and activism take place.[35] Most of the Hudson County groups were formed within the last 10 years in response to a variety of local community problems. Their first actions were on these issues, thereby preparing themselves for the larger energy siting battles that followed. Generally, the groups are not the traditional environmental organizations with narrowly focused goals, although environmental quality is of increasing concern. In the complex urban setting in which they operate, the groups were formed and have continued to respond to a wide variety of pressing urban crises. Most are general civic organizations rather than environmental groups in the narrower sense. Thus they are involved in activities such as preservation of historic landmarks, beautification programs, preservation of parkland, and issues of taxation. Their flexibility of operation, ability quickly to muster large numbers of their own members and to magnify these efforts by a "call to arms" to other groups—an indication of the large human resource upon which citizens in dense urban populations can draw—have been hallmarks of their operation. Although the groups range in size from perhaps 30 to 500 members, most have a leadership core of a dozen or so people, in the form of a board of directors or steering committee. In some respects total formal membership is irrelevant, since on an issue with broad appeal, such as opposition to a proposed energy facility, the citizen groups can generate thousands of signatures on petitions and can induce almost a thousand people to show up at a public hearing. These manifestations of community opposition are far more impressive to the political structure than are formal group membership numbers.

The groups' image is enhanced by their ability to rouse the usually "silent majority." Their formation of the "Ban the Tanks" Coalition, including poorer residents from the local neighborhoods closest to the energy facilities, was a precursor to their formation in February 1977 of the Waterfront Coalition of Hudson and Bergen Counties.[t] This coalition differs in that it is not a response to an actual siting proposal, but is instead a formal recognition that regional planning to preclude unwanted development is far better than fighting constant crises.

In seeking an institutional mechanism for regional planning,[u] the groups have exhibited some differences of opinion as to the form and extent of political authority that a regional agency should have. Having been successful in influencing their elected officials, these citizens are wary of any autonomous commission or authority (like the Hackensack Meadowlands Development Commission, geographically adjacent to their communities) that would diminish or eliminate their leverage in the decision-making process. This concern is particularly evident with some group members in Jersey City, by far the largest municipality in the county, with the largest amount of waterfront land. Although generally agreeing that regional planning is preferable to the fragmented proposals embodied in the energy siting controversies, this issue has caused dissension among the groups.

[t]This organization was predated by an even earlier entity, the Hudson Environmental Coalition, now defunct. This coalition was formed in 1972, when the first of the energy facilities was rejected, and consisted of most of the same groups in the current coalition. Its prime focus at the time was inclusion of the Hudson and Bergen County waterfronts in the then-proposed Coastal Area Facilities Review Act (CAFRA). This law, passed in 1973, excluded this geographical area as well as other urban coastal zones on the Delaware River.

[u]In a report issued to New Jersey Governor Brendan Byrne in December 1977 on development in and around Liberty State Park, a panel of the Urban Land Institute (ULI) urged the formation of a special planning and development management agency in a coordinated strategy for the waterfront area extending above and below Liberty State Park—possibly as far north as the George Washington Bridge and as far south as Bayonne. ULI suggested that the commission members could be appointed, elected, or a combination of both.[36] In 1966 the Regional Plan Association also recommended a regionalized approach to waterfront planning for the lower Hudson in New York City and New Jersey.[37] In March 1979, by executive order, Governor Byrne created the Hudson River Waterfront Study, Planning, and Development Commission encompassing 15 municipalities in Hudson and Bergen counties. This 34-member commission has representatives from municipal, county, and state government, as well as citizens outside government. Its purpose is to examine options for management and development of approximately 14 miles of the waterfront in the area suggested by ULI.

Motivations, Concerns, and Aspirations

Although the citizens opposed these siting proposals primarily because of the facilities' pollution and safety hazards, the emerging broader issue is that of land use. Living with urban blight and other urban assaults to their sensibilities, these citizens have introduced a new sense of values to challenge the existing "business as usual" fiscal planning. They see their urban community as not just an economic entity, but as a place where large concentrations of people require protective measures at least as stringent as those used for less populated rural areas. They feel that urban dwellers are an "endangered species" that must be protected, along with the whooping crane and bald eagle.

Access, diversity, and use of the waterfront to balance the heavily industrial nature of the area are the major goals of these citizen groups. In this desire they join with citizens and planners in other cities (including those in Canada and England) that are experiencing urban waterfront revitalization activities. The energy facility siting proposals were seen as contrary to this new perception and as a first step for the petrochemical industry eventually to dominate the waterfront. Citizens are aware of the rural versus urban siting dichotomy that has emerged from national and state coastal zone management legislation, and they are determined that their interests be considered along with the prevailing rural preservationist coastal focus.

Formula for Success

As indicated, several converging factors led to the extraordinary success that these citizens groups experienced in their siting battles. The inherent source of their strength resulted from forging a pluralistic coalition of citizens so that the expressed concerns and actions were not interpreted by political leaders to be narrow and elitist in nature. By joining with residents in the poorer neighborhoods closest to the unwanted facilities, they developed alliances whose numbers and political strength could not be ignored by elected officials. This basic strategy was combined with other politically sophisticated tactics, including use of the mass media to educate the public and to stimulate local and outside editorial support. Other factors included the experience of some of the groups in previous political confrontations, most with successful results; their ability to generate attendance of large numbers of citizen opponents at public meetings and to obtain thousands of petition signatures; and use of volunteer professionals to serve as expert consultants on technical issues.

That professionals and poorer residents alike were willing to join the citizen groups in their siting confrontations is indicative of another fundamental reason for their victories. The groups apparently tapped a vein of broad discontent over facility siting proposals that were seen as a bad bargain for the area from almost all viewpoints. Citizens were convinced that while pollution and safety hazards would be intensified by existence of the facilities, the community would not gain very much in return. These energy facilities are not labor-intensive. Tax benefits, in at least two of the cases, were in question because of the tax abatement mechanism; and the valuable waterfront would return to industrial use likened to that of the railroad era, precluding citizen access and enjoyment of the water's edge as well as repelling "cleaner" more labor-intensive commerce.

Anomaly or "Wave of the Future"?

Because of their deep-seated distrust in government's ability or willingness to serve them, citizen activists in Hudson County appear determined to help guide the future of their area by continued intervention in the decision-making process. Having rejected the paternalistic "father knows best" attitude of previous city bosses, these citizens have become sophisticated in using the political system to their advantage. In their attempts to bring about waterfront land use that more closely parallels their hopes for upgrading this valuable area and their community as a whole, they have been and continue to be willing to expend extraordinary efforts to affect planning and siting decisions.

Most of the citizens have lived in this urban area much of their lives and expect to remain here. Many are the survivors who chose not to flee the city during the exodus of the white middle class that began in the 1950s. They have experienced a long list of assaults on urban life and have now established limits at further degradation of the waterfront of their metropolis. Recent arrivals to the area have chosen urban life more for the hope it offers than the current reality of complex problems. They are a new breed of urban dweller, with a measure of economic mobility, who could help reverse the flow of middle-class residents from the cities for a better quality of life elsewhere. These citizens comprise one element representative of the future. If this infusion of new vitality is discouraged because urban living is too inhospitable, hope for revival of the cities may be out of reach.

Society's decisions, large and small, will determine whether our cities are to be national cultural treasures or so-called dumping grounds. The Coastal Zone Management Act's mandate "to restore and enhance the resources of the nation's coastal zone" and give "full consideration to ecological, cultural, historic and aesthetic values as well as to needs for economic development"[38] can readily apply to Hudson County and other urban coastal areas badly in need of restoration. Citizens in Hudson County are focusing attention on the hopeful possibilities they see for their troubled community. They are not likely to fade away, although dissension and fragmentation certainly could diminish their effectiveness. Because of their long record of successful civic involvement, they must be seen as serious actors in shaping the destiny of their community and certainly not as a transitory anomaly.

Whether the special chemistry of citizen action in this community can be projected to other areas cannot be certain. Some clues from urban citizen opposition to unwanted development are presently apparent (e.g., the Westway highway in New York City). Current moves to revitalize urban waterfronts in several cities throughout the nation offer further clues to changing values that could breed citizen opposition to energy and other polluting facilities. Many of these citizens would agree with William L. Slayton of Urban America, Inc., when he stated:

> The goal is the creation of an urban society that retains a continuing association with the natural world. This is achieved not by opposing all development, but by insuring that it is channeled into forms that are in harmony with the natural environment. . . . Even in our crowded urban regions of the future, there is a place for nature and a place for man.[39]

NOTES

1. Interview with Raymond Daly, Principal Labor Market Analyst, New Jersey Department of Labor and Industry, Jersey City, January 3, 1978.
2. Hudson County, *Hudson County Combined Employment and Training Administration FY 1977*, August 1976, p. 4.
3. Ibid.
4. David Morell, *Who's in Charge?—Governmental Capabilities to Make Energy Facility Siting Decisions in New Jersey* (Princeton: Princeton University, Center for Environmental Studies, Report no. PU/CES 48, July 1977), p. 81.

5. Interviews were conducted in November and December 1977 with the following Hudson County (and Bordentown) leaders involved in the siting controversies.

Rachel Budd, President, Bayonne Against Tanks, Bayonne
Theodore Conrad, President, Citizens Committee of Hudson County, Jersey City
James Dette, Chairman, Weehawken Environment Committee, Weehawken
James Drago, President, Save the Palisades Association, Union City
Joseph Duffy, President, Historic Paulus Hook Association, Jersey City
Helen Manogue, Chairman, Hoboken Environment Committee, Hoboken
James Parker, Co-Founder, Help Our Polluted Environment, Bordentown
Leo Pia, President, Union City Citizens League, Union City
Dr. Joseph Weisberg, Chairman, Jersey City Environmental Protection Committee and Chairman, Dept. of Geoscience and Geography, Jersey City State College, Jersey City

These interviews generally lasted from one-and-a-half to two-and-a-half hours each. A series of set questions were asked of each person; where different issues were more relevant to some rather than others, they were pursued on that basis.

In addition to contact with the citizen groups in Hudson County, an interview was conducted with a representative of a similar organization in Bordentown on the Delaware River in central New Jersey. Because of the similar nature of the opposition of this group to chemical storage tanks and because of Bordentown's riverfront location, it was felt that an interesting comparison of similarities and differences could be made with the Hudson County situation.

6. The following 23 groups formed the Waterfront Coalition of Hudson and Bergen Counties:

American Littoral Society
Sandy Hook, Highlands, N.J.

Association of New Jersey Environmental Commissions
Mendham, N.J.

Bayonne Against Tanks
Bayonne, N.J.

The Center for the Hudson River Valley
Wappingers Falls, N.Y.

Central New Jersey Lung Association
Clark, N.J.

Citizens Committee of Hudson County
Jersey City, N.J.

Historic Paulus Hook Association
Jersey City, N.J.

Hoboken Environment Committee
Hoboken, N.J.

Hudson County Citizens for Clean Air
Jersey City, N.J.

Jersey City Environmental Protection Committee
Jersey City, N.J.

League for Conservation Legislation
Teaneck, N.J.

League of Women Voters of Jersey City
Jersey City, N.J.

New Jersey Audubon Society
Franklin Lakes, N.J.

New Jersey Citizens for Clean Air
Short Hills, N.J.

New Jersey Conservation
Foundation
Morristown, N.J.

Puerto Rican Congress of
New Jersey
Trenton, N.J.

Regional Plan Association
New York, N.Y.

Save the Palisades
Association
Union City, N.J.

Scenic Hudson Preservation
Conference
Hewlett, L.I., N.Y.

Sierra Club, North Jersey Group
South Orange, N.J.

Union City Citizens League
Union City, N.J.

Weehawken Environment Committee
Weehawken, N.J.

West New York Concerned Citizens
West New York, N.J.

7. Interview with Daly, op. cit.
8. Interview with Myron Solinakas, Tax Assessor, City of Bayonne, January 9, 1978:

   The other companies are Bayonne Terminal Warehouse, a Division of Bayonne Industries and Howard Fuel Company. These five companies are part of 120 industries in Bayonne.

9. Interview with John Lane, Senior Planner, Hudson County Office of Planning, January 13, 1978.
10. Hudson County Planning Board, *Economic Baseline Study*, October 1974, pp. 12 and 13; and interview with Louis Carnevale, Hudson County Office of Planning, January 11, 1978.
11. *Economic Baseline Study*, ibid., p. 16.
12. Lynn Rosellini, "Reform in Jersey City," *Reader's Digest* 102, no. 610 (February 1973): pp. 85-88 (article condensed from *Parade* magazine).
13. Ibid.
14. Regional Plan Association, *The Lower Hudson*, December 1966, p. 69. The Regional Plan Association (RPA) is a nonprofit citizen organization that has been working since 1929 on planning and development of the metropolitan region surrounding the Port of New York. This area encompasses 31 counties in New York, Connecticut, and New Jersey including Hudson County.
15. 21.3 percent of Hoboken's population is below the poverty level. Median annual family income in Hoboken is $7,786 compared to $9,305 for Hudson County, $11,403 for the state, and $9,957 for the nation. The median school years completed is 8.7 compared with a national figure of 12.1 (Hoboken, N.J.: Stevens Institute, Center for Municipal Studies and Services, *Waterfront Redevelopment Project Report No. 1: Existing Conditions*, 1976), pp. 3, 30, and 31. Hoboken's low income rate is in large measure due to its high percentage of poor Puerto Rican residents who make up 22 percent of the population as compared to the 15 percent average for Hudson County as a whole. Language barriers and low literacy rates have caused a poor employment record for this group.
16. Ann Breen Cowey, "The Urban Coastal Zone: Its Definition and a Suggested Role for the Office of Coastal Zone Management," Master's Thesis, School of Government and Business Administration, George Washington University, May 1976, p. 93.

17. Robert Hanley, "Weehawken Split over Proposed Housing for the Aged," *New York Times,* January 5, 1978.
18. Gwen Shrift, "Group Claims Zoning Was Changed to Suit Dow," *Trenton Times,* February 26, 1978.
19. Gwen Shrift, "Dow Company Ponders Pull Out," *Trenton Times,* January 11, 1978.
20. Michael J. Hall, "Garden State Attitudes Show Regional Flavor," *Trenton Times,* July 10, 1977.
21. *Environmental Attitude Survey,* conducted by The Environmental Protection Committee of Jersey City and the Urban Institute of Jersey City State College, 1973.
22. Hudson County, *Hudson County's Economic Development Program,* 1976, p. 60.
23. A Rand Corporation study concluded that "The pervasive problem is not simply a loss of people in general, but the loss of middle class working people in particular, these being the ones who normally bear the principal tax burden. . . . Households are attracted by cities that also offer a comfortable climate and pleasant physical surroundings, and there is evidence that jobs may follow people to such areas contrary to the old maxim. Therefore, policies that affect the quality of local amenities; pollution abatement, the provision of cultural and recreational facilities, for example, will also lead to changes in the distribution of the urban population." Rand also found that "local fiscal incentives do not seem to play a major role in the location of industry." For a summary of the Rand study, see Mark J. Kasoff, "The Urban Impact of Federal Policies," *Nation's Cities,* November 1977, pp. 25-32.
24. Seymore Eichel, Assistant Professor of English, Jersey City State College, "Letter to the Editor," *New York Times,* January 2, 1976. © 1976 by the New York Times Company. Reprinted by permission.
25. Phyllis M. Walker, Jersey City, Letter to the Editor, *Jersey Journal,* December 10, 1975.
26. WNBC-TV Editorial, "Superport II" by Editorial Director Joe Michaels, August 4, 1976.
27. "Not Worth It," Editorial, *Jersey Journal,* October 2, 1976.
28. Laura Lewis and David Morell, *Nuclear Power and Its Opponents: A New Jersey Case Study* (Princeton: Princeton University, Center for Environmental Studies, Report PU/CES no. 39, May 1977), p. 102.
29. Joseph D. McCaffrey, "3 Seen Smoking on Tanker Deck Just Before Blast," *Philadelphia Bulletin,* April 20, 1974; and Gerald McKelvey, "11 Believed Dead on Tanker," *Philadelphia Inquirer,* April 11, 1974.
30. "Fire Rips Refinery in Philly," *The Dispatch* (Hudson County), October 13, 1975.
31. "Brooklyn Oil Tank Blaze," *The Dispatch* (Hudson County), January 6, 1976.
32. Charles O. Jones, *Clean Air: The Policies and Politics of Pollution Control* (Pittsburgh: University of Pittsburgh Press, 1975), p. 144.
33. *Ibid.*
34. *Ibid.*
35. Stan L. Albrecht, "Legacy of the Environmental Movement," *Environment and Behavior* 8, no. 2 (June 1976): 148.
36. The Urban Land Institute (ULI), *Liberty State Park—An Evaluation of Development Potential in and Around the Liberty State Park Site—for The Liberty State Park Study and Planning Commission,* a panel service

report by ULI, Washington, D.C. (panel convened in Newark, October 3-7, 1977).

37. *The Lower Hudson*, op. cit., pp. 7, 8.
38. Public Law 92-583, Coastal Zone Management Act, October 27, 1972.
39. *The Lower Hudson*, op. cit., p. 32.

Chapter 3

The Urban Waterfront: Planning Perspectives and Energy Facility Siting

Peter Denitz

One of the more fascinating, and certainly one of the least appreciated, facets of the redevelopment challenge facing American cities is occurring on the waterfront. Only in recent years has the popular perception of the urban waterfront changed, to the point where many urban dwellers no longer accept their waterfronts as the unattractive, unproductive, and polluted places they often are.

To the extent that the collective consciousness has been so raised, the time seems opportune to develop plans of imagination and substance to direct reuse of the urban waterfront. However, for many of the cities contemplating revitalization of their waterfronts, several potential problems are significant. One is the need for strategically sited onshore service facilities for the offshore oil industry. The emergence of energy self-sufficiency as national policy and major offshore explorations in the Baltimore Canyon, Georges Bank, and other new areas point to the likely need to locate major new onshore support activities. Critical issues of economic, social, and aesthetic impact require coastal cities to determine exactly what constitutes the highest and best use of their waterfronts.

To date, coastal cities have addressed the problems and opportunities of waterfront redevelopment in various ways. To understand these variations, 11 cities on the Atlantic Coast were surveyed.[1] All are old, industrial cities that have suffered decline in recent decades. Attempts at redevelopment were identified, with specific reference to the extent to which energy facility siting requirements were related to their planning and decision making. Broader perspective was then gained through an examination of the regional context of waterfront development in Hudson County, New Jersey. Special attention was paid to the attitudes of cities, the county, regional planning agencies, and various advisory boards and activist groups regarding the feasibility and acceptability of creating a regional strategy for waterfront planning.

THE CASE STUDY CITIES

The oil explorations to be conducted at Georges Bank and the Baltimore Canyon on the North Atlantic's Outer Continental Shelf (OCS) raise many questions about the siting of various onshore facilities and the advantages or disadvantages that might accrue to recipient communities. Although the ultimate land and facility requirements of the oil development process vary according to size and type of find,[a] all of the case study communities are so situated as to be of potential value to oil developers. Some places, such as New Bedford, Massachusetts, are capable of providing a full range of onshore services, while the port capabilities of places such as Trenton, New Jersey, are considerably more limited.

In this context, representatives of each case study community were asked:

To describe their existing waterfront

To discuss current and proposed land use plans in general, and specifically the extent of special waterfront planning

To describe what, if anything, has already occurred in the way of waterfront redevelopment

If in proceeding with or in contemplating waterfront plans, to discuss whether the city had considered the possible impacts of OCS-related development

To explain whether the city was actively encouraging or discouraging onshore service facilities, and why

To discuss their view of the potential role of regional planning in waterfront planning

[a]See Appendix A.

Jersey City, New Jersey
(1976 Estimated Population: 259,790)

Jersey City's seven-mile-long waterfront has proved to be hard to manage and, despite ambitious urban renewal plans dating from 1971, hard to develop.[b] The existing waterfront is characterized by "marginal" industrial uses, a moderately sized (97 acres) containership facility, and large expanses of vacant or underutilized land (about 2,000 acres). Two major, ongoing waterfront projects are of particular interest.

The northern portion of the city's waterfront has been designated an urban renewal area; multiuse development is envisioned, with industrial, commercial, and residential uses. Although intensity of use projections for this 600-acre strip have been revised downward, plans call for construction of 5,000 to 8,000 residential units, the accommodation of 45,000 office workers in 8 million square feet of office space, and industrial uses accommodating 10,000 workers. Developers are being sought under the auspices of the city's economic development office.

The Liberty State Park project for 600 acres (35 acres of which have been developed to date) of Jersey City's southern waterfront has attracted regional and national attention. The report of the Liberty State Park Study and Planning Commission recommends a balanced combination of "active and passive, structured and unstructured, recreational activities."[2] While designed primarily as a "green" waterfront park, plans include rehabilitation of the old Jersey Central Railroad passenger terminal, development of a wide variety of exhibition spaces, a possible golf course, and ferry service to Ellis Island and Liberty Island. Several problems of conflicting uses were identified by the study commission. These include inadequate vehicle access, and the existence of the Liberty Industrial Park to the south, which the commission regards as an incompatible use.

The city planning office indicated no interest in OCS development, pointing to the rejection of major energy facility proposals in recent years. The city explicitly intends to reject new energy-related proposals as incompatible with its waterfront redevelopment plans.

Hoboken, New Jersey
(1976 Estimated Population: 46,567)

Hoboken is the only Hudson County community examined whose waterfront (approximately one mile long) is built up right to the

[b]See Chapter 2 for a detailed examination of Jersey City.

river's edge. This waterfront, once devoted exclusively to railroads and industry, now houses only two major industrial users (Maxwell House Coffee and American Can Company). The Erie-Lackawanna Passenger Terminal is a major waterfront facility, recently designated as a national historic building and the recipient of a $5-million federal grant for rehabilitation. This active station (28,000 commuters pass through it daily)[3] is regarded as a catalyst for commercial and residential revitalization along the entire Hoboken waterfront. The Stevens Institute of Technology and three waterfront piers (all in good condition, although only one—owned by the Port Authority—is active) are other waterfront uses. Redevelopment plans for this waterfront area anticipate a combination of apartment, hotel, office, retail commercial, and conference center development.[4]

Despite formidable economic problems, severe lack of open space, and pressures for incompatible land use, Hoboken has been active in housing, waterfront, and general economic development efforts. The city benefits from an unusually well-preserved and low-priced stock of brownstone buildings, unsurpassed views of midtown Manhattan, and excellent public transportation; it has been successful in attracting an increasingly affluent and involved citizenry to its areas near the waterfront.[5]

Hoboken planners and citizens express much concern that potential waterfront uses be harmonious with the city's redevelopment plans. Accordingly, future energy facility proposals will be opposed, as they have been in the past.

Bayonne, New Jersey
(1976 Estimated Population: 73,635)

The Bayonne waterfront is characterized by heavy industrial uses along its eastern side and primarily park and recreational uses along the western waterfront. The western shore is planned for the right-of-way for a new highway along Newark Bay to connect the Bayonne Bridge and State Highway 440, although this alignment has been opposed by the Regional Plan Association as obstructing views and use of the bayfront. The city maintains two large parks on the bay-front, along which faces most of the city's housing. A 20-acre park, now half complete, is situated on the southern waterfront (Kill van Kull). City officials note that this park is accessible to nearby low- and moderate-income housing projects and public transportation.

According to city planners, OCS development has been considered in its planning process, and unofficial policy at this time is that Bayonne would be receptive to "appropriately scaled" onshore service facilities along its industralized eastern shore. These considerations have not gone beyond the level of "in-house" discussions, however.

Elizabeth, New Jersey
(1976 Estimated Population: 114,795)

The Elizabeth waterfront is characterized by several major industrial uses. Pittsburgh Plate Glass Company and the Singer Company account for 50 percent of the waterfront; underdeveloped land and vacant structures account for most of the remainder. As is the case with many of the 11 cities studied, Elizabeth owns only a small portion of its waterfront, including a small play lot situated between two industrial sites. The city has attempted to have itself designated as a regional entity by the Army Corps of Engineers in order to become eligible for financial and personnel support for a waterfront cleanup effort.

One city planner indicated that while the city had no specific plan for the waterfront at this time, he believed that this area would emerge as one of primary concern. He suggested that the unimplemented 1968 plans for Elizabethport—combining park and marina development with housing and rehabilitation—would serve as the basis for a new waterfront planning effort. In addition, tentative interest was expressed in consolidating the scattered waterfront for industrial uses, although the feasibility of such a plan is considered problematic at best. Identification in early 1979 of the serious safety and pollution hazards posed by the 50,000(+) barrels of toxic and hazardous wastes stored at the defunct Chemical Control Corporation facility on the Elizabeth waterfront brought renewed (and long overdue) attention to this area.

The planning office was aware of no energy facility proposals that might involve Elizabeth. Local planners did not believe the city would be interested in any new onshore uses that would be counter to the "interests of waterfront renewal."

Linden, New Jersey
(1976 Estimated Population: 42,150)

Linden, which has no full-time planning staff, owns none of its waterfront. The Exxon Corporation's large Bayway refinery is the primary waterfront presence. The city engineer indicated that "the Federal government has been looking for fuel oil storage sites. . . . Linden was recently inventoried as part of that search." This engineer indicated that the city's receptivity to any such proposal would depend on "exactly what would be stored, how much would be stored, and how many people would be involved." He summed up the city's attitude as one of "wait and see."

Asbury Park, New Jersey
(1976 Estimated Population: 16,775)

The planning board secretary of Asbury Park, which apparently has no planning staff, was reluctant to discuss waterfront planning matters. It appears, however, that the city has no waterfront plan and has taken no position on OCS-related development.

Camden, New Jersey
(1976 Estimated Population: 105,600)

Camden's economic development director described that city's waterfront—directly across the Delaware River from downtown Philadelphia—as an important part of its overall community and economic development efforts. The tangible manifestations of this interest to date are a $10-million waterfront park, which will be constructed soon, and a $10-million extension of the Beckett Street Terminal facility. These plans will not affect uses along that portion of the waterfront (approximately 2.5 miles) now actively utilized.

City officials expressed interest in attracting OCS-related onshore facilities, particularly for ship repair and small ship construction (there are currently two such firms in Camden). In preparing both general and energy related waterfront plans, the city has been cooperating with Camden County, NJDEP, and Rutgers University.

Trenton, New Jersey
(1976 Estimated Population: 106,625)

Although most of the Trenton waterfront is separated from the rest of the city by Route 29, several recent proposals point to a possible revival in port, manufacturing, and recreational uses. The city's 40-acre marine terminal area is the subject of a study to determine whether the facility could once again handle shipping. A city planner indicated that "if the study finds the terminal can be used as a port, the South Jersey Port Corporation would be invited to lease it and operate it." A negative feasibility study will probably lead to city efforts to use the property for industrial uses (apparently private companies have expressed interest in the terminal facility).

City officials indicated "no strong feelings" regarding energy facility siting. The precise character of future waterfront uses and the city's response to specific proposals will depend greatly on the outcome of the marine terminal study.

With regard to recreational use of the waterfront, two groups—the Coast Guard Auxiliary and the Puerto Rican Community Association—have offered to take over areas south of marine terminal for boat launching and inspection and picnic area development, respectively. The city appears inclined to enter into an agreement with these groups pemitting nonprofit and public uses while stipulating that they could be turned out on notice.

Chester, Pennsylvania
(1977 Estimated Population: 51,000)

With "little new" reported along the industrialized Chester waterfront, the city is attempting to retain existing industry and encourage new industry. Approximately half its three-mile waterfront is in active use, with Sun Shipbuilders and Scott Paper the primary facilities. Approximately one-half mile of waterfront is inactive, containing scattered warehousing and the Delaware County Sewage Treatment Plant. The remaining mile of waterfront is being incrementally acquired (over 100 separate ownerships are involved) by the Philadelphia Electric Company for an unspecified future use (it is speculated that the utility sees this as the site of a fossil fuel or nuclear generating plant). This land is being cleared as acquired, and it will remain vacant indefinitely. Because of the lack of current alternative uses the city has not resisted Philadelphia Electric's acquisition, although locating a large power plant at this site is considered to be a long-term detriment to Chester's economic development. Removal of this tract is felt to preclude any new heavy industrial uses along the waterfront. There are no recreational areas along the Delaware waterfront; and no such plans are under consideration.

City planners do not believe that Chester is a likely recipient of OCS-related onshore facilities, due to a generally shallow waterfront unable to accommodate deep draft vessels. While the city would like to conduct landfill operations to the pierhead line, cost considerations have prevented any action on this proposal.

New Bedford, Massachusetts
(1977 Estimated Population: 100,000)

The newly established 200-mile fishing limit, interest in the Georges Bank and Baltimore Canyon as a possible location for offshore oil development, interest in establishing tourism as a local industry, and interest in strengthening overall economic development have led the city of New Bedford and neighboring town of Fairhaven to develop a joint master plan for the harbor. The New Bedford-Fairhaven Harbor is the area's most important economic and natural resource. The harbor is being planned to reinforce its role as a major fishing and cargo port, and to be used as a center for water-related manufacturing, a support base for offshore oil exploration and production, a tourist attraction and revitalized downtown, and the residence for more than 1,600 people. These uses are regarded by the city as mutually reinforcing, and they are being vigorously pursued. Vacant buildings and undeveloped land—constituting over 25 percent of the 637-acre harbor land area—are considered assets because the city wishes to accommodate new and expanded uses. To protect the fishing industry, which is the city's livelihood, the city will attempt to guide OCS-related development to sites meeting oil industry needs while causing the least conflict with existing harbor uses.

New Bedford and Fairhaven are actively seeking OCS development. The mayor's committee on offshore oil is the center for broad-based citizen participation, assessing the possible impacts of OCS development and serving as an advocacy group for both the city and the harbor. Factors favorable to OCS development in New Bedford are its wide and deep harbor, its relative proximity (under 130 miles) to both exploration areas, extensive vacant and rehabilitated dock and warehouse space, major shipyards and specialized marine services, the third largest airport in Massachusetts, and an adequate, skilled labor pool. Furthermore, to the extent that local receptivity is a significant factor in attracting the oil industry (often, of course, this is a critical factor), New Bedford has shown such interest and initiative. And although New Bedford does not seek regional assistance in waterfront or OCS planning, the coordination and cooperation between New Bedford and Fairhaven are impressive and mutually beneficial.

New Haven, Connecticut
(1970 Population: 137,707)

The 16-square mile New Haven harbor is an important chemical and oil port and a less important dry cargo and container port. It is also the site of major oyster farming operations. A consultant's study of the harbor has recommended improvement of open spaces (both for recreational use and development of warehousing) as well as mixed commercial and residential development.

Two primary reasons are cited why New Haven is not a likely site for OCS-related development: the city is located too far into Long Island Sound to attract such development, and the state of Connecticut has demonstrated an "absence of enthusiasm" for major oil-related development.

THE REGIONAL CONTEXT OF WATERFRONT DEVELOPMENT

Waterfronts, by their very nature, are regional entities. The effect of development along the riverbanks can be felt for miles upstream and downstream. Waterfronts need special attention.[6]

Throughout this research, city consideration of the possible benefits from regional cooperation in waterfront planning and development was noticeably absent. Of the 11 cities examined, only 6 had strong sentiments—pro or con—about regional cooperation; the other 5 were neutral.

Jersey City questioned the effectiveness—actual and potential—of the official regional planning agency: the Tri-State Regional Planning Commission. However, Jersey City chose to rely on its own staff and on special interest groups (such as the Waterfront Coalition of Hudson and Bergen) to address local waterfront planning concerns.

Hoboken, while also unhappy with the performance of Tri-State, would like to see greater regional cooperation. The city believes that the plans and actions of its neighbors will be important factors in the ultimate success or failure of Hoboken's own waterfront redevelopment efforts. The Regional Plan Association (RPA), while a private and unofficial voice, has had a great effect on Hoboken's efforts. The RPA's *Lower Hudson Plan* in 1966 identified Hoboken as "a special place" with exploitable assets in location, housing, and character.[7]

Elizabeth, too, seeks greater regional cooperation in waterfront development, at this stage primarily to test proposals and identify possible development funding sources. In its waterfront planning, Camden has sought cooperation with the county, NJDEP, and Rutgers University.

Chester has cooperated with the Delaware Valley Regional Planning Commission in the early stages of the coastal zone management (CZM) study. However, the city believes that if and when the CZM study is completed, state regulatory legislation would probably follow, abrogating the city's land use powers. Chester does not wish to surrender its home rule and land use planning prerogatives.

New Bedford places little currency in the ability of its regional planning entity, the Southeastern Regional Planning and Economic Development District (SRPEDD), to address regional development concerns. The city believes that any existing regional planning agency should not be involved in implementing development plans or in resource management. Furthermore, given the competitive nature of attracting OCS development, SRPEDD is thought to be unable to mediate between New Bedford-Fairhaven and Fall River, Massachusetts, the latter also pursuing OCS-related development. Finally, in cooperating with Fairhaven, New Bedford feels that the entire harbor area already is being planned in a unified, sensitive, and effective manner.

Hudson County presents an unusually pronounced but nevertheless instructive example of the need for regional cooperation. The contiguous Hudson County communities share a remarkable commonality of interests and problems: high unemployment, poor housing, high density, inadequate transportation, and insufficient park and recreational facilities. Despite these and other common concerns, interjurisdictional cooperation does not yet characterize planning in Hudson County.

In response to the call for a regional planning mechanism, New Jersey's Governor Brendan Byrne in April 1979 created the Hudson River Waterfront Study, Planning and Development Commission, encompassing 15 municipalities in Hudson and Bergen counties. This 34-member commission has representatives of municipal, county, and state government, as well as knowledgeable citizens outside government. Its purpose is to examine options for management and development of approximately 14 miles along this urban waterfront.

The urban waterfront represents a special confluence of local and regional and public and private interests. In this multiplicity lies both the problem and the opportunity. Most municipalities are loathe to surrender to any larger jurisdiction their long-standing home rule authority to plan and manage growth. Privately owned industrial, warehouse, or transportation facilities, while perhaps inactive or in serious disrepair, represent a potential resource for reuse. Such lands and facilities, contrary to appearance, are not always "soft" real estate. Conflicting and mutually misunderstood goals among the many agencies and jurisdictions with waterfront interests also pose problems.

To date, New Jersey's coastal management effort has been able to prevent only the most serious degradation of the urban waterfront in Hudson County.[8] Although the opening of Liberty State Park and the cleanup of harbor debris in this area have offered some hope of future improvement, the lack of application of the federal Coastal Zone Management Act, except through riparian statutes, and exclusion of the area from the state's Coastal Area Facility Review Act (CAFRA) leave Hudson County communities with little protection from faulty land use proposals.

The record of existing regional agencies in guiding waterfront planning is also not encouraging. The Tri-State Regional Planning Commission, in its *Coastal Zone Management Perspectives*,[9] tends toward oversimplification of waterfront and land use problems and solutions. While identifying the "unprofitable and archaic" character of much of the waterfront and establishing a "goal" of planning compatible with the marine environment, it is nowhere made clear whether "such a goal should be applied across the board, i.e., in urban economic clusters, or only in suburban areas."[10] Unfortunately, such a lack of specificity creates a planning vacuum, often with deleterious effects.

A study of the Hoboken waterfront illustrates how serious such generalizations can be. Hoboken was designated by Tri-State as a "Primary Urban Economic Cluster," a category that in effect sanctions almost any type of facility or development. This designation resulted in Hoboken—which has consistently resisted energy facilities in or near the city—being "assaulted by one heavy industrial proposal after another (including oil refinery, STOL-port, and tank storage facilities) because regional zoning permitted it."[11] Clearly, the need exists for land use designations to be consistent with the reality of the urban waterfront. This example underlines a primary defect of much regional planning; namely, the inability to guide development at the project scale and a tendency to resort to land classifications so broad as to be misleading or inappropriate in the specific applications.

Hudson County's *Land Use Study and Plan* is likewise misleading.[12] Reflecting the Tri-State designations, large areas of the Hoboken waterfront are classified for development of industrial, transportation, and utility facilities. Nearly the entire Hudson County river waterfront is so designated, quite surprising in light of repeated calls from the Regional Plan Association and the Waterfront Coalition of Hudson and Bergen Counties for public acquisition of these lands for park and recreational purposes, and in view of the rejection of several proposed energy facilities in this area.

The Regional Plan Association has been an influential and highly respected, if unofficial, voice in regional affairs. As noted earlier, RPA first identified the potential for waterfront redevelopment in

Hoboken as well as along New Jersey's entire Hudson River waterfront. In brief, the *Lower Hudson Plan* calls for public acquisition of all available land along the Palisades with continuous waterfront parkland and properly scaled residential and commercial development from the George Washington Bridge to the northern boundary of Hoboken. From Hoboken to the Morris Canal Basin in Jersey City, large-scale housing and park development is encouraged with commercial and residential uses proposed for Hoboken and retention of active industrial uses throughout (with proper buffering of incompatible mixed uses). From Jersey City south to Bayonne, harbor and industrial uses were considered most appropriate.

It seems clear that the functionally variegated but ecologically and conceptually singular character of the lower Hudson River waterfront requires that it be planned for and administered as a single environmental, social, and economic unit. Common concerns related to the river—water quality, erosion and sedimentation, fish and wildlife, energy and the environment, transportation and shipping, recreational needs, socioeconomic impacts—cannot be conclusively addressed by any one city. The river is now under a variety of controls and jurisdictions that have, as a rule, not functioned well on interrelated concerns. "Controls are imperfectly related because combining coastal uses with resource continuance and renewal has not been the guiding aim."[13]

Perhaps as many as 50 federal agencies have ownership and regulatory interests along this waterfront. Several interstate agencies—most notably the Port Authority—play a major economic coastal role. And, of course, regulation takes place at the local level, "where much building, digging, dredging, and filling is programmed and approved."[14] If individual agencies or jurisdictions were performing singular roles adequately, the case could be made for nonintervention. However, duplication of effort without coordination exists for almost every waterfront function, necessitating regional action of some kind.

The challenge in waterfront planning appears to be threefold: (1) understanding the changing character of the waterfront in both a local and regional context; (2) recognizing the roles of existing waterfront agencies; and (3) developing a regional governing mechanism to which would be assigned those functions properly addressed at the regional level.

The necessary conditions for such a regional arrangement are feasibility and acceptability. Costikyan has described the former as the determination of "which services are best provided within a... jurisdiction, which mechanisms are most appropriate for the planning and delivery of those services, and what the impact of these mechanisms would be."[15] Acceptability means accounting for the existing structures and, more importantly, understanding the reality of relationships among residents, local governments, counties, states, and the new coordinating body. With local attitudes toward regionalism running from cautious acceptance to apathy to outright antagonism, a strategy gradually to assume responsibility without the appearance of cooptation is of fundamental importance. This is underscored by the apprehension exhibited by many waterfront activists in Hudson County—a traditional source of support for comprehensive planning—who fear the effect of a locality-insensitive, autonomous regional authority.

Suggestions for an appropriately scaled regional body[16] have included utilization of existing regional agencies (such as Tri-State,[17] the Palisades Interstate Park Commission, the Liberty State Park Study Commission, and others), creation of a joint state-local design planning body,[18] and the establishment of the Waterfront Coalition of Hudson and Bergen Counties as a body responsible for protection, reclamation, conservation, recreation, general land use, and economic planning. The latter arrangement has been endorsed by the Liberty State Park Study Commission, and formation of the Hudson River Waterfront Study, Planning and Development Commission in 1979 was very much along these lines. This body consists of representatives of affected municipalities and state agencies, plus citizens. All of these various schemes regard the proper unit of analysis and management as the New Jersey waterfront from the George Washington Bridge to the southern tip of Bayonne. Although cooperation between New York and New Jersey would be informally encouraged, it is felt that the legal and coordinative problems of formal interstate arrangements preclude effective planning.

As Hudson County's waterfront is improved, consideration will have to be given to the spillover effects of renewal. In particular, the Liberty State Park Study Commission identified the dangers of real estate speculation and displacement of existing residents in neighborhoods near the waterfront (already occurring in parts of Jersey City and Hoboken). Early local and regional attention to such matters might help mitigate these negative spillover effects.

Apparently not yet fully considered are possible arrangements for the sharing of revenues and costs induced by new development, the type, magnitude, and location of which would be guided by regional planning. It is imperative that each municipality benefit from new growth in the region. Without some kind of tax-sharing mechanism, there is little incentive for cities to surrender their planning and development prerogative.

"The certainty of change and the uncertainty of the exact shape of the changes makes future requirements difficult to predict."[19] Hudson County has gone far in recent years to reduce the uncertainty accompanying change. Most local governments appear to be viewing their waterfront in new ways. Impressive renewal efforts are underway or contemplated in several places, with waterfront improvements serving as the catalyst for citywide redevelopment plans. Most promising is the emergence of articulate and involved citizen groups, whose efforts have been a principal force in the rejection of major industrial or energy facilities in Hudson County.[c] Their success has been nearly complete, and it has contributed to changing perceptions in Hudson County and elsewhere.

With major OCS-related facilities unlikely in Hudson County, issues of waterfront access and diversity have assumed high priority. There remains a need to fulfill critical open space needs while buttressing a declining local and regional economy. It is essential to acknowledge the special character of this Hudson River waterfront area with imaginative and sufficiently elaborated planning efforts so that it can be the nucleus for continuing and wide-ranging revitalization activities. Whether other energy facilities not related to OCS development have a place in such a future will depend upon the particular type of facility contemplated and such factors as its pollution potential, land use compatibility, and employment generation. Consideration of the ability to integrate energy facilities into the overall coastal setting is essential in judging the suitability of such operations for Hudson County as well as for many other coastal areas.

[c]See Chapter 2.

NOTES

1. The survey of case study cities was originally to be accomplished through a survey of master plans, zoning ordinances, and existing planning and development proposals. It soon became apparent, however, that many such documents, in addition to being out-of-date (and admittedly of little guidance to local officials), were primarily or exculsively concerned with nonwaterfront matters. Because of these deficiencies, telephone interviews became the primary means of gathering information. Discussions from five minutes to one hour were conducted, generally with the planning or community development directors of the case study cities and appropriate non-local jurisdictions. Secondary information sources included newspapers, public documents, advisory reports, and site visits.

2. State of New Jersey, Liberty State Park Study and Planning Commission, *Guidelines for the Development and Financing of Liberty State Park* (Trenton: December 19, 1977).

3. Helen Manogue, *Hoboken Waterfront Redevelopment Project Report No. 1: Existing Conditions* (Hoboken, N.J.: Stevens Institute of Technology, Center for Municipal Studies and Services, January 1976), p. 57.

4. Ibid., p. 59.

5. Vacant land and facilities also represent a potential means for public acquisition through foreclosure. In Hoboken, for example, tax liens exist and are liable for foreclosure action on 15.3 percent of the waterfront renewal area, ibid., p. 40.

6. William Shore, ed., *The Lower Hudson Plan* (New York: Regional Plan Association, December 1966).

7. Ibid.

8. New Jersey, Department of Environmental Protection, *Options for New Jersey's Developed Coast* (Trenton: NJDEP, 1979) and *State of New Jersey, Coastal Zone Management Program—Bay and Ocean Shore Segment* (Trenton: NJDEP, May 1978).

9. Tri-State Regional Planning Commission, *The Tri-State Coastal Zone: Management Perspectives* (New York: Tri-State, April 1975).

10. Manogue, op. cit., p. 55.

11. Ibid.

12. Hudson County Planning Board, *Land Use Study and Plan* (Jersey City: Hudson County Planning Board, December 1974).

13. Tri-State, op. cit., p. 46.

14. Ibid., p. 47.

15. Edward N. Costikyan and Maxwell Lehman, *New Strategies for Regional Cooperation: A Model for the Tri-State New York-New Jersey-Connecticut Area* (New York: Praeger, 1973).

16. The Costikyan model for regional cooperation (ibid.) envisions "a number of multi-purpose entities, each with sufficient planning and executive powers to deal with the regional matter entrusted to it." These functional areas include transportation, water supply and distribution, air quality control, water pollution and sewage control, solid waste disposal, parks and recreation, housing, planning and economic activity, and electric power supply.
    There are at least two deficiencies to this scheme in considering the Hudson County waterfront. First, the functional regions are too extensive to address project scale development (this objection is partially addressed by Costikyan in his suggestion that "sub-regional districts" be created to deal with matters affecting only part of the region). Second, organized around single functional areas, there is the tendency to view the waterfront in the uncoordinated manner in which it is currently regarded, rather than at a true tri-state scale. The systems complexity of the Hudson County waterfront would require cooperation and coordination among so many functional agencies that accountability and decisiveness would not be encouraged.

17. Costikyan (ibid.) envisioned Tri-State as the overall coordinating body for the regional cooperative body he proposes. The Tri-State Commission Chairman has recommended a major restructuring of the commission, feeling that it has not lived up to its potential as a force for improvement in the region.

18. Shore, op. cit., p. 47.

19. Ibid., p. 18.

Chapter 4

Air Quality and Urban Waterfront Development: A Review of Government Regulations and Attitudes

Thomas Ash

Air quality is one of the principal constraints to the siting of new facilities on urban waterfronts, especially those—typified by major energy facilities—with high levels of air pollution even when using advanced abatement technology. Many urban areas still fail to meet national ambient air quality standards.

Air quality issues in Hudson County illustrate this concern. Afflicted with one of the highest cancer rates in the United States, the county has been designated as a nonattainment area for almost every category of air pollutant. It is part of a region that the U.S. Environmental Protection Agency (EPA) has ranked second in priority nationally for pollution abatement. Hudson County is one of the most heavily industrialized areas in New Jersey, the most industrial state in the nation. And it is the locale for continuing pressures to site new energy- and petroleum-related facilities.

Certain onshore support facilities for OCS development, such as for oil storage, transfer, and refining, add a tremendous amount of pollution to the air. Some argue that these facilities should be banned in existing nonattainment areas. On the other hand, there is considerable sentiment favoring siting of such installations only in areas in which they already exist in order to preserve pristine areas from such deleterious impacts.[a] Such a rural preservationist policy makes Hudson County a prime siting candidate for such facilities.

Many Hudson County residents are opposed to the siting of OCS facilities. This opposition results from several unsuccessful attempts to locate oil storage terminals in the area.[b]

Air quality control in Hudson County is largely determined by governmental regulations, policies, and attitudes. There has been an increasing separation of stationary and mobile source regulation. In mobile source regulation, increasing interest is being devoted to emissions controls and less to forms of indirect pollution control inherent in land use regulation. EPA has backed away from transportation control plan (TCP) enforcement, and is now encouraging localities to develop their own TCPs, which are likely to be quite different from EPA's original proposals. All levels of government seem to have agreed to disagree on the subject of urban versus rural siting of major emission sources.

A HUDSON COUNTY AIR POLLUTION PROFILE

Hudson County is part of the New Jersey-New York-Connecticut Interstate Air Quality Control Region. This is a nonattainment area for national air pollutant standards in sulfur dioxide (SO_2), particulates, nitrogen oxides (NO_x), carbon monoxide (CO), and hydrocarbons (HC). Mobile sources account for approximately 90 percent of the carbon monoxide and 60 percent of the hydrocarbons in the ambient atmosphere. Petrochemical facilities emit large quantities of sulfur dioxide and hydrocarbons. The region contains many petrochemical facilities, particularly in Hudson County and in the Port Newark-Port Elizabeth industrial complex to its southwest.

Heavily industrialized Hudson County is a major contributor to the region's pollution problems. Yet many of the county's pollution problems arise not in the local area itself but from its regional and geographical location downwind from many industrial facilities. Exxon, Texaco, and Hess operate storage terminals in Bayonne. The Lincoln and Holland Tunnels contribute to high concentrations of vehicular activity, especially in Jersey City. Much of this traffic has its origin and destination outside of the county. According to John

[a]See Chapter 1.

[b]See Chapter 2.

Lane, a Hudson County planner, Hudson County could meet the ambient air quality standards if it were not for the Lincoln and Holland Tunnels and the New Jersey Turnpike Extension.[1]

Readings conducted by the Division of Environmental Quality of the New Jersey Department of Environmental Protection (NJDEP) indicate the severity of the Hudson County air quality situation. In Jersey City in 1975, air quality was rated "satisfactory" 22 percent of the time, "unsatisfactory" 52 percent of the time, and "unhealthy" 27 percent of the time. The air quality situation in Bayonne was better, rated "unsatisfactory" or "unhealthy" only 36 percent of the time in 1974.[2]

Tables 4-1 to 4-3 compare the national ambient air quality standards to the situation in Hudson County. As shown, the most serious pollutants in the area are hydrocarbons, carbon monoxide, and particulates. This has led to the general opinion that the control of mobile sources in the county, combined with continued regulation of stationary source emissions, can greatly reduce the pollution problem. New energy facilities in the area would intensify the hydrocarbon situation, and sulfur dioxide might become a significant problem as well.

One factor intensifying pollution in this area is the lack of space. By one estimate, 96 percent of Hudson County is built up.[3] Although this estimate may be somewhat high,[4] there are only two substantial open areas: the Hackensack Meadowlands and 2,000 vacant areas on the Jersey City waterfront.

AIR POLLUTION CONTROL IN HUDSON COUNTY

Federal Involvement

Pollution control measures can be divided into two categories: stationary and mobile source regulation. Stationary source regulation is based primarily on use of best available control technology (BACT) and recently on an "emission offset" approach in non-attainment areas.[c] Best available control technology requires that each source install equipment to reduce emissions to the maximum

[c]These policies have been modified in late 1979 by EPA, which instituted the "bubble" policy that allows each facility's manager to control individual stack emissions as long as the total emissions do not violate an agreed-upon overall standard for the facility.

Table 4-1. Summary of National Ambient Air Quality Standards[a]

Pollutant	Averaging Time	Primary Standards	Secondary Standards
Particulate matter	Annual (geometric mean) 24-hour[b]	75 $\mu g/m^3$	60 $\mu g/m^3$
Sulfur oxides	Annual (arithmetic mean) 24-hour[b]	80 $\mu g/m^3$ (0.03 ppm) 365 $\mu g/m^3$ (0.14 ppm)	
	3-hour[b]		1300 $\mu g/m^3$ (0.5 ppm)
Carbon monoxide	8-hour[b]	10 mg/m^3 (9 ppm)	(Same as primary)
	1-hour[b]	40 mg/m^3 (35 ppm)	(Same as primary)
Nitrogen dioxide	Annual (arithmetic mean)	100 $\mu g/m^3$ (0.05 ppm)	(Same as primary)
Photochemical oxidants	1-hour[b]	160 $\mu g/m^3$ (0.08 ppm)	(Same as primary
Hydrocarbons (nonmethane)	3-hour[b] (6 to 9 A.M.)	160 $\mu g/m^3$ (0.24 ppm)	(Same as primary)

Source: Air Quality Data—1975 Annual Statistics (Washington, D.C.: U.S. Environmental Protection Agency), May 1977.

[a]The air quality standards and a description of the Federal Reference Methods (FRM) were published on April 30, 1971, in 42 CFR 410, recodified to 40 CFR 50 on November 25, 1972. The new FRM for nitrogen dioxide was published on December 1, 1976, as 40 CFR 50, Appendix F.

[b] Not to be exceeded more than once per year.

extent practicable. Emissions offset means that for every increase in emissions from a new source, there must be a corresponding or greater decrease from existing sources somewhere else in the airshed.[d] Mobile source regulations are based on new car pollution control technology and on various transportation control measures. The general theory is that by cutting down as much as possible

[d]See Chapter 5.

Table 4-2. Air Pollution in Jersey City, 1975

Type of Pollutant	Relevant Measurement	Number of Observations	Minimum Observation	Percentiles							Maximum Observation	Violation of Primary Standard	Violation of Secondary Standard
				10	30	50	70	90	95	99			
Particulates	μg/m³ per 24 hours	27	45	58	65	87	94	152	157	160	160	Yes	Yes
Sulfur dioxide	μg/m³ per 24 hours	28	3	3	3	14	27	60	111	182	182	No	No
Carbon monoxide	mg/m³ per 1 hour	3771	.3	1.7	3.2	4.8	7.8	14.0	17.1	24.2	42.9	Yes	Yes
Carbon monoxide	ppm per 8 hours (1976)	—	—	—	—	—	—	—	—	—	20.4	Yes[a]	Yes[a]
Nitrogen dioxide	μg/m³ per 24 hours	25	10	14	28	37	43	56	61	68	68	No	No

Sources: Air Quality Data—1975 Annual Statistics (Washington, D.C.: U.S. Environmental Protection Agency), May 1977; and Air Quality in New Jersey Compared with Air Quality Standards—1976 (Trenton: N.J. Department of Environmental Protection), June 1977.

[a]There were 167 violations of the 8-hour CO standard in 1976.

Table 4-3. Air Pollution in Bayonne, 1975

Type of Pollutant	Relevant Measurement	Number of Observations	Minimum Observation	Percentiles							Maximum Observation	Violation of Primary Standard	Violation of Secondary Standard
				10	30	50	70	90	95	99			
Particulates	μg/m³ per 24 hours	28	24	40	52	72	88	114	119	129	129	Yes	Yes
Sulfur dioxide	ppm per 24 hours (1976)	—	—	—	—	—	—	—	—	—	.09	No	No
Carbon monoxide	mg/m³ per 1 hour	4235	.3	.7	1.1	1.5	2.0	3.1	4.0	7.2	12.6	No	No
Carbon monoxide	ppm per 8 hours (1976)	—	—	—	—	—	—	—	—	—	13.7	Yes[a]	Yes[a]
Nitrogen dioxide	ppm annual average (1976)	—	—	—	—	—	—	—	—	—	.029	No	No
Hydrocarbons	ppm per 3 hours	—	—	—	—	—	—	—	—	—	4.6	Yes[b]	Yes[b]

Sources: Air Quality Data—1975 Annual Statistics (Washington, D.C.: U.S. Environmental Protection Agency), May 1977; and Air Quality in New Jersey Compared with Air Quality Standards—1976 (Trenton: N.J. Department of Environmental Protection), June 1977.

[a]There were two violations of the 8-hour CO standard during 1976.
[b]The HC standard was exceeded on all days for which data are available.

on stationary source measures, pollution standards can be attained in nonattainment areas by reducing auto emissions and vehicle miles traveled (VMT) while still allowing for new growth. Emissions offset is meant to allow this growth while ensuring that pollution from stationary sources does not increase. According to one air quality official at EPA's Region II Office in New York City, energy facility development in Hudson County would not worsen the air quality there because any increase in emissions from these facilities would have to be matched by corresponding decreases elsewhere in the area.[5]

EPA was designated the principal actor in pollution control on the federal level by the Clean Air Act of 1967 and its subsequent 1970 and 1977 amendments. Federal financial and technical assistance are provided to state and local governments to establish and maintain pollution control mechanisms. The act recognized pollution control as a national priority, and its provisions were intended to enhance and protect the nation's air resources. The act authorized EPA to establish primary ambient air quality standards (to protect public health and welfare) and secondary standards to protect property. EPA was empowered to accept or reject state implementation plans (SIPs), which detail how each state planned to meet those standards. If a SIP were found unsatisfactory, EPA was to develop one of its own for the state.

The Clean Air Act called for air pollution to be controlled through better source controls, land use planning, and transportation control plans. Of these three aspects, only source controls and transportation control plans received any attention, and only source controls met with any acceptance. Both TCPs and land use planning intruded greatly into what is considered local prerogatives. For instance, the TCP for northern New Jersey, as developed by EPA, required improved public transit, bus-only lanes, controls and restrictions of on-street parking, park-and-ride lots, bicycle and pedestrian lanes, carpooling, staggered work hours and road user charges in addition to automobile inspection, retrofitting of pollution control devices, and reduction of emissions through improved traffic flow.[6] Any hope of implementing such a TCP died long before the plan was officially nullified by the 1977 amendments to the Clean Air Act.

The 1977 amendments came about as it was realized that the timetable for meeting national ambient air quality standards could not be met. The automobile emission standards deadline was extended from 1977 to 1978; the HC standard was delayed for two years, and the CO standard for three years. A delayed, lower final standard was set for NO_x. The emissions offset policy was officially incorporated into the act as a means of permitting industrial growth in nonattainment areas while moving toward attainment of standards by fixed, though delayed, deadlines. All states are to submit revised SIPs that use all "reasonably available control measures" to provide for attainment of standards by 1982. If a state demonstrates by 1979 that the standards cannot be met by 1982, the deadline for attainment may be extended to 1987. In this case, the SIP revision must contain provisions for alternate site analysis for new or relocating major emitters, a schedule for vehicle inspection and maintenance, and funding for mass transit.[7]

The 1977 amendments demonstrated a definite trend. All references to land use planning in pollution control were deleted, and indirect source reviews were no longer required. A state governor may, in times of severe energy shortages or high unemployment, suspend the SIP for a maximum of four months. Although TCPs were still encouraged, the initiative for developing them was returned to the states,[8] most of whom will rely on traffic control measures rather than land use controls or reduction of travel measures. In this sense, the 1977 amendments represented a modest decline in federal intervention in state and local politics.

In December 1978, in accordance with the 1977 amendments, NJDEP submitted its SIP to EPA. To achieve National Ambient Air Quality Standards (NAAQS), NJDEP relied on better source controls and transportation control planning (including its successful inspection and maintenance—I and M—program for motor vehicles). NJDEP expressly eliminated the emission offset mechanism, giving economic development as its reason. In early 1979 EPA rejected this approach because it felt that transportation controls were not imminent and the state's nonattainment areas, such as Hudson County, had to be protected from further air degradation.

State Involvement

NJDEP is responsible for attainment, maintenance, and enforcement of federal air quality standards in the state. Air quality regulation and enforcement here is characterized by an emphasis on attainment rather than maintenance of air quality, on emissions control of chimneys and automobiles rather than land use or transportation control, and on monitoring of ambient air quality.

New Jersey passed its first Air Pollution Control Code in 1954. The state legislation that most affects Hudson County, however, is the Air Pollution Control Act and the traditional riparian laws. The Department of Environmental Protection Act of 1970 created

NJDEP and consolidated the state's environmental efforts into this agency.[9] Pollution codes, originally under the administration of the New Jersey Department of Health, fell under NJDEP jurisdiction.[10] The new agency was authorized to set pollution standards and emissions limits. It was also granted power to issue permits, thus giving the agency the ability to enforce its standards. NJDEP was also responsible for developing the New Jersey SIP.

The Air Pollution Control Act grants NJDEP authority to determine where facilities cannot be located (negative authority);[11] the agency cannot, however, determine where facilities will be located without private initiative and municipal approval (positive authority). Any onshore OCS facility or other energy development in Hudson County must be compatible with the New Jersey SIP. This does not mean that such facilities would be excluded from Hudson County, however, for under emission offset policy some polluting energy facilities could obtain approval for construction. In fact, the Steuber storage facility proposed for the Jersey City waterfront obtained conceptual approval from NJDEP, though it was later denied its riparian permit.[e]

New Jersey's riparian laws may also affect air quality in Hudson County. Much of the available land in the county is affected by these statutes. In New Jersey, all riparian lands belong to the state, which may convey the rights belonging to the land in question through grant, lease, license, or easement.[12] Since all OCS facilities and many other energy facilities require a physical intersection between the tidal waters and the land, potential facilities must obtain riparian permits from the state through NJDEP's Division of Coastal Resources and a tidelands conveyance through the Natural Resources Council.[13]

New Jersey has discretionary authority over riparian lands. Riparian approval may therefore become a major factor in pollution control. In the Steuber case, for example, failure to obtain riparian approval from the state ended any possibility of the facility's construction. The riparian approval process, like any other, is subject to political pressure. As long as citizen opposition to development of new energy facilities in Hudson County remains active and visible, riparian permits for these facilities will be difficult to obtain. Should public involvement decrease, however, riparian approvals could become more sensitive to other corporate and political pressures.

NJDEP must coordinate its air quality activities with the New Jersey Department of Transportation (NJDOT). NJDEP is responsible

[e]See Chapter 2.

for regulating stationary source emissions, while NJDOT handles mobile source controls. Lou Carnevale, staff member of the Hudson County Planning Commission, claimed that NJDOT does not even want to hear about air quality. According to Carnevale, many programs compete for scarce dollars, including subsidies for rail and bus transit. He questioned the extent of state commitment to mass transit, much less to programs affecting air quality more directly.[14]

Perhaps the most crucial factor influencing future air quality in Hudson County is the debate over siting of major polluters such as energy or OCS facilities in urban or in rural areas. Residents of urban areas, especially those designated as nonattainment areas for air quality, favor rural siting, arguing that the air in urban areas has far exceeded its carrying capacity for pollutants. Such an argument is extremely forceful when applied to Hudson County. On the other hand, rural residents wish to restrict any new facilities to areas—predominantly urban—where they already exist. They point out the equity issue involved in placing a major pollution source in a rural area when the majority of the facility's customers live in urban areas. In this debate, the state or federal government cannot avoid assuming the role of arbiter.

As in many states, NJDEP's position in this debate has not been spelled out very well, with the possible exception of the CAFRA coastal regulatory zone. Several decisions, however, suggest that NJDEP tends to favor urban siting of major polluting facilities in Hudson County or other urban areas. Prevention of significant deterioration regulations, sentiments against removing land from agricultural use, and restrictions on development in the CAFRA zone all combine to place substantial obstacles to construction of new facilities in rural locations. Furthermore, urban sites are less conspicuous than their rural counterparts in many, though not all cases, and therefore might arouse less opposition from the political public. This may be especially true in the Linden-Port Newark-Port Elizabeth industrial complex to the southwest of Hudson County. Perhaps because of strong political pressure from urban areas, NJDEP has resisted taking a firm public stance on the rural-urban siting issue. Paul Arbesman, NJDEP assistant commissioner in charge of air quality programs, suggested that some new energy facilities might finally have to be located in northwestern New Jersey, where there is sufficient water for cooling[f] and the air has not reached its carrying capacity. On the other hand, Arbesman believes that OCS oil and gas, if discovered in significant quantities off the

[f]Some New Jersey environmentalists would challenge this assertion.

state's coast, "has got to be brought ashore someplace." The best location, he suggested, would be as close to existing facilities as possible (i.e., in urban areas).[15]

Required by the EPA, Air Quality Maintenance Planning (AQMP) is fundamentally a state responsibility. This program, undertaken on a county basis, requires an analysis of air quality problems as the basis for development of a statewide strategy to maintain ambient air quality standards once they have been attained. Energy facilities impact on local air quality and thus play a major role in determining whether air quality in an area may violate the standards. Once an AQMP is completed,[16] it may be difficult to site those facilities where HC or SO_2 is already a problem, as in Hudson County. Where HC, CO, or NO_x is a problem, construction of new automobile facilities, such as a highway or a parking lot, will also be difficult. This may tend to encourage investments in mass transit or to soften attitudes toward transportation control plans.

According to the original timetable, analysis of future air quality problems and compilation of the existing emissions inventory were to have been completed by July 1977; by July 1978, NJDEP was to have developed its statewide strategy. Progress was slow in terms of air quality maintenance plans.[17] The Tri-State Regional Planning Commission originally began this work, but its contract was canceled by New Jersey. It seems likely, therefore, that a statewide strategy will not be developed before the early 1980s.

Arbesman said the slow progress in AQMP was not because of lack of interest, but rather because AQMP and 208 areawide water quality studies originally were supposed to dovetail. Thus, the two programs were run concurrently, with the result that most of the funding went to the 208 studies to the detriment of AQMP. By mid-1979 the AQMP analysis, based on estimates of future conditions, an emissions inventory, and diffusion modeling, had been completed for the two metropolitan areas centered in New York and Philadelphia. The former area includes Hudson County. Owing to NJDEP's concentration on other pressing demands, including meeting the requirements of the Clean Air Act for prevention of significant deterioration in cleaner areas, further work on AQMP had to be set aside.

Local Involvement

Although responsibility for regulation and enforcement rests at the state level, success requires cooperation from local and regional levels. One gets the impression that the problem of air quality has not been attacked seriously at the local level, at least not in Hudson County.[18]

Day-to-day enforcement of stationary source emission limits is the responsibility of the Hudson Regional Health Commission. This organization is fiercely independent and regional in scope; however, it lacks initiative and plays only a "watchdog" role while enforcing the Air Pollution Code.[19] Air quality control planning on the local level is primarily carried out by the Hudson County Office of Planning and the Jersey City Division of Planning. The Tri-State Regional Planning Commission has nominal responsibility for air quality planning in Hudson County, but most of its work has been delegated to local planning agencies within the county. In addition, both the Hackensack Meadowlands Development Commission and the Port Authority of New York and New Jersey frequently influence the air quality situation in Hudson County by their decisions on land use and transportation.

The Hudson County Office of Planning will be including air quality data in its transportation and other planning to meet the requirements of the Clean Air Act. Its interest in air quality, however, may be better revealed in another report prepared concurrently on potential OCS impacts on Hudson County. This report contained very little on the air quality impacts of OCS facilities, although it did proffer the recommendation that only "clean" facilities—temporary and permanent service bases, repair and maintenance yards, steel platform installation service bases and pipelines—be introduced into Hudson County. This may indicate that Hudson County is more concerned with the aesthetic disadvantages of tank farms, refineries, and transfer facilities than with these facilities' air emissions. This is not to say that Hudson County finds air pollution unimportant, only that this problem appears to involve less political salience than aesthetic considerations.

Jersey City's Division of Planning has addressed the problems of emissions from mobile sources. However, its 1977 report, "Air Pollution from Vehicular Sources in Jersey City," seemed to avoid more than attack the problem of transportation-related pollution. The original TCP promulgated by EPA for northern New Jersey focused on land use management and measures to reduce VMT. The TCP developed by the Jersey City Division of Planning instead focused on measures to facilitate traffic flow. Seven of the eight improvements specifically mentioned are devoted to improving the traffic circulation system; only one is aimed at reducing VMT: provision of park-and-ride lots at PATH mass transit stations. The report reduces the importance of bus service and vehicle inspection to the category of "other factors to be considered." While it is true that traffic congestion produces higher concentrations of pollutants in the atmosphere, especially CO, it is also true that facilitating traffic flow will inevitably increase VMT, which will result in increased pollution, primarily HC and oxidant/smog. Moreover, models predicting VMT have historically underestimated mileage induced by traffic flow improvements.

The Jersey City transportation report is not unique in its attempt to satisfy requirements without including anything controversial. Nevertheless, it fails to respond to the magnitude of the air quality problem in Jersey City and, if carried out, would not solve the pollution problem nor even significantly reduce the amount of pollution emitted by mobile sources. Instead, it preserves the status quo while telling the careful reader that Jersey City still is not prepared to face up to its air quality problems.

A more helpful attitude is seen in the Jersey City zoning ordinance, which regulates land use in accordance with the city's master plan. The zoning ordinance specifically prohibits the "processing of petroleum into fuel oil, or other products," and the siting of new tank farms.[20] While it is of course possible that a variance from this ordinance could be obtained, the Steuber proposal for a deepwater terminal and storage facilities for bulk fuel oil and chemicals never received a variance from the city council because of strong citizen opposition. Again, however, prohibition of such uses appears to stem more from aesthetic and safety factors than from a desire for pollution control. Furthermore, a zoning ordinance is only useful as long as a vigilant citizenry continues to insist that its provisions are observed. This was true in the Steuber case, but it requires long-term citizen activism. Finally, this zoning ordinance can only affect stationary source emissions, not air pollution from mobile sources.

Much of western Hudson County is part of the Hackensack Meadowlands in which development must be approved by the Hackensack Meadowlands Development Commission (HMDC). This agency was formed by the New Jersey legislature in the hope of stopping piecemeal development of the Meadowlands. The HMDC has developed a comprehensive land use plan for the area, and tight zoning restrictions will probably prevent any "dirty" energy facility from locating there. In addition, the marshy nature of the ground (in much of the Meadowlands the depth to bedrock is over 100 feet)[21] may make construction of such facilities uneconomical.

For these reasons, large energy facilities are more likely to be built along the county's eastern waterfront than in the Meadowlands.

In addition to operating mass transit through the county and the tunnels to New York through which so much traffic flows, the Port Authority of New York and New Jersey also controls industrial land in the Port Newark-Port Elizabeth complex. The Port Authority favors building any needed storage tanks and transfer facilities for petroleum in this area, to provide a "psychological boost" to northern New Jersey.[22] These facilities, however, would be upwind of Hudson County and thus would increase the HC and SO_2 concentrations in the county.

THE FUTURE OF AIR QUALITY
IN HUDSON COUNTY

According to John Lane, there is no way Hudson County can meet federal ambient air quality standards by 1982, with the possible exception of the SO_2 standards, which could be met if coal were not used to fuel the county's power plants.[23] Within this overall constraint, how might Hudson County's air quality situation change in the future?

Both stationary and mobile source emissions must be considered when accounting for the future state of air quality in the county. Each factor contains elements that will tend to reduce pollution in the future as well as elements that will tend to increase future pollutant concentrations.

In general, energy and OCS facilities seemed a dirty word to all parties involved in all levels of government. Those interviewed consistently gave the impression that such facilities would be resisted. Present plant and storage capacities are considered to be sufficient, and presumably OCS discoveries would replace foreign oil, not serve as an addition to it.[24] Citizen opposition to energy facilities in Hudson County is fervent and well organized. Five proposals for petrochemical storage and processing have been rejected, and none was accepted. As long as this situation exists, state riparian grants or leases and local zoning variances will be difficult to obtain. Furthermore, there seems to be no slackening in the intensity of opposition to these kinds of facilities.

Land in Hudson County is scarce. Severe zoning restrictions in the Meadowlands decrease the possibility of major energy facilities being located there. Hoboken has little land available for refineries or tank farms. In addition, Hoboken's waterfront has extremely poor road access. Although Bayonne "permits anything and everything,"[25] it does not have significant available land. The Texaco and Exxon facilities there could expand, but not by much. Land would be difficult to clear; it is all industrial on Bayonne's Hudson River side, while the west side has poor road access. Jersey City has a significant amount of waterfront land, but storage terminals have been zoned out and it is unlikely that a zoning variance could be obtained, at least in the near future. On the other hand, there is a possibility that landfill or a more intensive use of Port Jersey, on the border of Jersey City and Bayonne, could create room for waterfront energy facilities.

In contrast, factors encourage development of OCS bases and other energy facilities in Hudson County. The increasing unemployment, the decreasing labor base, and fleeing companies are undercutting the county's tax base. If other uses cannot be attracted to the waterfront, or if those uses cannot afford a waterfront location, tank farms and transfer facilities might be the sole remaining opportunity for income from the waterfront areas. If this pattern persists into the 1980s, petrochemical concerns eventually might become increasingly acceptable to the municipalities in Hudson County.

Major energy and OCS facilities may have nowhere else to go but urban areas, including Hudson County. Even if facilities were built in the Port Newark-Port Elizabeth-Perth Amboy area, prevailing winds would carry the pollution to Hudson County. Therefore, if new facilities are built in New Jersey, and if they are not located in rural areas, Hudson County will probably end up with a good share of the added pollution. Thus the county's future air quality depends to a great extent on the ultimate outcome of the urban-rural siting controversy and on implementation of the emission offset concept.

Mobile source emissions will be influenced by changes in technology and in land use. Hudson County is blessed with one of the nation's best mass transit systems, including excellent bus service, PATH trains, and several commuter railroads. Thus in this area, more than almost anywhere else, there is a possibility of large-scale shifts from automobile to mass transit travel without constructing new infrastructure. In Hudson County, TCPs aimed at reducing VMT could be successful, since well-established alternatives to automobile travel exist. In fact, if a TCP aimed at restricting traffic volumes cannot succeed in Hudson County, it is doubtful if it could succeed anywhere outside of very dense central cities.

On the other hand, the prevailing do-nothing attitude toward TCPs suggests that localities will not be willing voluntarily to commit themselves to politically unpopular on-street parking bans or other types of parking restrictions, for instance. If this is the case, EPA may have to resort to litigation, which would result in very slow implementation of TCP regulations.

These conflicting influences on both stationary and mobile source pollution are aggravated by the general confusion that seems to beset New Jersey's approach to air quality in Hudson County and elsewhere. This confusion is a result of the problem of coordinating pollution control between NJDEP, NJDOT, and the New Jersey Department of Energy (NJDOE), the lack of a definite policy on urban-rural facility siting, the horizontal fragmentation of positive siting authority on the municipal level, and the absence of an effective air quality planning process on state and regional levels. Generally the result of confusion is inaction, or at best slower action than would be the case if objectives and authority were clearly defined.

The most probable scenario for air quality in Hudson County will be a steady decrease in pollution from stationary sources, while pollution from mobile sources either remains at its present level or even increases somewhat. Particulates in the ambient atmosphere will decline as better emissions control equipment is put in place. New source performance standards and emission offset will combine to restrict pollution associated with new facilities. Hydrocarbons in the atmosphere will probably remain at about their present levels, with increases in VMT being offset by improvement in stationary source emissions and new auto emission controls. Carbon monoxide may increase, however, as increased VMT may more than offset automobile emissions controls, as has happened in Southern California.

The air quality situation will be aggravated by at least two factors: less open space in the Meadowlands and increased industrial development upwind of Hudson County. If the HMDC land use plan is carried out, much of the Meadowlands will be built upon. This will decrease existing buffer zones, providing less room for diffusion of pollution. Possible industrial development related to energy and OCS facilities in Port Newark and Port Elizabeth would provide increased background pollution in Hudson County.

The impact of Baltimore Canyon OCS development on Hudson County remains unclear, dependent on how much oil or natural gas is discovered, the type of crude oil found, the mix of foreign and domestic oil that is processed, and the ability of existing facilities to absorb OCS development. The impact of transportation on air quality is much less hypothetical. Unless attitudes change, the amount of pollution emitted from motor vehicles will become even more intolerable than it already is.

There is no indication of any shift in favor of VMT restrictions over traffic flow mechanisms in attacking transportation emissions. This change must be made if these pollutant levels are to decrease. Yet Tri-State is proposing another highway along Hudson County's waterfront. Suggestions for carpool-only or bus-only lanes have met with little success, while parking restrictions have met with no success at all. Any change in existing attitudes will come slowly, probably through response to legal mandates.

The key to improving air quality in Hudson County lies in citizen awareness of and involvement in the problems of air pollution. As long as citizen opinion remains as active as it has been in the 1970s, little in the way of new energy or OCS facilities will be sited in the county. Unfortunately, transportation problems are not as dramatic or as obvious as the problems resulting from a large waterfront tank farm. It is unlikely that citizens will be willing to view themselves or to judge themselves as critically as they viewed and judged the Steuber Company's proposal.

NOTES

1. Telephone interview with John Lane, Hudson County Planning Commission, December 1977.
2. "Air Pollution from Vehicular Sources in Jersey City—Winter 1976" (Jersey City: Jersey City Division of Planning, 1977), pp. 5, 36.
3. David Morell, *Who's in Charge?—Governmental Capabilities to Make Energy Facility Siting Decisions in New Jersey* (Princeton: Princeton University, Center for Environmental Studies, 1977).
4. Telephone interview with Lou Carnevale, Hudson County Office of Planning, December 1977.
5. Telephone interview with Bill Baker, U.S. Environmental Protection Agency, New York, December 1977.
6. *Code of Federal Regulations* (Washington, D.C.: U.S. Government Printing Office), Title 40, part 52, subpart FF—New Jersey.
7. "President Carter Signs Clean Air Act Amendments," *Congressional Record* (Washington, D.C.: U.S. Government Printing Office, August 3, 1977), pp. H8507-H8541.
8. *Congressional Record*, ibid., p. H8510.
9. Lewis Goldshore, "A Flood of Environmental Legislation: An Analysis of the New Jersey Experience 1970-1975," *Seton Hall Legislative Journal*, 1, no. 2 (Summer 1976), pp. 1-19.
10. "Air Pollution from Vehicular Sources...," op. cit., p. 5.
11. Morell, op. cit., p. 9.
12. Lewis Goldshore, *Riparian Rights Handbook* (Trenton, N.J.: NJDEP, 1978).
13. Morell, op. cit., pp. 19-27; also see Hannah Shostack, *Federal Preemption and Energy Facility Siting: The Power of State Riparian Statutes* (Princeton: Princeton University, Center for Energy and Environmental Studies, August 1979).

14. Carnevale, op. cit.
15. Telephone interview with Paul Arbesman, Assistant Commissioner, New Jersey Department of Environmental Protection, Trenton, December 1977.
16. Morell, op. cit., pp. 63-64.
17. Telephone interview with Dr. Ray Dyba, New Jersey Department of Environmental Protection, Trenton, December 1977; and Lane, op. cit.
18. Telephone interview with John Filippelli, Jersey City Division of Planning, December 1977.
19. Telephone interview with Joe Statile, Hudson Regional Health Commission, December 1977.
20. "Zoning Ordinance—City of Jersey City" (Jersey City: Division of Planning, 1974), pp. 88, 94.
21. *Hackensack Meadowlands Comprehensive Land Use Plans* (Carlstadt, N.J.: Hackensack Meadowlands Development Commission, 1970), p. 11.
22. Interview with Edward S. Olcott, Port Authority of New York and New Jersey, December 1977.
23. Lane, op. cit.
24. Dyba, op. cit.
25. Carnevale, op. cit.

Chapter 5

EPA's Emission Offset Policy and Energy Facility Siting

Barry Merchant

Hudson County, New Jersey, with its prime waterfront location has traditionally been chosen by industry as the site for petrochemical and energy facilities serving the greater New York area, and indeed the whole Northeast. In recent years, however, concern about seriously high concentrations of petrochemical oxidants (smog) and other airborne pollutants has caused a backlash among county residents.[a] As described in Chapter 4, Hudson County has one of the highest overall cancer mortality rates in the country. It is clear that the petrochemical and energy facilities in and near the county (along with mobile sources) are the major emitters of hydrocarbons, sulfur dioxide, and particulates, which comprise the bulk of the area's air pollution problem.

With exploratory drilling for oil and gas underway off New Jersey's coast, pressure for new facilities in Hudson County and the surrounding area seems likely to increase. New Jersey's Department of Environmental Protection (NJDEP) has already adopted policies that would encourage needed new facilities to locate in the developed industrial areas of northern and southern New Jersey, rather than risk degrading the state's recreational and resort coastal beach

---

[a]See Chapter 2.

areas. But can new growth be accommodated in Hudson County—and in other nonattainment urban areas—without further decline of air quality? Such degradation would be in violation of the Clean Air Act, and it would run counter to recently articulated local demands for improved air quality controls.

In coping with the challenge of building new facilities in non-attainment areas, which include most of the country's urban waterfronts, the U.S. Environmental Protection Agency (EPA) has developed an "emission offset" policy designed to allow sufficient flexibility in implementing the Clean Air Act so as to permit "needed" growth to occur.[b] Because of the vital importance of this policy to energy facility siting in urban coastal areas throughout the country, this chapter is devoted to examination of the EPA policy, perusal of the reasons for its adoption, and analysis of its probable impact. A case study of the Hudson County area is used as the basis for speculation as to the policy's possible implications.

EMERGENCE OF AN
OFFSET POLICY

Under the Clean Air Act of 1970, primary (health-related) national ambient air quality standards (NAAQS) were to be attained as expeditiously as practicable, but not later than July 1975;[c] secondary (welfare-related) standards were to be achieved within a "reasonable time." So that the requirements of the act could be carried out and attainment timetables met, EPA in August 1971 ruled that all state implementation plans (SIPs) had to require preconstruction review and disapproval of new or modified major point sources that would "interfere with" attainment of national standards.

By 1976, however, EPA found itself in a dilemma in attempting to enforce the Clean Air Act. In order to carry out the act's legal requirements, the agency would have had to bar any new major emission sources in nonattainment areas. So long as attainment of the standards was to be achieved in a relatively short time, this

[b]In late 1979, EPA modified the emission offset policy with its "bubble" policy allowing each facility's managers to control individual stack emissions as long as the total emissions do not violate an agreed-upon overall standard for the facility.

[c]Extensions were later allowed to July 1977. The 1977 CAA Amendments granted further extensions, pushing back to as late as 1987 the attainment date for many polluted areas.

stance would not have caused serious hardship. But with the original 1975 deadline past and with achievement of the standards not yet in sight in most nonattainment areas, the automatic barring of any new major point source became unacceptable both politically and economically.

The Hampton Roads Energy Company Case

The seriousness of EPA's implementation problems was brought to a head in late April 1976, when EPA's Regional Office in Philadelphia (Region III) took an unexpectedly strong stand against a new refinery proposed by the Hampton Roads Energy Co. (HREC) for a site in Portsmouth, Virginia. The Virginia Air Pollution Control Board had already granted all necessary air permits to HREC on the grounds that the new refinery would more than meet all existing point source emission requirements. All necessary construction and operating permits had already been granted by the state; only a dredging permit from the U.S. Army Corps of Engineers was still needed before the project could get underway. It was at the public hearing on that permit that EPA spoke out against the HREC project. EPA contended that the refinery was "environmentally unacceptable" because it would add to an already serious photochemical oxidant problem in Virginia's Tidewater region.[d] According to a spokesman for the EPA Regional Office,

> It is not reasonable to allow new sources into an area where standards are being violated 200 to 300 percent.[1]

While EPA had no direct legal authority to deny operating approval to HREC, the effect of its eleventh-hour objection was to delay the Army Corps' decision on the dredging permit until a further review of air quality problems could be undertaken.

The political repercussions for EPA were immediate. Until that time, business interests had assumed that new facilities employing the best available technology should and *would* receive approval. Now, however, it was clear that the best pollution control techniques were no longer necessarily enough. Even when the most advanced technologies were to be employed to keep emissions far below state

[d]Portsmouth had been in violation of primary oxidant standards on 205 days in 1975. The HREC project's EIS estimated that the refinery would increase hydrocarbon levels in the Tidewater area by 1.2 percent.

and federal requirements (as was HREC's intention), a facility still might not be approved if the overall air quality in its region were found to be unacceptable. In a formal response to EPA's position, HREC raised the following question:

> The photochemical oxidant (ozone) standard is presently being exceeded in every Virginia air quality control region in which it is measured. Does this mean that no new industries, no new automobiles, and no new economic development can be permitted in Virginia until the . . . standard is met?[2]

The state quickly joined HREC and the city of Portsmouth in attacking EPA's "no-growth" decision, and within a week EPA agreed to give the whole matter further consideration.[3]

Wider Implications of No Growth Feared

The implication of EPA's stand, however, clearly had an impact well beyond the Tidewater region or the state of Virginia. HREC Project Manager, Robert Porterfield, charged that if EPA opposed construction of the refinery simply because of the prevailing hydrocarbon problem, then

> it means that the EPA is declaring that the entire East Coast is a no-growth area. . . . I think this is the way EPA chose to tell Congress that the present law is unacceptable and cannot be enforced.[4]

This belief appeared to be shared by several federal agencies. The Commerce and Treasury Departments both openly supported the refinery proposal and expressed reservations about the apparent no-growth implications of EPA's stand. Particularly strong concern was voiced by the Federal Energy Administration (FEA), now part of the U.S. Department of Energy, which feared that the policy would seriously discourage other refinery siting attempts. No new East Coast refinery had been approved in a decade,[e] and the only other current proposal—a refinery at Eastport, Maine—was experiencing serious problems. HREC's president had recently built a "clean" refinery in Hawaii, where he had won the begrudging respect of many environmentalists for his willingness to go well beyond existing abatement requirements in installing the most advanced

[e]See Chapter 9.

technologies available.[f] FEA worried that rejection of HREC's refinery bid could effectively end any hope of building, within the foreseeable future, the new refining capability that it believed the East Coast badly needed.

A Compromise Emerges

Environmental groups that lauded EPA's stance pressed for continuation of existing regulatory policy regardless of its implications for growth; in sharp contrast, business interests argued that any new facilities employing the best available control technology should be approved. EPA considered both positions unacceptable. The former, by ignoring the potential economic hardships and dislocations in various industries and locales, threatened to destroy what was left of the Clean Air Act's fragile political support. In contrast, the latter view failed to consider the serious health issues that were the reason for the act's existence. Out of this political morass, EPA sought a compromise ruling that would add enough flexibility to implementation plans to allow for some growth without slowing progress toward the goal of eventually attaining national air quality standards.

In a meeting in Philadelphia with officials of HREC and the Virginia Air Pollution Control Board, EPA agreed to reverse its opposition to the refinery on two conditions. First, HREC had to prove that it was in fact using the best available control technology in all of its operations. Second, the state would have to develop a program to reduce overall hydrocarbon emissions in the Tidewater area so that a "tradeoff" could be achieved. EPA had previously suggested to state environmental control agencies that they adopt emission reduction programs as a means of allowing construction of major new point sources;[g] but the political controversy arising out of the HREC showdown forced EPA publicly to announce a national emission tradeoff policy. The new policy was unveiled in late May 1976, following EPA's initial negotiations with HREC and just prior to the start of debate in Congress on amendments

[f]This individual had already fought one long battle to site a refinery in Machiasport, Maine. That unsuccessful attempt in the late 1960s prompted several attempts by other developers (also unsuccessful) to site refineries in New England. His third choice, Savannah, Georgia, was eventually discarded as unfeasible.

[g]Such a tradeoff was proposed in 1975 in the Steuber case documented in Chapter 2. Though the plan received conceptual approval from NJDEP, the project was rejected because of strong citizen opposition.

to the Clean Air Act. It was not until December 1976, however, that a tradeoff policy was officially published in the *Federal Register.*

THE EMISSION OFFSET RULING

The emission offset ruling drafted by EPA in December 1976 was an interim measure allowing new pollution sources to locate in nonattainment areas if the additional emissions were "offset" by reductions in the amount of pollutants being released by other sources in the area. Owing to the limited capabilities of reviewing authorities and the "insignificant impact" of many small pollution sources, the EPA ruling restricted the offset requirements to "major" new sources, originally defined as having an emission rate of 100 or more tons a year of any pollutant (1,000 tons of carbon monoxide). (EPA later adopted a new definition of 50 tons a year—500 tons of carbon monoxide.) Recognizing that such a cutoff was somewhat arbitrary, the ruling encouraged states to utilize a lower cutoff number, but did not legally require them to do so.

The object of this policy was to allow growth in nonattainment areas while standards were being attained, but only under certain strict conditions. The primary requirements of the ruling were as follows:

A major new source seeking to locate in a non-attainment area must meet the "lowest achievable emission rate." In no instance could the limit exceed the applicable new source performance standard set by EPA under the Clean Air Act.

Offset credits could only be accepted for reductions not required in revised SIP's. Offset credits were allowed to new sources only for emission reductions from existing sources "which would not otherwise be accomplished as a result of the Clean Air Act." All states had to submit revisions of their SIP's to EPA by July 1, 1979. Until those SIP revisions were officially approved by EPA, the "baseline" for determining appropriate offsets was to be the "reasonably available control measures" which all revised SIP's were required to include.

More that one-for-one offsets were required in order for progress to be made toward attainment of NAAQS. The ruling was not to be a status quo measure. However, no numerical standards for net emission reductions were specified.

It was the responsibility of the proposed new source, not the state, to arrange an offset. Nevertheless, states if they so chose could play an active role in working out appropriate offset plans.

Because the oxidant problem in many areas was a consequence of transport of pollutants from other locales, for these pollutants the policy was limited to areas where the source of the problem was concentrated: metropolitan areas of over 200,000 population.

Emission offsets were allowed only at the discretion of local and state government. Even if an offset were arrived at which met the criteria of the ruling, the new source could be prohibited if:

1. a more acceptable site were available
2. the proposed offset would not be in the public interest, or
3. the new source would not be in the public interest.

The appropriate geographical boundaries of the offset area were to be determined on a case-by-case basis until EPA was able to formulate specific guidelines.

An offset agreement need not necessarily take the form of a SIP revision if another means were available to make it legally binding.[5]

Under the ruling, three basic alternatives were available to major new sources seeking an offset arrangement. First, a company could install controls more effective than those required by law. This could be done either by retrofitting existing facilities owned by the company in the area, or by devising controls for the new facility that were tight enough to bring emissions of each pollutant below the 50 tons per year threshold. Second, a company could buy an existing source and either shut it down or install additional control equipment. Third, and finally, if a company did not own other facilities in the nonattainment area and if it could not buy any pollution sources large enough to provide an offset, the company could seek state aid in reaching a settlement. The state could either reduce emissions from its own facilities and operations or place tighter controls on new or existing sources through revision of its SIP. EPA's stated belief was that even if these options should prove unworkable in some locales, their use should not be denied to other areas.

THE IMPLEMENTATION RECORD

To what extent do these implementation alternatives actually work when put to the test? This question is difficult to answer given the policy's relatively short existence, for success or failure may depend as much on the level of demand for investment in new facilities as on the opportunities for realistic offset agreements. With the overall level of business investment still sluggish, it is difficult to say what the future experience might be. Nevertheless, a sufficient number of companies have attempted to site new facilities under the offset ruling so that some of the likely possibilities and pitfalls have now become apparent.

Internalization of Offset Reductions

The first implementation alternative is clearly the simplest to achieve, because emission reductions are internalized within a single firm's operations. It is not surprising, then, that most of the successful offset arrangements touted by EPA have involved this option. Many of these offsets were in fact built into companies' investment programs. For example, the Koppers Company was granted permission to build a new coke oven in Birmingham, Alabama, and Allied Chemical Corporation was allowed to do the same in Ashland, Kentucky, in exchange for shutting down antiquated polluting facilities they were operating. There is every reason to believe that the new modern ovens had always been intended as replacement facilities. This process in fact corresponds to the model of emission reduction ascribed to by business even before the advent of a formal emissions offset policy. It was generally believed that pollution control is essentially a process of replacing old polluting facilities with new efficient ones. However, what the offset ruling has done is to make construction contingent for the first time on just such a replacement program. It is too soon to say whether the policy has significantly accelerated this process.

In other cases, companies have chosen to retrofit some of their existing operations in order to construct a new facility. The instances to date in which this has occurred are difficult to evaluate, however, because there is frequently an advantage to retrofitting, apart from being allowed to build a new facility. The petroleum industry has shown itself willing to retrofit old oil storage tanks with floating roofs to reduce hydrocarbon emissions. This is largely due to the economic benefit that also accrues from reducing costly evaporation losses. Conoco, Champlin Petroleum, APCO Oil, and Sun Oil Company all agreed voluntarily to install floating roofs on their storage tanks in the Oklahoma City area so that General Motors Corporation could receive sufficient offsets for the hydrocarbon emissions from its proposed new automobile plant. It is not surprising, then, that this alternative was turned to by the Steuber Company in its attempt to build a major oil transfer and storage terminal in New Jersey. In order to allay concern about the hydrocarbon emissions its facility would produce, Steuber proposed to install floating roofs on oil storage tanks it leased in nearby Carteret, New Jersey, thereby attaining a marginal (2 percent) net reduction in overall hydrocarbon emissions in the region.

Critics have charged that reductions such as those achieved by installation of floating roofs should be required of *all* existing sources, rather than only as part of the offset agreements allowing new sources to be built. Roger Strelow, then EPA Assistant Administrator for Air and Waste Management, however, contended that:

> there is significant potential for further emissions reduction at facilities such as steel mills and petrochemical complexes which are very unlikely to be realized. . . (because) states either cannot or will not require certain emission reductions. . . . There is considerable emission reduction potential throughout private industry that is "real" but which neither EPA nor a state could prove adequately in a court of law if a regulation was challenged. . . [6]

EPA hoped that its emission offset policy would bring about many of these "real" potential reductions, and that once demonstrated to be feasible, they could then be incorporated into future emission control regulations.

Perhaps of more serious concern should be another kind of "built-in" emissions reduction. By making minor or moderate design alterations, or by installing more sophisticated abatement technologies, companies can sometimes reduce emissions below the threshold stipulated in EPA's policy. This was true for the Philadelphia Gas Works, which adopted an improved double sealing system for its new storage tanks and thus was able to bring the projected evaporation below the original limit of 100 tons a year, thereby avoiding the need for an offset. Similarly, Dow Chemical Company, denied an offset by California in its attempt to build a new chemical plant in Solano County,[h] chose to expand existing facilities in Illinois, Louisiana, Texas, and overseas in order to avoid having to negotiate an offset agreement.[i] Expansion of Dow's existing facilities

[h]California offset regulations are more stringent than EPA's. California refused to let Dow build its new plant in exchange for reducing emissions at its nearby Pittsburg, California, plant.

[i]Dow's proposal for a $30-million chemical transshipment terminal in Bordentown, New Jersey, on the Delaware River, was thwarted in 1978 because of strong citizen opposition; see Chapter 2.

produced new emission loads at each site that were below the offset threshold. Texas has challenged EPA directly over the offset issue.[7]

If an emission offset had been required of either company, their new facilities would have brought about a net reduction in emissions (however small) in their areas. But by avoiding the offset requirement, they were able in fact to produce an actual net increase in emissions. This is particularly disturbing as the increase in emissions could be well above the new threshold of 50 tons a year of any pollutant. Moreover, if one result of the offset policy is to substitute incremental plant expansion for construction of new facilities, the goal of replacing old and antiquated plants with new efficient plants might actually be retarded. Furthermore, the sum of many new so-called minor sources of this kind may produce pollution loads as high or higher than those of a few new major sources (with or without the offset ruling). In short, just because major sources are clearly a bigger problem than minor sources does not mean that it is either reasonable or wise to treat them as if they are the only problem.

Purchasing Emission Reductions

Buying emission reductions from neighboring facilities is much more difficult. Many offsets that are theoretically available are either too costly to implement or are impractical to administer legally.

The Standard Oil Company of Ohio (Sohio) negotiated with EPA and California for five years in an attempt to reach agreement on an offset plan that would allow it to build a landing and storage facility for Alaskan crude oil at Long Beach. Sohio offered to pay for reductions in hydrocarbon emissions from dry cleaning establishments in the Long Beach area and to reduce emissions from a glass manufacturing plant. The most serious emission problems, however, were the more than six tons of sulfur dioxide that the new terminal would emit daily. One proposal called for Sohio to finance the installation of pollution scrubbers at a Southern California Edison power plant, whereby 1.2 pounds of sulfur dioxide emissions would be eliminated from the Edison plant for every pound the Sohio terminal would produce. A deadlock existed on how much Sohio would spend to bring the Edison facility up to the necessary emission standards and whether use of very low sulfur fuel could avoid the need for scrubbers. The state wanted Sohio to spend $120 million to fulfill its commitment on the scrubber scheme. This sum amounted to at least 20 percent of the more than $500 million Sohio planned to invest in its terminal. Sohio abandoned its plans in

March 1979. Similarly, EPA initially asked HREC to spend $50 million to retrofit a nearby Amoco refinery in Yorktown, Virginia, in order to achieve an offset for its hydrocarbon emissions. That would amount to 20 percent of the projected $350 million cost of HREC's Portsmouth refinery.[j]

The serious implications of this cost problem need to be addressed. First, are the costs feasible for companies to bear?[k] Sohio's position was not entirely clear, as the company's only alternative was to ship its Alaskan oil through the Panama Canal, a costly proposition in itself. HREC, on the other hand, made it clear that it was unwilling to accept proposed costs of that magnitude and instead sought other offset opportunities.

Second, given extraordinary costs, where should the burden fall? The U.S. Department of Energy has identified both the Sohio and HREC projects as important components of its national energy policy. The Sohio terminal was believed critical to the efficient movement of Alaskan crude oil to refineries in the Southwest and Midwest. The HREC project was seen as the current best hope for increasing the East Coast's refining capacity. Assuming that these companies are doing everything technically feasible to minimize emissions from their own facilities, should they be expected to bear the full cost of reducing pollution from other sources, for which they are not responsible? Or does such a policy penalize firms seeking to build new facilities employing advanced abatement technologies while providing little incentive for existing inefficient and polluting firms to adopt effective controls? What are the implications for economic growth, which is ultimately reliant on a sufficient level of investment in new capital formation? Resolution of these policy issues is critical to formulation of siting and urban waterfront renewal policies.

State and Local Government Intervention

The most difficult cases are those in which a state or local government must actively intervene if a company is to achieve an acceptable offset. Unless the governing body can find suitable offsets in its own activities, it must either place tighter restrictions on other private sources or seek voluntary cutbacks. The former is of questionable legality unless a clear overriding public interest is at stake.

[j]The projected cost has now escalated to over $550 million.

[k]See Chapters 9 to 11.

The government may not regulate one private interest solely for the benefit of another. The latter option is unlikely to succeed unless the government is willing and able to defray a large portion of the abatement costs, or unless some economic benefit can be derived from voluntary reductions (such as limiting evaporation losses).

In only two cases can the state (or localities) be said to have played such an active role in arranging an offset agreement. In the first case, Pennsylvania undertook to reduce emissions from its road paving operations in the southwestern quarter of the state to allow the Volkswagen Corporation of America to operate a large new automobile assembly plant at New Stanton.[8] The Volkswagen facility was originally predicted to emit as much as 898 tons of hydrocarbons a year from its paint spraying operations, worsening the already serious photochemical oxidant problem in the greater Pittsburgh area. Yet Pennsylvania had already committed $76 million to road improvements and other amenities around New Stanton in order to woo Volkswagen, with its 5,000 jobs and $80 million in tax revenues (over five years), to an economically depressed area of the state. The state was therefore determined to ensure that an offset was reached.

The final agreement called for a net reduction in existing hydrocarbon emissions of 1,025 tons per year to offset the Volkswagen plant's emissions. This net reduction was to be achieved through a requirement that the Pennsylvania Department of Transportation (Penn DOT) restrict its use of "cutback" nonmethane hydrocarbon based asphalt, substituting a water-based emulsified solvent in its place. The restriction would limit the use of cutback asphalt to 20 percent of the total asphalt used in a 16-county area (the southwestern quarter of the state). In addition, Volkswagen had to agree to phase in the use of a water-based high solids paint in its paint spraying operations and to cut nonmethane hydrocarbon emissions to 280 tons per year over a three-year period.[1]

The Volkswagen agreement has been roundly criticized as a "quick fix," designed for political purposes rather than air quality. Why, it has been asked, was Penn DOT not already planning to use emulsified asphalt for road paving, since it is cheaper than cutback asphalt and does not require constant heating to apply? Or, if the state already had plans for such a change, did that not negate the intent of the offset ruling? After all, emulsified asphalt is now the preference of the Federal Highway Administration and is recommended for use throughout the country.

---

[1]Volkswagen had already made other changes in its operations that had cut projected emissions from 898 to 620 tons per year.

The second case involved Virginia. After a year of unsuccessful attempts by HREC to find an appropriate offset for its hydrocarbon emissions, the state, at the suggestion of EPA, turned to the asphalt solution that had proved successful in Pennsylvania. The agreement called for the state to undertake a partial conversion from cutback to emulsified asphalt in the southeastern third of the state, reducing hydrocarbon emissions by 1,351 tons a year to offset the 1,285 tons to be produced by HREC. On the basis of this agreement, the Virginia Air Pollution Control Board voted unanimously to extend HREC's air permit.[m] The Air and Hazardous Materials Division of EPA's Region III Office, which had originally blocked the HREC project on air pollution grounds in 1976, endorsed the arrangement as "proper and reasonable," but stated "we have very little hard scientific data on which to base a decision."[9] Earlier EPA had maintained that it could not accept an agreement unless there were "a genuine cutback that was not already in the works. If it was already a Highway Department program, then it could be a problem."[10] It was not clear what kind of assurance EPA required on this important point. Yet John Daniels, Assistant Director of the Virginia Air Pollution Control Board, stated after contacting the Virginia Highway Department that "they already had a program underway . . . so it just worked out that we killed two birds with one stone. . . . I want to emphasize that the Highway Department is not doing this just to benefit HREC."[11]

Clearly, then, the agreement represented a violation of the intent, if not the letter, of EPA's emission offset ruling.[n] It raises serious questions about the Pennsylvania agreement and the precedent that EPA had thereby allowed. EPA seemed to have recognized its mistake in the Virginia case by again voicing formal opposition to the Army Corps of Engineers in its deliberations on the final dredging permit. But by waiting to voice its concern until the Virginia Air Pollution Control Board had already granted an air permit extension, EPA lost any opportunity it had had for constructive participation. Having given the state the clear impression that the asphalt tradeoff was reasonable, EPA again put itself into the role of a "spoiler."

In fact, the evidence suggests that EPA decided to oppose the HREC project because the possibility of serious oil spills in Hampton Roads and the Lower Chesapeake Bay represented an inordinate danger to the Virginia shellfish industry (already suffering from

[m]The original permit, granted in 1975, would have expired in 1977 if construction on the project had not commenced.

[n]Conversion to emulsified asphalt was not required in either the Virginia or the Pennsylvania SIP.

kepone contamination). Strong opposition on the water quality issue allowed EPA to express continuing concern about air quality in the Tidewater area, without letting it be this issue that might defeat the project. The Corps of Engineers approved a dredging permit on December 28, 1979. On January 25, 1980, EPA issued the Prevention of Significant Deterioration permit and approved the Virginia SIP, effectively ending federal opposition to the project. The proposal still faces a legal challenge from a group based in Norfolk, Citizens Against Refinery Effects (CARE).[12]

CONCLUSIONS: IMPLICATIONS FOR URBAN COASTAL AREAS

Experience with emission offset has shown that the photochemical oxidant problem, serious nationwide, continues to defy solution, even with the offset provisions. Prevailing winds carry pollutants for hundreds of miles, making localized efforts to deal with the problem practically futile. Yet states have proven unwilling to undertake the comprehensive statewide regulatory controls necessary to cope with this problem. Competition for new industry and public opposition to meaningful traffic controls have foreclosed most state initiatives. The asphalt solution adopted by Pennsylvania and Virginia is of questionable compliance with EPA's emission offset ruling, and in any case it is a one-shot conversion process that will not be available to deal with future development pressures. Many touted potential offsets, such as vapor recovery controls at gasoline stations and reduction of emissions from dry cleaning establishments, have proven unfeasible in most cases because the large number and small size of such businesses have made legally enforceable administration of any such arrangement a nightmare. Only the retrofitting of oil storage tanks has proved readily feasible and effective. This option is easier for firms with multiple facilities in an area (such as the Steuber Company) than for independent operators (such as HREC) who must buy emissions reductions from other sources.

The implication for Hudson County, New Jersey, is that, with some exceptions, energy and other facilities are unlikely to be significantly easier to site under an offset arrangement than in its absence. New Jersey, like most other states, has been unwilling to address its air pollution problems seriously, particularly the problem of photochemical oxidants. Apart from numerous petrochemical and energy facility emitters of hydrocarbons, Hudson County is plagued by serious levels of hydrocarbon emissions from motor vehicles. The bulk of this pollution comes from the New Jersey Turnpike and the approaches to the Lincoln and Holland Tunnels. The latter are among New Jersey's main links to New York City. Yet, the state has failed to enforce a transportation control plan for Hudson County, much less for the dense northern New Jersey region, from which much of Hudson County's traffic emanates. In fact, NJDOT has not appeared to be seriously committed to air pollution reductions through transportation controls.[o]

The only other feasible alternative for achieving significant emission offsets for hydrocarbons would appear to be the retrofitting or closure of old petrochemical and energy facilities. The latter is unlikely to involve many possibilities, as pressure for new facilities is expected to come from a demand for greater capacities in the area (especially if offshore oil and gas supplies are developed in the Baltimore Canyon, off the state's coast) rather than from normal replacement of outmoded capital stock. Retrofitting of existing facilities, then, can be expected to provide the bulk of offset possibilities. Whether this alternative provides sufficient flexibility is contingent on the level of controls now in existence and planned. Few (outside the industry) would contend that there are not still means of tightening existing controls in petrochemical facilities. But with the state becoming increasingly concerned about its high cancer mortality rate and its growing reputation as "cancer alley," there may be cause to doubt whether potential emission reductions will be as great 5 or 10 years hence, the time when the greatest pressure for new oil facilities may well occur.

The emission offset policy expired in July 1979. After that date, if a revised SIP has not been approved no new sources will be allowed to locate in nonattainment areas. The implication for Hudson County and other urban areas is clear. Even now, a state can obtain a waiver from the requirements of the policy if it has adopted an approved statewide plan.[p] However, some form of offset policy will have to be adopted by most states in order to maintain NAAQS once the standards are achieved. In Hudson County, for example, in the absence of new technologies or state efforts to adopt strict transportation controls, the possibilities for future offsets do not look promising, and future siting of major new energy facilities remains in doubt. This will probably be true for many nonattainment urban coastal areas.

[o]See Chapter 4.

[p] Texas attempted to obtain a waiver, but it was rejected by EPA.

NOTES

1. "Additional Air Pollution Said Unacceptable Threat," *Virginian Pilot* (Norfolk), April 20, 1976.
2. Ibid.
3. "EPA Will Reassess Refinery Statement," *Richmond Times-Dispatch*, Richmond, Va., April 29, 1976.
4. "Corps Awaits EPA Refinery Statement," ibid., April 21, 1976.
5. *Federal Register*, 41, no. 240 (December 21, 1976).
6. "Doing a Balancing Act With Air Quality," reprinted from the May 31, 1976, issue of *Business Week* (no. 2434), pp. 68-70, by special permission, © 1976 by McGraw-Hill, Inc. All rights reserved.
7. "The Texas Rebellion Over EPA's Air Rules," ibid., no. 2461 (December 6, 1976), pp. 97-98.
8. "Pollution May Kill VW's Rabbit Plant," ibid., no. 2473 (March 7, 1977), p. 26.
9. "Refinery Gets Permit Extension," *Richmond Times-Dispatch*, Richmond, Va., October 4, 1977.
10. "Plan to Advance Refinery Proposed," *Virginian-Pilot* (Norfolk), August 20, 1977.
11. Ibid.
12. Interview with Kenneth Dunn, Liaison Officer, Office of Environmental Review, U.S. Environmental Protection Agency, Washington, D.C., April 24, 1980.

PART II

Alternative Patterns of Development: Energy Facility Siting in the Gulf Coast Region

Chapter 6

Case Study of a Refinery Sited in Louisiana

*Research and Planning
Consultants, Inc.*

In the early 1970s, companies that had been involved in marketing, transporting, or utilizing large volumes of energy products foresaw the need to expand their production facilities within the United States. Owing to the decreasing availability and increasing price of energy products, these companies anticipated profitable returns on their investments in new domestic energy facilities. However, though many firms considered diversification, few committed themselves to the extent of proposing a $300-million refinery as its first venture of this kind. One that did was the Ingram Corporation, a closely held nonpublic corporation formed under the laws of the state of Delaware but with its headquarters in New Orleans, Louisiana. Through its subsidiaries, Ingram was principally engaged in transport of petroleum products and construction of pipelines.[1]

In 1972, officials at Ingram became convinced of the need for a refinery to process high-sulfur crude oil into low-sulfur residual oil.[a] Most U.S. refineries processed "sweet" domestic crudes (less than 0.5 sulfur by weight); they lacked the desulfurization equipment required to refine Middle Eastern and South American oil.[2] Ingram

---

[a]"Resid" is fuel oil that remains after removal of valuable distillates such as gasoline. Industry is the principal user of residual oil.

believed industrial firms and utility companies would serve as a strong market for desulfurized fuel oil.

The company sought a partner for its refining project and by early 1973 found one: Northeast Petroleum Corporation, a wholly owned subsidiary of Northeast Petroleum Industries, Inc. This subsidiary is the largest independent marketer of wholesale and retail gasoline and fuel oil in New England and the second largest on the East Coast. The two partners formed the Energy Corporation of Louisiana. In the summer of 1974 a subsidiary of this institution, ECOL, Ltd., began construction of the largest independent refinery (200,000 barrels per day) in the United States. The process of siting this facility in St. John the Baptist Parish, Louisiana, resembles the process employed to build many major energy facilities in recent years. However, the $300-million facility was designed, sited, and constructed in a relatively short period of time—less than five years—and the plant was welcomed by state and local officials.

In fact, this favorable political climate was one of the factors that led ECOL to select a Gulf Coast site. The Northeast is the major fuel oil market in the United States. While the partners would have preferred to locate their refinery along the East Coast in order to be nearer this market, they did not seriously consider siting in this region. To quote James O'Neill, executive vice-president of Ingram, "time was of the essence"; delays anticipated in permitting and constructing the plant discouraged ECOL from attempting to site in this region.[3]

ECOL's selection of a Gulf Coast site followed existing trends. Historically, the oil and gas fields of Texas and Louisiana stimulated construction of processing facilities nearby, thereby contributing to geographic separation of refineries and principal markets. Intense land and population pressures have restricted the siting of new refineries on the East Coast in recent years. As a result of these two factors, approximately two-thirds of the products that emanate from U.S. refineries and are marketed on the East Coast now come from Gulf Coast refineries.[4]

ECOL considered 30 sites before choosing its final location, along the banks of the Mississippi River 35 miles west of New Orleans. Each site was evaluated relative to 10 basic requirements:

Minimum area of 1,000 acres
Minimum deep water river frontage: 3,000 feet
Stable river bank

    Adequate distance from heavily populated areas, hospitals,
    schools, and convalescent homes
Ample availability of public utilities
Adequate drainage
Proximity to the major existing and proposed pipeline systems
Adequate availability of skilled labor
Cooperative attitude of state and local governments
Adequate highway and railroad accessibility.[5]

In addition, in its attempt to select "the best possible site" the corporation considered a number of other factors, including "economic resource procurement, marketing, design criteria, labor, tax structures and environmental impacts."[6]

The original list included 30 sites in South Carolina, Mississippi, and Louisiana. It was then narrowed to 11, 10 along the Mississippi River in Louisiana and the other near Pascagoula, Mississippi. The sites in South Carolina were dropped because of anticipated opposition from environmental groups. The remaining 11 sites were carefully scrutinized by officials of the firm. Four were rejected because of navigational hazards, revetment problems related to construction of dock facilities, or both; and for a number of others, land prices were above the amount ECOL was willing to pay.

After months of internal corporate discussions and external negotiations, ECOL selected 2,440 acres of land, known as the San Francisco Plantation, that met all of its basic requirements and also offered clear advantages. After the site was acquired and construction plans were formalized, ECOL submitted applications for the necessary permits to the appropriate local, state, and federal agencies. Construction and (later) operational permits were obtained with only one recorded objection to the facility.

The official ground-breaking ceremonies were held in October 1974, and 22 months later the first tanker docked at the ECOL plant. However, the Federal Energy Administration's (FEA) rulings on fuel oil entitlements in early 1976 greatly affected ECOL's production and marketing plans.[7] Officials of the firm became concerned over the economic feasibility of their refining project and were receptive to Marathon Oil Company's offer to purchase the entire facility. ECOL agreed to sell Marathon the plant for approximately $400 million, and the sale was completed in September 1976. Thus, within a period of four years ECOL had built and sold the largest refinery every constructed in a single phase in the continental United States.

THE COMPANY

Although the ECOL siting process was similar to that employed by many industrial firms, each siting process is unique to some extent, depending on three factors: the administrative entity or political-legal jurisdiction in which the facility is to be located; the type and demands of particular industrial activities; and the personality of the company.[8] The last variable is particularly relevant to a discussion of the ECOL siting process. Had another firm sought to site a similar refinery in Louisiana, the siting process might have resulted in a rather different outcome. Not only might the site ultimately selected have been different, but also the tone and character of the interaction between the company, government officials, and private citizens might have been altered.

A company's previous experience and preferences are major determinants of its personality, and certainly the ECOL siting process reflects the importance of the experience and preferences of the two partners in the project. For example, the involvement of Ingram and Northeast in marketing and transporting energy products led them to consider expanding into refining; and Ingram, which played the lead role in formation of the partnership, expressed an early interest in siting along the Gulf Coast near the company's headquarters. The partners saw the major marketing area for their refined products as the Northeast, but they did not seriously consider siting in this region.[9]

ECOL was described by O'Neill as "a happy joint venture."[10] While geographic features of the various possible sites dominated the evaluation, local economic data and "the cooperative attitude of state and local officials" were also important. The new firm's management structure drew heavily from the two parent companies, reflecting the hybrid nature of the project. The chairman of ECOL's board of directors, F. B. Ingram, was also chairman of the Ingram Corporation. O'Neill, later executive vice-president of the Ingram Corporation, at the time served as a director on the ECOL, Ltd., board. One of ECOL's vice-presidents was a former employee of Northeast Petroleum. Both ECOL's president and senior vice-president were members of the board of directors. These individuals set the tone of the project and were responsible for the siting decision.

THE SELECTED SITE

The site ultimately selected by ECOL is within an area

called the New Orleans River Region, comprised of seven parishes:[b] Orleans, Jefferson, Plaquemines, St. Bernard, St. Charles, St. James, and St. John the Baptist (see Figure 6-1). This region has published brochures detailing its advantages and encouraging energy facilities to investigate siting within the New Orleans–River Region area. Generally, state and local officials have joined in encouraging industries to site within these parishes.

The region's obvious center is the city and port of New Orleans. With the general increase in industrial activity in this area, demand for riverfront property in New Orleans has outpaced supply. Companies seeking large tracts of waterfront property have thus been encouraged to look for sites within the larger River Region, enabling them to draw on the city's skilled labor supply and other resources. Figure 6-2 shows some of the vast number of facilities that have located in this region.

ECOL was the first major industrial facility to site in St. John the Baptist Parish. Local officials were pleased by ECOL's decision, and have worked to encourage other industrial firms to site within the parish. Their efforts have been successful. Since the siting of the ECOL plant, two other major facilities have been sited in the area, a petrochemical complex and a steel mill.

Local government officials' positive attitude toward siting of the facility in this parish was definitely a factor in ECOL's selection of the San Francisco Plantation site. The site contained 2,440 acres of land and approximately 6,100 feet of frontage along the east bank of the Mississippi River. Construction of dock facilities at this site would not interfere with normal navigation along the river. A substantial portion of the property had been cleared and well drained to allow for cultivation of sugarcane.

As shown on Figure 6-3, the site offered access to two major railroads and a major highway. ECOL did construct one major access road along the site's eastern boundary.

Adequate supplies of water and utilities were available. Louisiana Power and Light Company had sufficient reserve capacity to supply the facility from their main generating station located about 15 miles from the site. In fact, a transmission line already crossed the San Francisco property, and electric supply to the site was both immediately adequate and accessible. Potable water could be purchased from St. John the Baptist Parish and also processed at the plant. Untreated water from the Mississippi River could supply the refinery's water system.

[b]Louisiana parishes correspond with the county level of government in many states.

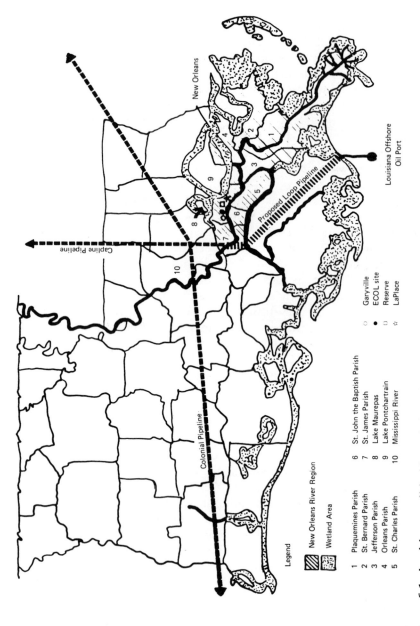

Figure 6-1. Louisiana—political boundaries, offshore port, and major pipeline systems. *(Source:* Louisiana Offshore Terminal Authority, *A Summary: The Effects of Superport Development on Louisiana Refining, Petrochemical and Related Growth,* New Orleans: no date, p. 27).

Legend

New Orleans River Region

Wetland Area

1 Plaquemines Parish
2 St. Bernard Parish
3 Jefferson Parish
4 Orleans Parish
5 St. Charles Parish

6 St. John the Baptist Parish
7 St. James Parish
8 Lake Maurepas
9 Lake Pontchartrain
10 Mississippi River

○ Garyville
● ECOL site
□ Reserve
☆ LaPlace

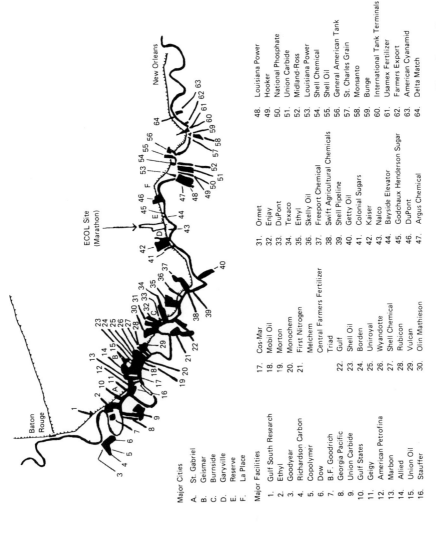

Baton
Rouge

ECOL Site
(Marathon)

New Orleans

Major Cities

A. St. Gabriel
B. Geismar
C. Burnside
D. Garyville
E. Reserve
F. La Place

Major Facilities

1. Gulf South Research
2. Ethyl
3. Goodyear
4. Richardson Carbon
5. Copolymer
6. Dow
7. B.F. Goodrich
8. Georgia Pacific
9. Union Carbide
10. Gulf States
11. Geigy
12. American Petrofina
13. Marbon
14. Allied
15. Union Oil
16. Stauffer

17. Cos-Mar
18. Mobil Oil
19. Morton
20. Monochem
21. First Nitrogen
   Melchem
   Central Farmers Fertilizer
   Triad
22. Gulf
23. Shell Oil
24. Borden
25. Uniroyal
26. Wyandotte
27. Shell Chemical
28. Rubicon
29. Vulcan
30. Olin Mathieson

31. Ormet
32. Enjay
33. DuPont
34. Texaco
35. Ethyl
36. Skelly Oil
37. Freeport Chemical
38. Swift Agricultural Chemicals
39. Shell Pipeline
40. Getty Oil
41. Colonial Sugars
42. Kaiser
43. Nalco
44. Bayside Elevator
45. Godchaux Henderson Sugar
46. DuPont
47. Argus Chemical

48. Louisiana Power
49. Hooker
50. National Phosphate
51. Union Carbide
52. Midland-Ross
53. Louisiana Power
54. Shell Chemical
55. Shell Oil
56. General American Tank
57. St. Charles Grain
58. Monsanto
59. Bunge
60. International Tank Terminals
61. Usamex Fertilizer
62. Farmers Export
63. American Cyanamid
64. Delta Match

Figure 6-2. Industries along the Mississippi River. (*Source:* Kim Rhodes, "ECOL Refinery... First Grass Roots Project in U.S.," *Louisiana Contractor*, March 1976, p. 11).

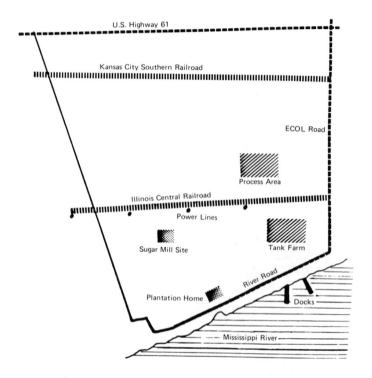

Figure 6-3. The ECOL site. (*Source:* ECOL, Ltd., *Environmental Assessment, ECOL, Ltd., Energy Refinery, St. John the Baptist Parish,* Baton Rouge: Louisiana State University School of Environmental Design, 1975, plate 2.3-1.)

The site provided excellent proximity to major existing and proposed pipeline systems. The Colonial pipeline, the most important products pipeline system in the United States, is within 60 miles. The proposed pipeline from the Louisiana Offshore Oil Port (LOOP) passes within 15 miles of the selected site on its route to connect with the Capline pipeline system at St. James, Louisiana. The Capline system, a major one, extends north to Illinois. A spur line can be built from the ECOL facility to the LOOP pipeline (see Figure 6-1).

The LOOP project, the first phase of which is scheduled to be operational in 1980, will be the first deepwater "superport" in the United States. LOOP, Inc., a venture of a number of oil companies, is constructing a private oil terminal in the Gulf of Mexico 19 miles south of the mouth of Bayou LaFourche. The port is designed to accommodate very large crude carriers (VLCCs) at initially three, and eventually six, single point mooring buoys. The initial capacity of LOOP is estimated at 1.4 million barrels of crude oil per day, with an ultimate projected capacity of 3.4 million barrels per day.

There is little doubt that the proximity of LOOP and its associated pipeline system proved an added incentive for ECOL to select the San Francisco Plantation site. LOOP would allow for direct unloading of Middle Eastern crude arriving on VLCCs, and the docking facilities at the plant would handle cargoes that had been moved from VLCCs to smaller vessels in the Bahamas. In fact, in ECOL's environmental assessment the point is made that "only two other refineries of significant size are as well located with respect to LOOP."[11] It is also reasonable to assume that the refinery's location contributed to Marathon Oil Company's interest in purchasing the facility, especially since one of its subsidiaries, Marathon Pipeline Company, is a partner in the LOOP project.

Finally, the selected site was removed from heavily populated areas, hospitals, schools, and residential neighborhoods. It did, however, pose a "historic" problem. Located on the property is an antebellum mansion, built before 1860. One of the few mansions left to reflect the rich history of this region, the decaying house was "a fantasia on a steamboat theme with Gothic overtones."[12] ECOL pledged to restore this mansion to "its original splendor," and after financing a reported two million dollars to meet this pledge, the firm turned the project over to a nonprofit foundation.[13]

In summary, the ECOL siting process was similar to many others in its basic components. The firm decided to construct a facility and sought sites that would satisfy certain requirements. After evaluating numerous potential sites, ECOL selected one based not only on the needs of the proposed industrial activity, but also on the experiences and preferences of the firm.

However, this process does not end with a firm's selection of a site. There is another important variable: the political-legal jurisdiction in which the firm seeks to receive siting approval. While admittedly ECOL, like many other firms, discussed its plans with local and state officials before purchasing a site, it was not until the firm received the necessary government permits that construction could begin. Although the possibility that government agencies or citizen opposition may prevent a firm from constructing a facility on a particular site is increasingly prevalent today in many areas of the country, ECOL encountered no major problems in obtaining the required permits.

THE FEDERAL AND STATE PERMIT PROCESS

The ECOL facility was originally designed to yield maximum quantities of residual fuel oil and middle distillates and smaller quantities of unleaded gasoline and asphalt. Table 6-1 details the planned daily product output. In addition to the processing units and blending facilities that constitute the major portion of the refinery, ECOL also built two docks on the Mississippi River, storage tanks for crude products, utility boilers, and river and wastewater treatment facilities. The original storage capacity of the tank farm was 7,296,000 barrels.

Before beginning construction and operation of the refining plant and its support facilities, ECOL was required to meet certain state and federal standards. In Louisiana, a firm must obtain a construction permit from the parish government before seeking state and federal approval of its plans. St. John the Baptist Parish not only issued ECOL the necessary construction permit but also offered to supply pollution control devices for the facility, an agreement that will be discussed in greater detail in the next section.

When the parish permit was obtained, ECOL, under the laws of Louisiana, was required to obtain state approval of the facility's solid waste disposal operations, wastewater discharges, and air emissions. The facility also had to meet federal air emission standards

Table 6-1. Projected Daily Output of the ECOL Refinery

Product	Barrels
Residual fuel oils	95,743
Home heating oil	40,000
Unleaded gasoline	31,912
Chemical feedstocks	13,460
Asphalt and industrial flux	10,000
Plant fuels and process loss	8,885
Total	200,000

Source: Louisiana Department of Commerce and Industry, *Monthly Report* 1, no. 1 (January 1975), p. 1.

and obtain permits for its wastewater discharges and any dredging or alteration of the Mississippi River.

It is important to understand the relationship between these two levels of government in Louisiana, which, unlike Texas, relies heavily on its powers of comment on federal permits to protect its natural resources. The Louisiana statutes evince a purpose and intent of nondegradation of a particular resource and then give an agency control over the specific resources. These statutes are organized by agencies rather than natural resources and do not spell out how this control is to be exercised. These agencies do not issue permits, but certificates of approval or letters of no objection instead. Certificates or letters are generally issued by an agency's staff without a public hearing. If enforcement is required, the agency must prove that the facility was responsible for the specific violation of a standard. Proof may be difficult because the agencies feel they must show this facility alone to be responsible, given the vagueness of the statutory language. For example, a facility discharging wastewater into a stream must be shown to be singularly responsible for the stream's failure to meet the ambient standards.

Much of the slack created by the weak statutory language is taken up by state agencies' ability to request changes in federal permits. Generally, federal agencies request that appropriate state agencies comment on the federal permit application, and most federal agencies will not issue permits over the objections of state agencies. Louisiana relies heavily on this comment power of its state agencies.

State Solid Waste "Permits"

The ECOL facility planned to dispose of much of its solid waste by contracting with a licensed waste disposal operation. Thus although ECOL did not need a permit to dispose of solid waste through a commercial operator, the state agency controlling the commercial operator would require the operator to get a waste characterization form from ECOL. These forms are essentially a report of what ECOL gives to the commercial operator and in what quantities.

ECOL did plan to dispose of some solid waste, specifically bauxite (a spent catalyst) and sludge. Its landfill operations required a letter of approval from the secretary of the Louisiana Health and Human Resources Administration (HHRA). Neither Louisiana law nor HHRA's administrative rules give detailed and specific information as to how plans for landfill operations will be evaluated by the agency or what standards an applicant must meet.

Anyone who wants to operate a disposal plant sends in an

operational plan and maps. According to agency personnel, the maps are sent to the Louisiana Office of Conservation for evaluation of the geology of the disposal site. For disposal of industrial and hazardous solid waste, the geology of the area is looked at much more carefully, and the agency prefers at least 100 feet of clay beneath the site. The agency also requires a waste characterization form for each type of material placed in the site. The agency does not hold public hearings; therefore, there is no public input on site selection other than the parish police jury's comments,[c] which are limited to public health and environmental considerations.

State Water Quality Approval

Before ECOL could discharge waste into state waters, the Stream Control Commission (SCC) had to evaluate the type of wastes to be discharged and the treatment plans for the discharge. The SCC issues letters of no objection for discharges into the waters of the state. Applicants for such a letter must submit standard forms that are evaluated by SCC staff. The six-member commission, membership of which is determined by statute, holds a hearing and decides whether or not to issue a letter of no objection. SCC also promulgates water quality criteria for the state. Those criteria include the following:

> The Louisiana Stream Control Commission will disapprove any waste discharge that will cause water quality degradation of interstate waters and intrastate waters, portions thereof, and the coastal waters of Louisiana below the standards adopted by the State of Louisiana and approved by the United States Environmental Protection Agency without complying with the Federal and State of Louisiana laws applicable to the attainment of water quality standards. Any industrial, public or private project of development that would constitute a new source of pollution or an increased source of pollution to any of the waters in Louisiana will be required, as part of the initial project design, to provide the highest and best degree of waste treatment available under existing technology consistent with the best practice in the area affected under the condition applicable to the project or development.[14]

According to agency personnel, the normal rule is that on bigger streams the SCC uses EPA guidelines, while on smaller streams

---

[c]Louisiana parishes are generally governed by police juries, the members of which are elected from wards for terms of four years. However, many officials, such as the sheriff, clerk of courts, assessor, school board, and coroner, are not controlled by the police jury.

it enforces stricter requirements on total suspended solids and turbidity.

SCC has control of "waste disposal, public or private, by any person, into any of the waters of the state or any tributaries of drains flowing into any of such waters, for the prevention of pollution thereof tending to destroy fish life or to be injurious to the public health, the public welfare, or to other aquatic life or domestic animals or fowls."[15] It is specified that the Stream Control Commission:

1. Shall establish such pollution standards for waters of the state in relation to the public use to which they are or may be put as it deems necessary;
2. May ascertain and determine for record and for use in making its order what volume of water actually flows in any stream and the high and low water marks of waters of the state affected by the waste disposal or pollution of any person;
3. May by order of regulation control, regulate, or restrain the discharge of any waste material or polluting substance discharged or sought to be discharged into any water of the state;
4. May prohibit any discharge resulting in pollution which is unreasonable and against the public interest in view of the existing conditions in the waters of the state.[16]

HHRA has jurisdiction "over the handling, storage and disposal of waste materials, including solids and liquid residues, and disposal of sewage."[17]

The Bureau of Environmental Services (BES) must approve plans and issue permits for public and private sewerage systems and industrial wastes. BES must issue a permit if industrial waste is to be discharged into state waters used as a source of a public water supply. According to agency personnel, BES issues a letter of approval without a public hearing. In September 1975, SCC sent ECOL a letter of no objection granting the company permission to discharge waste as long as "the discharges will not violate water quality standards of the State of Louisiana."[18]

State Air Quality Approval

ECOL received a certificate of approval from the Louisiana Air Control Commission (ACC) to construct its facilities. ECOL was required to demonstrate compliance with ACC regulations and control technology for emissions of smoke. particulates, volatile organic compounds, and sulfur.

ACC has specific rules and regulations concerning emission standards and application requirements. The agency requires applicants to submit:

1. A brief statement describing the action which is proposed.
2. A statement giving the location of the industrial plant or manufacturing establishment, or a map showing such location.
3. A statement giving the location of sources of emission of air contaminants as defined in Section 4.4, the size of the outlets of such sources, the rate and temperature of the emission from such sources, and the composition and description of the air contaminants being emitted from said sources. Fugitive emission shall be determined from test results or best available technical data.
4. A statement giving a description of the air pollution abatement measures which will be utilized, and if no facilities within the definition of this term are contemplated, the steps which will be taken to prevent the emission of sufficient quantities of pollutants to result in undesirable levels.
5. An estimate of the extent to which the emission from the proposed facilities will alter or affect the quality of the air of Louisiana. This estimate should, considering new and existing emission sources, predict the cumulative maximum worst case ground level concentration of each pollutant involved. If said maximum occurs within plant site boundaries, cumulative maximum property line value should also be determined.
6. At the discretion of the Technical Secretary, a more detailed ambient analysis may be requested. The analysis will involve predicting maximum ambient air concentrations using emissions from all sources within an area defined by the Technical Secretary. Emissions data will be made available by the Department.
7. Such other pertinent data as may be necessary for a good understanding of the proposal which is being made.[19]

According to agency personnel, the application is sent to the air control district in which the facility is to be located to be reviewed by the public. After 30 days and a staff review, the application is submitted to ACC for approval or denial. Louisiana law requires ACC to consider several things when reviewing a new emission source, including the character and degree of injury to, or interference with, the health and physical property of the people; the social and economic value of the source; the priority of location in the area involved; and the technical practicability and economic reasonableness of reducing or eliminating the proposed emissions.[20] The Louisiana Air Control Law states that:

It is the intent and purpose of this law to maintain purity of the air resources of this state consistent with the protection of the health and physical property of the people, maximum employment and the full industrial development of the state.[21]

Federal Permits

The refinery also required several federal permits. Although ECOL did not have to have an EPA permit for air emissions, the facility did have to meet the federal agency's performance standards that limited sulfur oxide emissions from process heaters burning refinery fuel gas and also limited hydrocarbon evaporation losses from storage vessels by specifying the type of storage vessel allowed for crude oil and various petroleum products.

ECOL required a National Pollutant Discharge Elimination System (NPDES) permit from EPA. The facility was in EPA's petroleum refinery category, topping subcategory.[22] ECOL had to provide best available demonstrated control technology on startup and best available technology economically achievable by 1983. The NPDES permit included effluent limitations in pounds per day for Biological Oxygen Demand (BOD), Chemical Oxygen Demand (COD), Total Suspended Solids (TSS), oil and grease, phenol, ammonia, and sulfide.

Any alteration of the Mississippi River, including construction of dock facilities, required a permit from the U.S. Army Corps of Engineers. The corps has extensive authority over activities occurring in or affecting navigable waters. An entity that wants to construct, reconstruct, or conduct major renovation of a structure in, on, or under navigable water must obtain a Section 10 permit from the corps.[23] Section 404 of the Federal Water Pollution Control Act Amendments of 1972[24] requires the corps to use a permit system to regulate the discharge of dredged or fill material into navigable waters.

THE LOCAL GOVERNMENT
AND THE COMMUNITY

For decades, St. John the Baptist Parish, like many other areas along the Mississippi River, was primarily agricultural. Since before the Civil War, cotton, sugar cane, and other cultivated crops have been grown in the parish and then shipped down the river to New Orleans for sale. However, as the market for these products declined and industrial activity in New Orleans expanded, significant changes occurred. Robert Becnel, Secretary-Treasurer of the parish government, described the parish as now being "a bedroom community to New Orleans."[25]

Becnel distinguished the two catalysts involved in this change, which he feels began in about 1974 with the arrival of the ECOL facility. First, completion of interstate highway 10 connecting Baton Rouge and New Orleans made the parish more accessible to both of these cities. Second, while a number of industrial facilities were located within the parish, including an E.I. du Pont de Nemours and Company plant, a Kaiser Aluminum and Chemical Corporation plant, sugar refineries, and grain elevators, the ECOL siting in that year marked the real beginning of the parish's switch to a more industrial economy. Local government officials accelerated their promotion of industrial development. In 1977, Shell Chemical Company announced its plans to build a $500-million ethylene manufacturing plant in a parish across the river from St. John the Baptist. More recently, a European company met with parish officials and agreed to locate a steel mill in the area. Government officials are pleased with such siting decisions and apparently feel the positive economic benefits outweigh any negative environmental impacts.

Becnel stated that the parish will probably continue to encourage development along the river, but it will discourage or constrain siting outside of this corridor. As a result, industrial facilities will be concentrated away from the sensitive wetlands in the northern and southern portions of the parish. Becnel reported that many individuals favored restricting development in these wetland areas in order to maintain them as major hunting and fishing grounds.

Louisiana parishes have the authority to zone outside of the jurisdictions of municipal governments. However, St. John the Baptist Parish, like many other parishes, does not currently exercise its land use powers. Becnel foresees the parish beginning to use its zoning authority within the next few years, but mainly as a means of controlling commercial and residential development rather than industrial facilities.

Presently, the requirement that facilities obtain a construction permit from the parish government is seen as sufficient to control industrial siting in the area. Louisiana parishes also provide a variety of public services to industry, such as water and road maintenance. A parish's permitting authority and its provision of services encourage firms to contact local officials early in the siting process, and parish officials favor this early notification.[26]

Residents of the parish also appear to favor industrial development in the area. The downturn in the market for sugar cane has left many farmers who owned riverfront property happy to sell their acreage and use the money to "buy new homes and travel."[27] Industrial facilities offer employment either directly or through spinoff jobs. Approximately half of the parish's work force was employed outside of the parish in 1970, and development will certainly increase local employment opportunities. In addition, in 1970 the income of two-thirds of the families in the parish was below $10,000; 18.5 percent of the families had incomes under $3,000. Industrial development not only offers employment but it also offers relatively well-paying jobs.

Certainly, the absence of local land use pressures has influenced residents' attitudes. Although the parish covers 188,271 acres, in 1970 approximately 85 percent of its 23,813 residents lived in its three towns: Garyville (2,474), LaPlace (5,953), and Reserve (11,900). Even with growth of industrial development in the parish there is still abundant open space and recreational land. The availability of land for various uses, which has influenced industries' decisions to site in parishes near New Orleans rather than in the city, is probably an additional factor in the pro-development attitude of the residents in many of these communities experiencing industrial growth.

However, this pro-development attitude of residents involves more than just employment opportunities and lack of land use conflicts. Generally, individuals in Louisiana, as in Texas, simply do not find industrial facilities offensive and are not overly concerned with the effects of these facilities on its environment. Perhaps the long history of energy development and production in these states has contributed to this attitude.

The siting of the ECOL facility, then, far from being opposed by local officials and residents in St. John the Baptist Parish, was welcomed. Becnel discussed only one negative impact in connection with this specific facility: traffic congestion when shifts are changed at the plant. He affirmed that the parish government was "very pleased with ECOL."[28] In fact, the parish government offered to lease pollution control equipment to the company under a buy-back agreement. This equipment, including installation costs, was to be financed by St. John the Baptist Parish through sale of tax-exempt bonds to private investors. The refining company would then lease the equipment over a period of 25 years, at which time ownership would be transferred to the company. Upon acquiring the facility, Marathon accepted the parish's offer to install the pollution control equipment.

Sale of these bonds thus benefited both the firm and the parish.[29] The parish not only benefited environmentally but also financially. Industrial facilities are exempted from local property taxes for a period of 10 years in Louisiana, and this moratorium can place economic burdens on local governments. However, according to Becnel the pollution control lease agreement was designed to help the parish government finance any needed expansion of services.[30] Since the parish offers this equipment to the company, thus allowing the company to realize a federal tax savings, the parish requests the company to agree to make in-lieu-of-tax payments to the general fund. For Marathon, this amounts to approximately $17,000 per year.

Environmental Impacts

Although the only negative impact of the ECOL facility identified by Becnel involved traffic congestion, the ECOL environmental assessment does present a number of other impacts, both positive and negative. According to the assessment, the refinery would have little impact on wildlife, basically because the site's natural environment had already been heavily modified through continued cultivation. Wetlands would also not be impacted because the facility itself was to be away from the marshes.

Noise is a potential problem with most major industrial facilities. The ECOL refinery is designed to minimize this impact. Even on the grounds of the restored plantation house, noise associated with the refinery is not noticeable.[31]

Although the plant was designed to operate within primary and secondary ambient air standards, there has certainly been some detectable deterioration in air quality. However, the plant's design also made use of fragrant vegetation to reduce industrial odors.

Treatment of waste waters meets or exceeds the EPA's 1983 standards. However, the only recorded opposition to the facility involved the plant's waste treatment system. At least two environmental groups, the St. Charles Environmental Council and the Louisiana Wildlife Federation, objected to the discharge of waste water into Lake Maurepas, located in a critical wetland area nearby (see Figure 6-1). According to the environmental assessment, the firm investigated three alternative ways to dispose of its treated waste waters. Considered, but ruled out from the beginning, was the possibility of injecting waste water into the subsurface aquifers. Primarily because of the energy required and the fact that pumping into an aquifer removes the buffering of natural filtration, this was not an acceptable solution. The Mississippi River was also considered as a receiving body.[32] The major disadvantage to this alternative was that it would require continuous use of energy-consuming equipment to return the water to the river. There was also the psychological problem of discharging treated waste upstream from the intake to a community water supply. Lake Maurepas was the receiving body selected. The treated waste waters from the facility would enter a system of ditches, canals, and bayous that flow into the lake.

Under this plan, it was proposed that this system would provide for natural dilution of the facility's effluent from ground and surface waters before the wastes reached the lake. Maurepas, a lake deprived of overbank and crevasse flow from the Mississippi River,[d] which was one of its natural sources of replenishment, would be aided by this additional water flow (according to the ECOL environmental assessment).[33] However, this document also listed as one of the favorable environmental impacts of the project the reduction of the amount of waste water entering Lake Maurepas from 7,000 to 800 gpm because of the closing of the old sugar mill. This mill had used the same system of canals and bayous flowing into the lake for disposal of its waste water. According to ECOL's assessment, this reduction of 6,200 gpm would also produce a more favorable dilution ratio with surface and ground waters entering the system of canals and bayous.

Upon receipt of notice of ECOL's NPDES application concerning discharge into Lake Maurepas, the St. Charles Environmental Council and the Louisiana Wildlife Federation wrote a letter of protest to the SCC expressing concern over the impact of the discharge on the lake. SCC replied that it had issued a letter of no objection several months before. These groups offered no further protest to the facility.

The letter had been issued after SCC's technical staff had reviewed the ECOL permit application. SCC supported ECOL's choice of Lake Maurepas rather than the Mississippi River as the receiving body for its waste water. The staff noted that effluent limitations contained in the Louisiana permit are more restrictive than those contained in the EPA permit. In addition, the effluent limitations proposed were more restrictive than those called for by EPA in 1983. It was the judgment of the technical staff that the treatment planned for ECOL wastes would exceed the best practicable treatment anticipated by SCC to be required as of 1983, and no objection was made.

[d]Crevasse flow is the water that flows through a break in a natural or artificial levee system during high-water periods. With the strengthening of the artificial levee system of the Mississippi River, Lake Maurepas is now dependent on drainage from the watershed and rainfall replenishment and does not receive floodwaters from the Mississippi.

The refinery did, in fact, win an award for Distinguished Service in Environmental Planning in 1977 from the Industrial Development Research Council (IDRC) and Conway Publications. In constructing the refinery, more than $15 million had been spent on pollution control systems. Extensive use of air cooling was employed to minimize water use, thereby providing an effluent of a quality that exceeds EPA guidelines. Sour gas from the refinery operations is treated and sulfur removed in a sulfur recovery plant. Vented hydrocarbons from the process area are collected in a closed system and burned in a smokeless flare.

Had the refinery more directly threatened the broad issues of concern to organized environmental groups such as the American Lung Association of Louisiana, it is possible that it would have met more opposition. Likewise, had the refinery been sited in a less remote area, that is, closer to either New Orleans or Baton Rouge where the groups are centered, people might have been more concerned.[34] Thus siting had a direct impact on lessening the chances of citizen opposition.

Local opposition might also have been greater if the circumstances surrounding the ECOL facility had been different. It is apparent that citizens in the area are prone to organize when concerned about a facility that may adversely affect their lives. For example, there was much local opposition to the possible construction of grain elevators in the vicinity. The grain elevators, however, were proposed to be located near a residential area. Residents in the neighborhood feared the grain elevators posed a safety hazard because of the possibility of explosion.[35]

The ECOL refinery, in contrast, met the conditions for further industrial development along the Mississippi River, where industry is being strongly promoted. While representing a change in land use away from agricultural production, ECOL also was to be located away from major residential areas. Thus, it was not seen as presenting a threat to the lives of any local citizens.

Economic Impacts

As discussed previously, the economic impacts associated with the ECOL facility are seen as positive by most local residents. Construction of the facility provided approximately 2,500 temporary jobs for skilled and unskilled workers. The plant was scheduled to provide 175 permanent jobs, many of which would be filled by local residents. The firm estimated the refinery's average annual payroll to be $3,345,000 [or an average salary per worker of over $19,000 per year]; "assuming an 8 times turn over of available monies (i.e., after deductions, taxes, and rent or house payment) the input into the local economy resulting from wages of the ECOL workers could run as high as $20,000,000 per year."[36] In other words, a multiplier of 5.97 was applied to the total wage payments. While the multiplier of 8.0 based on disposable income is probably realistic on a local regional level, for example, within the New Orleans River Region, this figure probably is high in terms of input into the local parish economy.

Of course, the actual number of jobs provided by the ECOL plant after construction is relatively small in relation to the land used and the capital expenditures. Dividing the 175 jobs into the total acreage acquired (2,440) produces a figure of only 0.071 job per acre; by calculating the number of acres actually used by the facility (540), one gets a figure of 0.324 job per acre. These figures, though, represent only the direct employment associated with the facility and do not include spinoff or indirect employment, which could be significant. Additionally, during the construction phase there were between 1.024 and 4.629 jobs per acre (depending on which acreage figure is used).

While the facility's direct and indirect economic impact on individuals living within the parish should be generally positive as the result of increased job opportunities, there will be certain negative economic impacts. Overall industrial development in the parish has led to an increased need for housing, and land prices have risen. There has also been an increased demand on public services such as schools, utilities, hospitals, and roadways. Because of provisions in state law, the local government will not receive tax revenues from the facility to aid in offsetting this increased demand on services.

Louisiana state law allows a facility to be exempted from local property taxes for a period of 10 years if a company agrees "to favor Louisiana manufacturers, suppliers, contractors, and labor, all other factors being equal."[37] The refinery built by ECOL and now owned by Marathon received this tax exemption; however, Marathon has agreed to make in-lieu-of-tax payments to help the parish finance expanded service needs. These yearly payments of approximately $17,000 per year are far less than the approximately $500,000 that would be owed in local property taxes and school taxes. (Table 6-2 gives the current taxing formulas of the parish government and the assessed value of the ECOL-Marathon refinery). As a result, the local government may experience some negative economic impacts caused by the expanded service needs.

Table 6-2. Local Government Taxing Formulas for the ECOL Refinery

---

St. John the Baptist Parish—Property Taxes
10% of assessed value of the property; subtract homestead exemption of up to $5,000;
1.11% of the remainder is the amount of taxes owed. Also 15% tax on the reported
inventory.

St. John the Baptist School Board—School Taxes
10% of assessed value of the property; subtract homestead exemption of up to $5,000;
the amount of taxes owed is $34 on every $1,000 of the remainder.

1978 Tax Assessments—Louisiana Refining Division of Marathon Oil Company
(formerly the ECOL facility)

Land assessment	$ 132,984
Inventory merchandise assessment	3,376,236
Total assessment	$3,902,220

Social Impacts

A number of social impacts have resulted from the location of the
ECOL facility. A definite change has come over the character of the
area, which the residents in general view as positive. Many people
who have lived in the parish for years are happy about the arrival
of industry. Because the sugar cane market has declined, plantation
owners have been willing to sell their property and enjoy the additional money; and people formerly employed as farmhands making
less than $2.50 per hour on the struggling plantations that line the
Mississippi River are glad to have jobs paying more than $8.00 an
hour in refineries such as ECOL. However, the ECOL refinery alone
will certainly not directly employ many of these individuals.

Some road improvements have also helped enhance the character
of the neighborhood by providing easier access to major highways
and removing through traffic from residential streets. For example,
a new connecting road was built from U.S. Highway 61 to State
Highway 44 that not only removed through traffic from the residential streets of Garyville and provided better access to the highways, but also alleviated some noise and air pollution from moving
vehicles. In addition, construction of a two-lane paved highway has
reduced travel on the gravel roads in the area, which in turn has reduced the dust and particulate matter.

The restoration of the San Francisco Plantation home is another
positive addition to the area as a result of ECOL. ECOL commis-
sioned an historical survey of the selected site by Robert Heck,
Professor of Architectural History at Louisiana State University. The

survey classified the San Francisco mansion as an historic house of national, state, and architectural significance. The Marmillion House, home of the plantation's overseer, was also recommended for restoration although categorized as of lesser historic and architectural importance. This house remains standing but has not been restored. Other buildings or areas recognized were the Old Millet House, the Adelord Millet House, and the Triche House, not for historic or architectural value but rather for visual interest. Bishops Cemetery was recommended for preservation, and the survey noted that an old nineteenth-century cemetery on the site had been destroyed in years past. The old sugar mill and certain live oaks surrounding the building were cited as being of some significance. Whenever possible these trees were saved and the cemetery was preserved; however, the sugar mill was sold and shipped to Panama.

There appears to be no problem with a change in the aesthetics of the area. Even today, driving along the Mississippi River on the River Road (LA 44) one sees few signs of the operating industrial facility. The high grass-covered bank prohibits a view of the river and the refinery's dock facilities, while a grove of trees and other plant cover located behind the restored plantation house restrict one's view of the refinery itself. In fact, the only real evidence of the facility are a bridge containing pipelines, which crosses over the road, and an occasional glimpse of the facility's storage tanks.

The increasing industrial development in the parish has certainly changed the lives of residents, who historically have lived in close-knit communities or on farms. Many of the people one saw on the streets or passed on the highway were close friends or kin. Undoubtedly industrialization of the area will change their communities and their relationships. In the long-term, then, their positive perceptions of the impacts of development on their lives may undergo certain changes. However, it would be impossible and invalid to attribute any such cumulative impacts directly to the ECOL facility alone.

SUMMARY

In April 1974, ECOL, Ltd., was incorporated under the laws of the state of Louisiana to construct and operate a petroleum refinery in the state. The corporation was formed as a result of the decision by Ingram Corporation and Northeast Petroleum Corporation to undertake a joint project. Within six months, ECOL began construction of the largest refinery ever built in a single phase within the United States.

Unlike most U.S. refineries, the ECOL facility was originally designed to produce residual fuel oil rather than gasoline. The market for the fuel oil produced by the ECOL facility was foreseen by the partners as primarily industries and utilities along the East Coast and in the Midwest.

From the standpoint of both raw product supply and finished product market, the ECOL principals would have preferred to site their proposed facility on the East Coast, but "time was of the essence" and anticipated delays in permitting and constructing the facility discouraged ECOL from attempting to site there. ECOL developed a list of 10 basic requirements and then sought sites that met these requirements. While most of these factors involved physical or geographic features, the company was also concerned about local and state economic and political climates. For example, taxing policies, labor availability, and the attitude of local officials were all considered in selecting a site. However, in contrast to the site selection criteria identified by Corpus Christi Petrochemical Company (see Chapter 7), ECOL did not specifically rank ability to obtain the necessary permits as a requirement. This is probably a function of the difference between these firms' siting processes. First, and most important, ECOL was sited two years before the Corpus Christi facility, and federal regulations and requirements vis-à-vis energy and industrial facilities were strengthened in this period. Second, the companies sought sites within different states that varied in their approach to regulating and permitting facilities.

After considering 30 different sites in South Carolina, Mississippi, and Louisiana, the company chose to locate on the San Francisco Plantation, with 2,440 acres of land and approximately 6,100 feet of frontage along the east bank of the Mississippi River. The site offered access to two major railroads and a major highway, excellent proximity to existing and proposed pipeline systems, and an opportunity to purchase electricity from the Louisiana Power and Light Company, which had an adequate supply to meet the additional demand.

The plantation is located in St. John the Baptist Parish, 34 miles from New Orleans and 46 miles from Baton Rouge. There was little local opposition to the facility. In fact, the parish government, which continues to seek additional industrial development in the area, worked closely with ECOL during the construction phase. The only opposition came from the environmental groups concerned about the dumping of waste water from the facility into a nearby lake. In the fall of 1976, ECOL, Ltd., sold the new facility to Marathon Oil Company, which now operates the plant through its

Louisiana Refining Division. This refinery is one of the largest now operating in the United States.

NOTES

1. Subsidiaries of the Ingram Corporation are engaged in "ocean transportation, inland waterways barge transportation of petroleum, chemicals, rock, sand and gravel, petrochemical marketing, and construction of oil and gas pipelines. The company also underwrites insurance, and has developed and now operates a . . . waste disposal transportation system for the city of Chicago, transporting sludge through a barge and pipeline complex." ECOL, Ltd., *Environmental Assessment, ECOL, Ltd.: Energy Refinery, St. John the Baptist Parish* (Baton Rouge: Louisiana State University, School of Environmental Design, 1975).
2. Many foreign crude oil reserves contain greater amounts of sulfur and some trace metals. Because of air quality standards, these foreign crudes must be desulfurized (which requires special processing equipment) for sale and use in the United States.
3. Personal interview with James O'Neill, Executive Vice President of the Ingram Corporation and a former director of ECOL, Ltd., May 30, 1978.
4. ECOL, *Environmental Assessment*, op. cit.
5. Ibid. and O'Neill, op. cit.
6. ECOL, *Environmental Assessment*, ibid.
7. The Federal Energy Administration on April 1, 1976, adopted several new provisions to the Mandatory Petroleum Allocation Regulations of the 1974 Entitlements Program. These new provisions severely affected ECOL and other petroleum companies that refined crude oil. Under one of these provisions, the volume in excess of the first 5,000 barrels per day of crude oil run to stills each month in or into the East Coast was reduced by 50 percent. These new provisions, according to FEA, did produce a certain degree of economic distortion for residual fuel oil prices. The result was depressed prices for this product on both the East and Gulf Coasts. The reduction in ECOL's entitlement benefits increased the company's costs and diminished its cash flow.
8. Research and Planning Consultants, Inc., *Siting Industrial Facilities on the Texas Coast* (Austin, Texas: RPC, September 15, 1978), p. 14, study conducted for the Texas Coastal Management Program and the General Land Office of Texas.
9. O'Neill, op. cit. ECOL's preference for Louisiana over Texas probably reflects the personality of the company and its past business experience in Louisiana.
10. Ibid.
11. ECOL, *Environmental Assessment*, op. cit.
12. Clarence John Laughlin, *Ghosts Along the Mississippi* (New York: Bonanza Books, 1961).
13. ECOL, *Environmental Assessment*, op. cit.
14. Louisiana Stream Control Commission, Water Quality Criteria.
15. L.S.A.-R.S. 56:1434. (Louisiana Statutes Annotated-Revised Statutes.)
16. L.S.A.-R.S. 56:1439.

17. L.S.A.-R.S. 40:5.
18. Letter from Louisiana Stream Control Commission to ECOL, September 26, 1975.
19. L.A.C. 14-11:6.3.1-6.3 (Louisiana Administrative Code).
20. L.S.A.-R.S. 40:2204.
21. L.S.A.-R.S. 40:2201 et seq.
22. EPA's regulations state: "The provisions of this subpart (topping) are applicable to discharges from any facility which produced petroleum products by the use of topping and catalytic reforming whether or not the facility includes any other process in addition to topping and catalytic reforming." 40 *CFR* Part 419.10 (Code of Federal Regulations).
23. 33 U.S.C.A. sec. 403 1970 (U.S. Code Annotated).
24. 33 U.S.C.A. 1251 et seq. (Supplement 1977).
25. Personal interview with Robert Becnel, Secretary-Treasurer of the Police Jury of St. John the Baptist Parish, May 30, 1978.
26. Ibid.
27. Ibid.
28. Ibid.
29. Ibid., and telephone interview with Don Albaugh, Louisiana Refining Division Manager, Marathon Oil Company, September 1978.
30. Becnel, op. cit.
31. Personal visit to site, May 30, 1978.
32. ECOL, *Environmental Assessment*, op. cit.
33. Ibid.
34. Five major environmental groups are active in New Orleans: Sierra Club, Orleans Audubon Society, Save Our Wetlands, American Lung Association of Louisiana, and Ecology Center of Louisiana. The first three groups mentioned largely concentrate on preserving the marsh and wetlands areas of the state and have opposed, even to the point of completely halting, projects that were seen as threatening to these areas. The Lung Association is interested in air quality, while water quality is one of the principal concerns of the Ecology Center.
35. Becnel, op. cit.
36. ECOL, *Environmental Assessment*, op. cit.
37. *Make Your Own Louisiana Purchase*, p. 14 (no date).

Chapter 7

Case Study of a Petrochemical Plant Sited in Texas

Research and Planning Consultants, Inc.

The same factors that led to the formation of ECOL, Ltd.—the decreasing availability and increasing price of energy products—led Champlin Petroleum Company, with headquarters in Fort Worth, Texas, to diversify into petrochemicals. In 1973, Champlin, a subsidiary of Union Pacific Corporation, was preparing a large expansion of its Corpus Christi refining facility so that it would be able to provide feedstocks to a new petrochemical plant.

After initial studies confirmed the project's feasibility, Champlin investigated several joint venture possibilities. In 1975, two European firms were identified that were interested in participating in the project. Both had U.S. subsidiaries that already utilized ethylene and propylene in their Texas manufacturing facilities. ICI United States, whose parent company is Imperial Chemical Industries Limited of the United Kingdom, operates a facility in Baytown, Texas; Soltex Polymer, whose parent company is Solvay and Cie. S.A. of Brussels, Belgium, operates a facility in Deer Park, Texas. The idea was for Champlin's expanded refinery to provide the feedstocks for a new petrochemical plant, with ICI United States and Soltex Polymer then using this plant's products in their existing Texas facilities.

In late 1975, the three companies agreed jointly to construct a

143

large olefins complex.[a] However, they did not enter into a formal partnership to construct and operate Corpus Christi Petrochemical Company (CCPC) until November 15, 1976. During this intervening 10-month period, the partners conducted engineering and design studies and sought a suitable site for the olefins facility. They agreed to use as a model an operational ICI plant in England; ICI's experience in construction of large, integrated plants significantly reduced the amount of time required to design the new facility.[b]

The partners had relatively little difficulty in locating a suitable site, a 1,200-acre tract of land 4.5 miles east of Robstown, Texas (see Figure 7-1). This is an urban fringe location, just outside the Corpus Christi city limits though within an area in which the city has authority to apply certain of its regulations (as discussed later). The plant site is in an agricultural area not being used by any major industries.

From the beginning of the project Champlin preferred to site on the Texas Gulf Coast.[1] Locating the plant in Texas would offer the partners proximity to their respective facilities and corporate offices. However, when the issue of a refinery tax was raised in Texas, the partners did temporarily investigate the possibility of siting in Louisiana, but they refocused on Texas when this policy was not enacted.[2] A number of Texas coastal sites were considered, including sites along the upper Houston ship channel, a site near Soltex Polymer's Deer Park plant, and one near the Baytown plant of ICI United States. These sites would have placed the plant near the major petrochemical market, an important consideration. Major constraints to locating the CCPC facility in the above areas were the possibility of permitting problems and availability and cost of land at certain of the sites.[3]

Four reasons contributed to selecting Corpus Christi over the other possible areas:

1. Ability to obtain necessary permits at the local, state, and federal levels

[a] A class of petrochemicals, olefins are defined as unsaturated open-chain hydrocarbons containing at least one double bond. Ethylene and prophylene are both olefins.

[b] The CCPC plant's reliance on naptha and gas oil as feedstock, rather than the liquefied petroleum gas traditionally used to produce ethylene, is directly related to the plant's large size and the variety of its products. Use of these new feedstocks increases both the required size of the facility and results in increased production of olefins other than ethylene. The term "integrated" refers to a facility's production of other olefins, such as propylene, butadiene, and benzene.

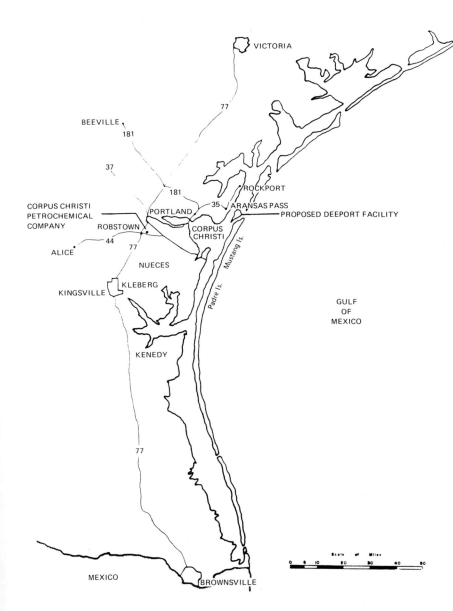

VICTORIA

77

BEEVILLE
181

37

181

ROCKPORT

CORPUS CHRISTI
PETROCHEMICAL
COMPANY

PORTLAND

35 ARANSAS PASS PROPOSED DEEPORT FACILITY

ROBSTOWN

CORPUS
CHRISTI

44

ALICE

77

NUECES

Padre Is.

Mustang Is.

KLEBERG

KINGSVILLE

GULF
OF
MEXICO

KENEDY

77

Scale of Miles
0 5 10 20 30 40 50

MEXICO

BROWNSVILLE

Figure 7-1. The lower coastal area of Texas (*Source:* Texas official highway travel map).

145

2. Availability of land
3. Port facilities
4. Proximity of raw materials[4]

The fifth and most important factor was the existence of Champlin's other operations in Corpus Christi.

After the partners agreed to locate the plant in the Corpus Christi area, a different set of factors was used to determine the specific site. By gradually eliminating various sites, the present site was chosen. According to Alstair Fleming, deputy facilities project director, all of the following factors, among others, were considered:

1. Access to raw materials (feedstocks)
2. Explicit permitting requirements
3. Safety
4. Land availability and cost
5. Soil characteristics
6. Access to waste water disposal streams or ditches
7. Subsidence and runoff patterns
8. Character of surrounding area
9. Availability of utilities[5]

In 1974, Champlin had purchased 500 acres near its refinery and the port and initially hoped to use this land for the plant site. Although for several reasons this acreage proved unsuitable, another Corpus Christi site was subsequently found. By gradually eliminating various areas, the present site was chosen.

In March 1977, the Corpus Christi Petrochemical Company began site preparation for its plant, which is designed to manufacture 1.2 billion pounds of ethylene per year as well as other ancillary chemicals. Official groundbreaking ceremonies were held three months later, and construction continued in mid-1979.

THE COMPANY

CCPC is a joint venture of Champlin Petroleum Company (37.5 percent), ICI United States (37.5 percent), and Soltex Polymer Corporation (25 percent). In general, joint ventures are attractive to both petrochemical firms and oil companies because the former can provide expertise in construction and operation of a plant and often a market for primary chemicals, such as ethylene, while the latter can provide feedstocks and the needed capital. Certainly both types of firms are drawn to the increasing profitability of petrochemical production. (Although exact figures on profitability of petrochemical activities could not be obtained, a CCPC official noted that an annual return on investment of 10 to 15 percent was expected.)

Usually the term "petrochemicals" refers to chemicals derived or isolated from petroleum or natural gas. According to Norman White-horn, author of a comprehensive economic analysis of the Texas petrochemical industry, both first-line raw materials and monomers as well as polymers and plastics are sometimes included under the rubric of petrochemicals.[6] Generally, though, petrochemical is not used to refer to fuel or energy products such as gasoline, natural gas, and kerosene. While the manufacture of numerous consumer goods such as drugs, fertilizers, and synthetic fibers depends heavily on petrochemicals, these end products themselves are also not generally thought of as petrochemicals. Here, therefore, the term is used to include raw materials, monomers, polymers, and plastics but not fuel, energy, or end products.

Petrochemical companies often have been led to consider joint ventures in the construction of new ethylene plants, both because of the relatively high cost of large ethylene plants and because of the importance of ensuring a steady supply of feedstocks. In the CCPC case, though, it was Champlin Petroleum Company that initiated the partnership. *Chemical Engineering* stated that Champlin hoped "to avoid seasonal fluctuation in production rates by sending excess products to the ethylene plant. And the company . . . (saw) more profit in the chemical markets."[7]

Champlin's two partners in the CCPC project both had international experience in petrochemical production. Solvay and Cie. have been involved in the production, processing, and marketing of petrochemicals through 100 subsidiaries in 15 countries. ICI has been a large manufacturer of chemicals, plastics, pharmaceuticals, and fibers as well as engaged in oil and gas exploration and production. In addition, ICI was one of the pioneers in production of ethylene from liquid feedstocks such as naphtha. *Chemical Age's* 1975 list of the largest chemical companies places ICI as third largest worldwide and Solvay as nineteenth.[8]

All of the principals of CCPC were loaned from the three companies involved in the joint venture. Many of the CCPC engineers and technical advisors came from a recently completed ICI facility in England. Richard Carlton, the facilities project director, is an ICI employee who has been involved in construction of a number of ICI facilities. Champlin also furnished engineers for the project team. Soltex provided an advisor-consultant and has several other employees involved in the project.

CCPC company policies are implemented through the executive committee, composed of one representative from each of the parent companies. This committee prepares items for submission to the policy panel, which is similarly constituted.

The project team was primarily responsible for construction of the plant. This team was involved in the original planning of the project and played the major role in the permitting process. The facilities project director and the deputy facilities project director led this team and were assisted by advisor consultants, managers (technical, construction, operations, and logistics), and engineers (pipelines, instrument-process, scheduling, process, and project).

The facilities project director has an office in Houston at the main CCPC office, and the deputy director is located in Corpus Christi at the construction site. CCPC chose to establish its main office in Houston because this is the center of the energy industry in Texas. The Houston location facilitated meetings between the principals of the company, since air transportation to and from this city is easier than to and from Corpus Christi.

THE SELECTED SITE

Champlin's preference for a Texas site was clear from the outset. By volume, this area has the greatest concentration of chemical plants in the United States, producing more than 40 percent of every basic petrochemical, 80 percent of the synthetic rubber, and 60 percent of the nation's sulfur.[9] Research conducted in 1977, during the initial phase of this study, indicated that there were 58 operational petrochemical plants in the Texas coastal area. At that time, at least 10 additional plants were proposed or under construction in this area.

The obvious center of the chemical industry in Texas is the upper coastal region, particularly the Houston area. Sites in this area, which would have placed the facility closer to its market, were considered by CCPC but were not chosen for reasons discussed previously.

While it is true that Corpus Christi is not currently a major market for ethylene and its associated chemicals, a large petrochemical pipeline network does extend up the coast from Victoria. CCPC had two options: build a pipeline to Victoria to hook into the present system[c] or construct a new pipeline to the Houston area.

[c]It is a common practice in the petrochemical industry to "swap" pipelined products. In effect, this means that CCPC or another company can introduce a given amount of ethylene into their end of a pipeline system, and a firm upline may buy this amount immediately.

The company chose the latter option, thus allowing for efficient transportation of the facility's products to this major market area.

Corpus Christi is the second largest port in Texas and a major U.S. port. These port facilities were one of the primary reasons for the company's selection of the Corpus Christi area for the plant. However, as can be seen from Figure 7-2, the selected site is approximately five miles from the port area. This choice of a land-locked site was necessitated by the lack of suitable land adjacent to the port facilities. The selected site was made feasible by the decision to pipe feedstock to the new facility from the Champlin refinery, adjacent to the port, and to buy 25 to 50 acres of dock space along the harbor for barge loading. Champlin's original plans to site the facility on a 500-acre parcel of land near its refinery were rejected by one of the partners because of the potential safety hazard posed by the site's proximity to airport flight patterns.[10] While this land was not within an area generally considered as potentially unsafe, one partner, based on its experience overseas, preferred to locate the plant elsewhere in the Corpus Christi area.

The company did not experience major difficulties in locating land suitable for the facility outside the port area. As shown in Figure 7-2, the selected site is just outside the Corpus Christi city limits. Historically, Corpus Christi has promoted industrial development outside its city limits and in the Corpus Christi industrial zone along the port. Industries in this area pay school taxes to the Corpus Christi Independent School District and county taxes to Nueces County, but they do not pay city taxes.

In a document entitled "Choices Facing Corpus Christi," the Corpus Christi Goals Commission stated that this unwritten policy of nonannexation of industrial areas began in the 1930s.[11] This document noted that industries attracted to the area make a significant contribution to the city's economic life. They provide jobs during the construction and operation of facilities. The city does not pay the cost of providing municipal services to the area. Although the city will sell gas and water to industries, industries must pay regular rates and bear the cost of bringing these services to their sites. The CCPC facility will purchase treated water, but not gas, from the city.

One city planning department official related that locating industrial plants outside the city had a positive effect on city management and staff requirements.[12] He based his statement on the fact that city building codes were not enforced in these facilities, thus reducing the cost of enforcement by the city. However, the director of the Department of Inspection and Operation, Bill Hennings, pointed out that large industrial facilities within city limits were also

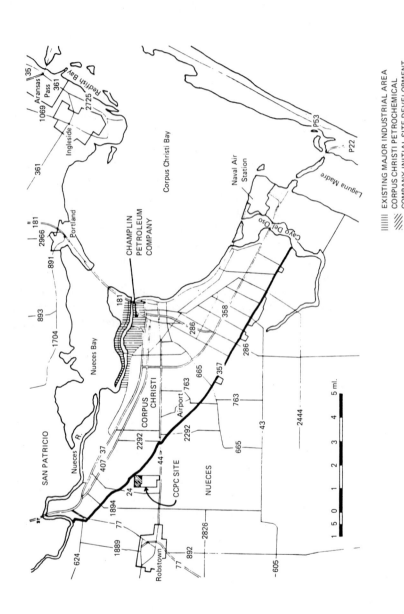

Figure 7-2. The Corpus Christi area (*Source:* Texas official highway travel map).

exempt from city building codes.[13] He stated that these facilities are covered under Occupational Safety and Health Administration (OSHA) requirements, and enforcement of city codes would result in duplication of codes enforced by OSHA.

Thus, the only generally acceptable reason given by Corpus Christi officials and chamber of commerce members for the existence of an industrial zone free of city taxes is that it provides an incentive for industries to locate in the area. Yet CCPC officials stated that this policy had only a small effect on their siting decision.[14] Certainly, though, given the size of the annual tax savings on a large facility, each year it remains outside of the city's taxing jurisdiction represents a substantial gain for the firm. In addition, this policy may play a greater role in the siting decisions of smaller firms with smaller capital bases.

After the specific area was chosen, local agents were hired to purchase the acreage. Use of a purchasing agent helped to protect the identity of the purchaser, since landowners will sometimes raise their prices if a large company is interested. Retaining local agents also reflects the tendency of companies to hire local specialists, including consultants and lawyers who are known and trusted in an area or who are acquainted with local and state officials.

The land surrounding the site purchased by CCPC is primarily agricultural, although there is some residential development within two miles. The site is within the taxing jurisdiction of two school districts. While CCPC owns 1,200 acres at the site, less than a third of this will be used for the facility (see Figure 7-3). It is likely that CCPC may offer sites to other companies, particularly companies that would buy CCPC's products.

FEDERAL AND STATE GOVERNMENT ROLES

The CCPC complex will ultimately include four distinct operations:

1. Ethylene plant
2. Barge dock, storage tank farm, and tank car terminals
3. Pipeline distribution facilities
4. Salt dome facilities

Construction and operation of each will require a variety of state and federal permits.

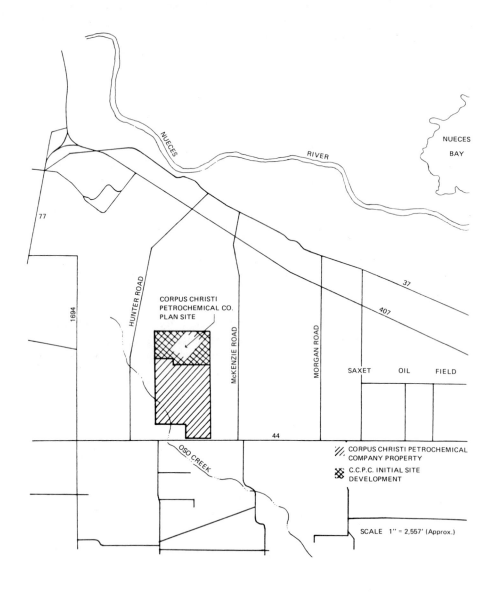

Figure 7-3. CCPC site and surrounding area (*Source:* Texas Department of Water Resources).

The company submitted applications to construct the ethylene plant at an early date, since this is the major operation and would require the most detailed permitting requirements. The focus of the following discussion is on the permitting of the ethylene facility, although the other support operations are discussed briefly. All construction permits have been applied for, and in most instances they have been received. Operating permits will not be applied for until construction is complete and operation is ready to begin.

One of the notable differences between the permitting process for CCPC's ethylene facility and the permitting of the Energy Corporation of Louisiana (ECOL) refinery discussed in Chapter 6 is the relationship of state and federal agencies. In Louisiana, federal agencies administer the federal statutes, and state agencies utilize their comment power rather than direct permitting authority. In Texas, the basic policy of state agencies has been to attempt to assume responsibility for administration of federal statutes. For example, the Texas Air Control Board applied for a waiver from EPA that would allow the state to administer the federal emission offset policy.[d] The board's request was turned down, however.[15]

CCPC encountered several problems in relation to the federal emission offset policy, in contrast to the ECOL facility, which received its air quality permits before this policy went into effect. CCPC was one of the first new facilities in Texas to be permitted under this EPA policy.

State Air Quality Permits

On October 13, 1976, Champlin Petroleum Company applied to the Texas Air Control Board (TACB) for a permit to allow construction of an ethylene plant in Corpus Christi. The plant is within Nueces County, which fails to meet the national ambient air quality standards for photochemical oxidants; in addition, small portions of the county near the port area (some six miles from the CCPC site) do not meet the standards for total suspended particulates. TACB, which is empowered by the state to require permits of facilities that will have air emissions, has historically tried to work with industry, providing advice on how to achieve the lowest possible emission rate by incorporating the best available control technology. TACB has disagreed with EPA on the need to reduce ozone pollution to the level of the federal ambient air standards and on the effectiveness of the hydrocarbon emissions control policy. To quote the view of

[d]See Chapter 5.

one petrochemical company official: "TACB has not rolled over and played dead to EPA."

On January 20, 1977, TACB issued a permit for construction of the CCPC plant. However, as discussed later, EPA required the permit to be revised and reissued in late 1977. In a letter to TACB, the Corpus Christi-Nueces County Department of Public Health and Welfare's Public Health Division, after review of the application, expressed concern over storage and handling of spent caustic. One of the special conditions of the CCPC permits, therefore, was a requirement that CCPC forward more detailed engineering data on spent caustic disposal (when they became available) and install abatement equipment approved by the TACB executive director before beginning operations.

There was only one known protest to TACB over construction of the plant. In a letter to this agency, Fred Burkhardt, Jr., an adjoining landowner, objected to the odors and fumes from the facility and the deterioration of his property's value. In a reply, TACB reported that a permit had been granted to the company three weeks before Burkhardt's letter was received. To quote TACB's reply: "It is our opinion that the impact upon existing air quality in the area will be minimal," but if TACB discovers a violation of its rules and regulations by this facility, "appropriate action will be initiated to insure compliance."[16]

In February 1977, Champlin requested that its permit be reissued in the name of Corpus Christi Petrochemical Company.[17] As modifications in the design of the plant were made, they had to be submitted for TACB review and incorporated into the permit. EPA's ruling on emission offset resulted in CCPC filing a revised permit application, which is discussed later. Within 60 days after achieving normal operation, the company must file for a TACB operating permit.

State Water Quality Permits

The discharge of surface water requires a permit from the Texas Department of Water Resources (TDWR, formerly the Texas Water Quality Board, TWQB). An application was made by CCPC to TDWR on March 10, 1977, for a permit to allow for discharge of sanitary waste and other waste water from its construction activities.

The permit was granted after a June 30, 1977, public hearing. Adjacent landowners Fred and James Burkhardt, and their lawyer Perry E. Burkett, protested the discharge of wastes into a ditch that crosses their property.[18] TDWR overruled the protests, citing the fact that this ditch already receives sewage. The permit approved on August 11, 1977, allows only for the discharge of treated domestic waste water from a package treatment plant into drainage ditches that flow into Oso Creek.

CCPC has also been granted permits to inject liquid waste in two deepwater wells on the plant site. These permits were issued by TDWR in 1979.

Federal Air Quality Permits

On June 3, 1977, the EPA administrator ruled that CCPC was in violation of certain parts of the Clean Air Act. Specifically, EPA maintained that the TACB construction permit was invalid since CCPC had not demonstrated that its air pollution emissions would be offset by equivalent or greater emissions reductions in the same area. CCPC was one of the first Texas companies to be held in violation by EPA under its emission offset requirements. However, this was probably more the result of the timing of the permit application than of the specific project.

On December 21, 1976, EPA had published its interpretive ruling prohibiting construction of new air pollution emission sources in areas where national ambient air quality standards had not been met, except where emissions from existing sources could be reduced by an amount greater than the new source emissions. CCPC argued that this emissions offset policy should not apply to its facility since the company had applied for its TACB permit before December 1976. EPA rejected this argument, stating that the facility was subject to the ruling since the company had not actually received its permit by this date.

A conference was held on June 29, 1977, at which both CCPC and EPA were represented.[19] Throughout the meeting, TACB staff members participated in the discussion only when asked specific questions. The meeting began with EPA outlining its authority to apply its offset policy to this project. EPA presented its findings from a dispersion modeling study for particulate emissions that showed a great impact on the surrounding area. Unfortunately, EPA's modeling had been based upon an incorrect plant location; this modeling error was indicative of a number of instances where the EPA's technical information appeared to be confused or inaccurate.

CCPC then presented the findings of its modeling, which showed minimal impact from the facility's emissions. CCPC argued that since the actual plant site was located in a portion of an air quality region that attained the federal standards for particulate matter, the facility should not be responsible for meeting the emissions offset requirements. While portions of the region did not meet federal standards, CCPC contended that the location of its facility would not impact these areas and, thus, would not threaten federal standards. Ultimately, EPA agreed that the facility's particulate emissions would not significantly impact air quality in these areas.

EPA agreed to reconstruct its modeling of particulate emissions. The federal agency requested CCPC to furnish further information on fugitive emissions of hydrocarbons (pumps, valves, compressors, and flanges) and to estimate the quantity of hydrocarbons that would be flared over a year. EPA also requested CCPC to complete a new TACB permit that showed revised hydrocarbon emissions.

In late November 1977, EPA broke off emission offset negotiations with all companies that had been held in violation (including CCPC) and instructed them to go through the appropriate state agency in order to obtain the necessary permits and to negotiate required offsets. On January 9, 1978, the TACB, after receiving preliminary approval from EPA, approved a change in the state regulations that was modeled on the EPA's interpretive ruling on emission offsets.[20]

In June 1978, a hearing was conducted by the TACB concerning a reduction of 246.6 tons of hydrocarbon emissions from Champlin Petroleum Company's Corpus Christi refinery, designed to offset the emissions resulting from CCPC's ethylene production and barge loading facility (188.7 tons per year). The proposed emission reduction would result from two changes. Removal from operation of a vacuum distillation unit capable of processing 12,000 barrels per day would eliminate at least 139 tons per year of hydrocarbon emissions from the Champlin refinery; and alteration of the fuels stored in a gasoline storage tank with a 300,000-barrel capacity would reduce hydrocarbon emissions by at least 107.6 tons per year.

The net hydrocarbon emission reduction of nearly 58 tons per year would represent progress toward attainment of national standards for photochemical oxidants and result in a positive net air quality benefit in Nueces County, which presently exceeds these standards. Champlin agreed to achieve its offered reduction before the new CCPC facility commenced operation.

TACB found that the hydrocarbon emission reduction offered by Champlin Petroleum Company complied with applicable state and federal laws and board policies regarding emission offsets in nonattainment areas. TACB thus issued an order to that effect. EPA has raised no objections to the revised permit.

Federal Water Quality Permits

The Federal Water Pollution Control Act requires that a National Pollution Discharge Elimination System (NPDES) permit be obtained in order to discharge any wastes into navigable waters. EPA administers the NPDES permit program in Texas, although it may delegate its authority to TDWR in the future. In 1978, CCPC received an NPDES permit allowing for the discharge of effluent into the inner harbor of Corpus Christi.

Other Permits

CCPC ultimately must apply to the National Flood Insurance Program for floodplain insurance for facilities within the 100-year floodplain and to the U.S. Army Corps of Engineers for a permit to construct a waste-water effluent structure below mean high tide. The latter permit will allow construction of a pipeline for the discharge of effluent into the Corpus Christi inner harbor. Permits of this type are required if a pipeline will intrude into a channel below the mean high tide. CCPC will probably also request the corps to make a site visit to ensure that the site is not within a wetlands jurisdiction area. Section 404 of the Federal Water Pollution Control Act gives the corps jurisdiction in this determination. It is unlikely that the site chosen will be defined as in a wetlands area.

In addition to the ethylene processing plant, the barge dock requires certain permits from the corps, which has determined that CCPC's plans comply with Sections 10 and 404 of the Federal Water Pollution Control Act. The barge-loading facility has also received a permit from TACB. To date, no permit application has been submitted by CCPC to TDWR. Other permits relating to pipeline distribution and the salt dome storage facilities are indicated in Table 7-1. To date, CCPC has not applied for any permits related to these activities.

THE LOCAL GOVERNMENT
AND THE COMMUNITY

Corpus Christi is called "The Sparkling City by the Sea." Gateway to the Padre Island National Seashore, the city enjoys

Table 7-1. Future Permitting of Associated CCPC Operations

Operation	Level of Permit and Applicable Regulations	Agency
Pipeline distribution facilities	Federal—Section 10 permit and Section 404 permit are required if pipelines cross rivers	U.S. Army Corps of Engineers
	State—easements for pipelines over state property and submerged lands	Texas General Land Office
Salt dome storage facilities	Federal—Section 10 permit and Section 404 permit are required if facilities are in wetlands areas	U.S. Army Corps of Engineers
	State—site-injection well permit	Texas Department of Water Resources
	State—approval of dikes or levees constructed	Texas Department of Water Resources
	State—permit to operate surface brine pits	Texas Railroad Commission
	State—construction and operating permits for sources of air contaminants	Texas Air Control Board

a mild climate and prevailing southeasterly winds, which result in a pleasant coastal environment. For these reasons, many tourists come to the area yearly.

This city with home rule and a 1970 population of 204,525 is located in Nueces County (237,544 population: 1970) and the Standard Metropolitan Statistical Area of Nueces and San Patricio Counties (298,800 estimated population: 1975). Compared to other parts of the country, the Nueces County unemployment rate (7.1 percent) is relatively low; but compared to Texas' 1977 average unemployment rate of 5.3 percent, the figure was relatively high. Aside from being a major seaport, Corpus Christi is a center for petroleum and petrochemical production, manufacturing, and agribusiness.

CCPC chose to locate in a largely agricultural area. Coupled with the effect of the prevailing winds, pollution from the plant probably will not adversely affect any residential areas. When the CCPC facility is in operation, it expects to provide 250 to 300 jobs, or roughly 0.62 job per acre (using the figure of 400 acres, the amount of land actually devoted to the facility).

The city of Corpus Christi is interested in supporting industrial facilities such as that proposed by CCPC. The Port of Corpus Christi has applied for a permit to develop a 72-foot deep channel and docking basin at Harbor Island, designed to handle very large crude carriers (see Figure 7-1). Champlin Petroleum Company and four other oil and petrochemical companies that are interested in importing crude oil through the Port of Corpus Christi have expressed willingness to give this Deeport project financial support.

In contrast with the numerous state and federal permits required, few, if any, local permits are necessary for the construction and operation of the CCPC plant. In general, few Texas cities require facilities to obtain environmental permits in order to build or operate within their jurisdiction. The environmental affairs coordinator for Champlin, who played a major role in the permitting of CCPC, reported that direct contact with city officials had been minimal.[21] Apparently, the staff of the Corpus Christi Industrial Commission worked with city officials in matters relevant to the CCPC proposal.

As discussed previously, the CCPC site is outside of the city limits of Corpus Christi, but within the city's area of extraterritorial jurisdiction (ETJ). Under Texas state law,[22] cities can utilize their ETJ powers to maintain control of certain areas outside their city limits. The size of this area depends on the city's population. Corpus Christi, with a population of over 100,000, has an ETJ extending out five miles.[23] A city can extend to its ETJ areas all rules and regulations governing plats and subdivisions of land. ETJ areas may be annexed by a city, or the city may choose not to annex but to create industrial districts within its ETJ. A city has the power to enter into contracts or agreements with owners of land within such an industrial district:

> ...to guarantee the continuation of extraterritorial jurisdiction status of such district, and its immunity from annexation by the city for a period of time not to exceed seven (7) years, and upon such other terms and considerations as the parties might deem appropriate. Such contracts and agreements...may be renewed or extended for successive periods not to exceed seven (7) years....[24]

Although the CCPC plant is not within the Corpus Christi industrial zone, the city has no plans to annex the CCPC site. (In fact, the city of Corpus Christi has annexed only a few hundred acres of land within the last few years.) Thus, the facility does not pay city property taxes.

LOCAL IMPACTS OF THE CCPC FACILITY

A variety of impacts, both positive and negative, could occur as the result of construction and operation of a large petrochemical complex. This discussion will focus specifically on the ethylene plant, since technical and locational information is not available on the other proposed operations (i.e., the tank farms, barge docks, pipelines, etc.). Siting of a similar plant in another community might raise an entirely different set of impact issues. A small, rural community would certainly be affected differently by such a facility from a large, metropolitan area such as Corpus Christi. With a population of nearly 300,000 in the metropolitan area and long-term experience with industrial development, Corpus Christi has knowledge of and some control over the possible effects of such a facility.

Changes in air and water quality in the area may result from operation of the CCPC ethylene plant. Certainly, petrochemical processing plants have negatively affected the air and water quality of some communities in the past. Recent legislation has, however, been directed at minimizing such impacts. EPA has the power to enforce federal air and water quality standards, and state agencies have the power to require industries to meet even more stringent standards.

The CCPC plant is equipped with its own water treatment facility, which should remove potentially damaging compounds from effluent discharges; as planned, the facility will not discharge a significant amount of treated effluent, if any, into the city's treatment system.[25] While the impact of the facility on water quality does not appear to be a significant issue, the question of water availability is worth discussion. The plant will purchase treated water from the city of Corpus Christi, which could experience shortages in the future if Choke Canyon Dam is not constructed. According to one concerned resident of the area, industrial development of this type constrains the future availability of water for residential use.[26] Facilities like CCPC also compete with industries that are less water-intensive but which provide more jobs per gallon of water use. However, should water shortages occur, the city's residential customers would have priority over industrial customers.

The impact of CCPC on air quality in the area is a more complex question. Air quality in this region fails to meet national standards, although the predominant winds tend to disperse air emissions over primarily nonresidential areas. Enforcement of EPA's offset policy is designed to ensure no further destruction of air quality in the area. Although CCPC has attempted to reduce emissions from the plant to an acceptable level, there will be some emissions. Of course, CCPC is not the only source of industrial emissions. There are numerous other facilities within five miles of the CCPC site; however, EPA's focus on new facilities has often led to tighter control over these sources than over existing emission sources.

A number of possible economic impacts may result from the location of the CCPC facility. Certainly, the plant will provide jobs for a number of local residents, although relatively few will be of long duration. Construction of the plant may provide up to 2,600 jobs for skilled and unskilled labor, but they will be only temporary. Once in operation, the plant should provide 250 to 300 jobs, but some of these positions will probably be filled by newcomers to the area. Without knowing the origin of residence and the time period of employment, the number of indirect jobs created by the facility cannot be calculated. However, large petrochemical complexes have generally resulted in numerous satellite industries. Thus, while the number of direct job opportunities may be relatively small, a significant number of induced jobs may be generated.

The location of the plant outside of the city limits has a number of economic advantages as well as disadvantages. While the plant will not be taxed by the city, it will purchase city water. The company is responsible for bearing the cost of extending this service to the site, but city-generated revenues for these sources will be slight. In general, it is difficult to detect any direct economic benefits to the city as a result of the plant's location.

The plant will be taxed by the county and two school districts, significantly increasing the districts' revenues (see Table 7-2). At the same time, it is doubtful that the school districts' enrollments will increase significantly because of the plant. In fact, it is likely that most new residents will locate within the boundaries of the Corpus Christi Independent School District, since this system serves most of the residents in the area. Thus, while Tuloso-Midway and Calallen may receive added tax revenues, the Corpus Christi district will probably receive most of the new students. However, given the small number of new residents associated with this plant, the number of new students should not dramatically affect the Corpus Christi school district.

The increased traffic in the area will probably require construction

Table 7-2. Local Government Taxing Formulas for the CCPC Facility

---

Nueces County—Property Taxes
65% of market value of the property; subtract assessed rate of 41.4%; the amount of taxes owed is $1.74 per every $100 of the remainder.

Tuloso-Midway Independent School District—School Taxes
Based on entire assessment and taxes at the rate of $1.75 per every $100 of property value.

Calallen Independent School District—School Taxes
Based on entire assessment and taxes at the rate of $1.33 per every $100 of property value.

---

of new roads and increased maintenance of others. Two state roads are adjacent to the site, but the remainder are the county's responsibility. Although construction of the plant will result in the need to expend funds on these roads, it is doubtful that the county will suffer a net negative fiscal impact.

The possibility of industrial growth negatively affecting the tourist industry in the area has been discussed previously. The alteration of the physical environment would probably reduce its appeal to tourists. Yet it is difficult to link this specific facility directly to any decline in tourism. The site is outside the normal tourist area, and CCPC's facility is only one plant of many. Nevertheless, the cumulative effect created by a number of similar facilities could have significant impacts on the region.

Given the population size and general characteristics of the Corpus Christi area, it is doubtful that the plant will have far-reaching social impacts on the community. This is a highly diversified community accustomed to industrial development. However, the specific site chosen for the CCPC facility does raise certain broad impact questions. Traditionally, industrial development in Corpus Christi had been clustered within the industrial zone near the port. Location of this plant in what has been basically an agricultural (and low-density residential) area may adversely affect the lives of nearby residents. While the value of their land may ultimately rise, there will be increased traffic, noise, and a certain amount of air pollution in the immediate area. The location of this plant may have a significant impact on land use patterns in the area by beginning a conversion to increased industrial development.

Citizens, however, have expressed little direct opposition to the siting of the CCPC facilities, with only two adjacent landowners protesting the location of the plant to TACB and TDWR. These are the only known instances of citizen opposition.

SUMMARY

Corpus Christi Petrochemical Company is representative of the growing trend for oil and chemical companies to diversify into the petrochemical sector. The plant's large size and its dependence on liquid feedstocks also make it illustrative of the future of the petrochemical industry. Like many other petrochemical plants, CCPC has chosen to site near its raw materials and markets. This proximity, the ability to obtain necessary permits, and the generally favorable business climate are probably the major incentives for a petrochemical facility to site in Texas. For CCPC, it is likely that the siting decisions were significantly affected by the location of the parent companies' facilities. The company's decision to locate near its feedstock source was certainly affected by Champlin's knowledge of and strong commitment to the Corpus Christi area.

The company appeared to make its siting decision on criteria not unlike those used by an average home buyer. It assessed its particular needs and sought a location where it could obtain land at a reasonable price. The facility required fresh water, power, and accessibility to transportation systems. The company looked for a site on which governmental agencies would allow it to build. In other words, ease of acquiring permits was an important consideration. Labor availability and construction and operating costs were also considerations. The area was seen as a nice place for employees to live. Thus, while CCPC's siting requirements and decision-making process were in certain ways unique, its general concerns are certainly mirrored in the siting decisions of other petrochemical companies.

NOTES

1. Personal interview with Richard Carlton, CCPC Facilities Project Director, October 1977.
2. Ibid.
3. Personal interview with Alstair Fleming, CCPC Deputy Facilities Project Director, November 1977.
4. Carlton and Fleming, op. cit.
5. Fleming, op. cit.
6. Norman C. Whitehorn, *Economic Analysis of the Petrochemical Industry in Texas* (College Station: Texas A&M University Press, May 1973), p. 8.
7. *Chemical Engineering*, August 30, 1976, p. 66.
8. Chemical Systems, Inc., *Structure and Competition Within the Petrochemical Industry and Economic Impact of the 1973-74 Petrochemical Shortage* (report prepared for the Federal Energy Administration, March 1976), p. 8.

9. Whitehorn, op. cit., p. viii.
10. Personal interview with Brody Allen, Corpus Christi Industrial Commission, October 1977.
11. Corpus Christi Goals Commission, "Choices Facing Corpus Christi," 1975, p. 210.
12. Personal interview with Larry Wengler, city of Corpus Christi, Department of Planning, October 1977.
13. Telephone interview with Bill Hennings, city of Corpus Christi, Director of the Department of Inspection and Operation, February 1978.
14. Carlton and Fleming, op. cit.
15. TACB favored a different approach to the air quality problem and sought to have facilities utilize the best available control technology. TACB disliked the offset policy and commented unfavorably on it. Chairman John Blair said that "the offset policy is untimely, may be inconsistent with the Federal Clean Air Act, encourages deceit, promotes waste and worst of all, promises what it probably will not deliver—cleaner air. "Current Developments", *Texas Natural Resources Reporter*, January 1978, p. 1.

    In August 1977, the United States Congress amended the Clean Air Act, Section 129, to allow EPA to waive its offset policy for any state. A state applying for a waiver was required to meet a number of requirements. In effect, these requirements demanded the state have a program similar in its intent and scope to the offset policy.

    The Texas Air Control Board passed a resolution to request a waiver from EPA. In December 1977, EPA denied TACB's request citing a number of deficiencies in the waiver application. TACB then adopted the offset policy as a state requirement.
16. Texas Air Control Board, CCPC file, 1976-1978.
17. Ibid.
18. Texas Water Quality Board, CCPC file, 1976-1978.
19. Minutes of this conference fill a 179-page document, which is on file at the Region VI EPA office in Dallas.
20. *Texas Natural Resources Reporter*, op. cit., pp. 1-3.
21. Personal interview with Jim Hutchinson, Environmental Affairs Coordinator, Champlin Petroleum Company, February 9, 1978.
22. Article 970a, Section 3, Vernon, Texas, Civil Statutes.
23. The ETJ rule is as follows:

City Population	ETJ Distance Outside City Limits
Less than 5,000	One-half mile
5,000-24,999	One mile
25,000-49,999	Two miles
50,000-99,999	Three and one-half miles
100,000 and above	Five miles

24. Article 970a, op. cit.
25. Hutchinson, op. cit.
26. Personal interview with Steve Frishman, Coastal Bend Conservation Association, October 1977.

Chapter 8

Energy Facility Siting on the Gulf Coast: A Policy Perspective

*Research and Planning
Consultants, Inc.*

New energy facilities may be needed; but so often people want them somewhere else, not in their own back yard. As a result, it is no longer sufficient for a company to consider only the economic viability of a potential site. Siting decisions must consider applicable environmental regulations and must take into account local attitudes toward the proposed facility.

The process of energy facility siting on the Gulf Coast has many similarities with the situation elsewhere in the United States, but it also shows several significant differences. Chapters 6 and 7 presented detailed case studies of two $300-million waterfront energy facilities recently sited in this region, one in Louisiana and the other in Texas. These case studies explored certain key issues pertinent to the siting process, including land use conflicts, environmental impacts, the effect of government regulations, corporate concerns in the siting process, the influence of citizen groups, and social and economic impacts of the facility. Texas and Louisiana, the Gulf Coast states producing the greatest amount of raw materials for energy production, were selected for an in-depth exploration of the similarities and differences between their siting processes. Based on these two case studies, and on other information gleaned from the research, conclusions may be drawn regarding energy facility siting on the Gulf Coast. These findings are summarized in the remainder of this chapter.

SITING INDUCEMENTS

Virtually every characteristic that makes a site attractive to industry—particularly to industries engaged in large, energy-related activities—can be found along the Texas and Louisiana coasts. These areas contain many physically and geographically suitable sites for major energy facilities. The strong economies of both states, public opinion, and the tone of governmental regulations favor further industrial growth. From a number of perspectives, therefore, these two states are as attractive today as potential locations for such new facilities as they have been in the past, when they attracted massive energy investments.

The qualitative and quantitative factors that enter into a corporate siting decision are numerous and varied.[1] Of particular importance to a company are the economic, political, and regulatory climates of the state and area under consideration, which must be balanced against the company's market for its products and need for raw materials.

Texas and Louisiana offer attractive sites that generally meet an energy company's physical requirements for transportation and raw materials. Sites in both states are accessible to a variety of transportation systems, including major port facilities, inland waterways, rail lines, pipelines, and highways. Utilities and fresh water, as well as skilled and unskilled labor, are also generally available. Historically, production of oil and gas in Texas and Louisiana has provided the raw materials for energy production. Further incentive for siting in these states now exists in that they are also considered to be major and expanding markets for refined and processed energy products. In addition to readily available raw materials and good transportation facilities, both states have relatively low tax rates and good business climates.

The people and governments of Texas and Louisiana have traditionally supported energy development, and the political climate encourages further development. As the number and scope of governmental regulations designed to protect the environment have grown, companies have been forced to assign increased weight to a state's regulatory climate in the site selection process. Some local governments, all state governments, and the federal government have laws and policies directed toward protection of the environment. The state and local regulatory climates of Texas and Louisiana reflect these two state's pro-development bias. According to corporate representatives, state and local regulatory laws and policies are administered in what they consider a reasonable manner. Energy facilities designed to meet state and local environmental regulations generally receive, without untimely delays, the nonfederal permits necessary for construction and operation.

STATE AND LOCAL APPROACHES TO SITING

On the Gulf Coast, the emphasis is upon "regulation," not "restriction." Although they have different management approaches, the policies of both state governments are oriented toward management of the impacts of energy facility siting rather than reassessment of industry's siting decisions.

Basically, the decision about where to locate an industrial facility is left to industry. Neither Texas nor Louisiana operates state-owned industrial parks, nor does either state specify areas as being suitable for industrial development. However, these states have effectively precluded the siting of major energy or industrial facilities along much of their coast either through public ownership of land or constraints on siting in ecologically sensitive areas such as wetlands.

In both states, local governments are vested with the power to control land use. State government enters the siting process only after a company has selected a specific location. At this point, the company must submit its plans, including engineering specifications, to a variety of state agencies responsible for protection or control of particular resources. No superagency controls all aspects of industrial permitting. In Texas, for example, a facility may require construction and operating permits from as many as seven state agencies.

While both states' policies emphasize management of impacts, as opposed to management of land use, each has adopted a somewhat different management approach. One of the most striking differences between Texas and Louisiana appears in the content of their statutes requiring state approval for any activity that might affect or deplete natural resources. Texas laws focus on specific natural resources, and each act delegates control to a specific agency. Statutes prohibit engaging in a particular activity without first receiving a permit from the appropriate agency. A Texas permit sets out in detail the requirements and specifications as well as its specific expiration date, thus allowing for tighter control over the state's natural resources. Should a state agency find a facility to be violating any of the requirements specified in the permit, it may revoke the permit, thereby immediately halting construction or operation.

Texas has strong requirements for public notice and public hearings before state agencies may promulgate rules and standards or issue permits. The procedure for most permit applications is to hold a public hearing presided over by a state-employed hearing examiner and attended by agency representatives, the applicant, and any other interested parties. The hearing examiner then makes a recommendation to the agency's citizen commission or board, which also hears arguments from the interested parties before reaching a permit decision.

In contrast, Louisiana statutes are generally organized by agencies rather than by natural resources. Although their declared purpose is the nondegradation of a particular resource, they do not specify how an agency's control is to be exercised, nor do they require public notice or hearings. Louisiana agencies issue letters of no objection or certificates of approval rather than permits. These letters or certificates usually do not contain a time limit, nor are they normally as specific as Texas permits. Given the unspecific nature of these letters or certificates, Louisiana agencies believe a facility must be found to be solely responsible for the violation of a stream standard, for instance, in order to halt construction or operation. However, the state's "weak" statutory language is supplemented by use of the state's ability to comment on federal permits. This is deemed preferable to operating a state permitting system, for most federal agencies will not issue a permit over the objection of state agencies.

Thus, their relationship to the federal permitting system is a major difference between the Texas and Louisiana approaches to impact management. Louisiana relies heavily on federal administration of specific permitting requirements, which saves the state the cost of maintaining large agency staffs and holding public hearings. Texas attempts to administer federal permits at the state level. Although Texas' permitting system has required larger agency staffs, it gives the state greater control over facilities and their impacts on natural resources.

These two major distinctions—the content of state law and the relationships between state and federal agencies—do not negate the two states' shared philosophy of impact management. Practically speaking, these different approaches appear to have little effect on the outcome of energy facility siting decisions. By concentrating the permitting process at one level of government (state for Texas, federal for Louisiana), both systems tend to reduce the time required to obtain necessary permits—an indisputable advantage from a corporate perspective.[a]

Local governments in both states have the authority to manage land use. However, they do not always make full use of this authority. In Louisiana, both parishes (analogous to counties) and cities may exercise land use controls. The Texas legislature has consistently rejected bills designed to give counties either general ordinance-making powers or land use controls.[b] Although a bill giving counties these powers on a local option basis was proposed in the 1979 legislative session, it did not pass. However, a Texas city can exercise its land use authority beyond its actual boundaries through control over its area of extraterritorial jurisdiction (ETJ). Similarly, cities in Texas can use annexation to extend their boundaries (and the boundaries of their ETJ).

Louisiana parishes and Texas cities do not always fully exercise their prerogative to control land use. As a case in point, St. John the Baptist Parish, where the Energy Corporation of Louisiana chose to locate its refinery, uses private deed restrictions (as in Houston). The parish does not zone land for a particular use.[c] Likewise, a number of Texas cities do not make full use of their zoning authority. For instance, Houston relies on private deed restrictions to control development, whereas Corpus Christi zones within its city limits but has a policy of using tax incentives to encourage industry to site in certain portions of its ETJ.

In both states, local governments influence siting through other mechanisms. A Louisiana parish government must issue a permit for a proposed facility. This permit must be obtained before state and federal agencies may review the project. Texas cities are generally given an opportunity to review and comment on permit applications at the state level. Texas counties may exercise informal control over siting through their authority over construction and maintenance of rural roads, for example. In sum, a range of informal controls,

[a]See Chapter 11.

[b]Three Texas counties have been given limited ordinance-making powers through special legislation. The purpose is to regulate recreational development around a major reservoir and on South Padre Island.

[c]Robert Becnel, a parish official, predicts that the parish will begin to make use of its zoning authority in the near future.[2]

particularly those related to public services, allows local governments to influence siting.

Industry's concern with community acceptance of a facility and maintenance of good community relations is also relevant. Given the availability of land in Texas and Louisiana, industry has generally been able in these states to select a site for a major energy facility that is acceptable to all interested parties. Thus, local governments have not yet felt the need to wield their authority to manage land use. However, as population density increases and the amount of suitable land in coastal areas decreases, citizen opposition to siting may emerge, and local governments may begin to exercise more fully their existing legal authority to control land use.

LAND AVAILABILITY ON THE URBAN FRINGE

Suitable land is increasingly scarce near major port facilities and within traditional industrial areas along the Texas-Louisiana coast. Although in other states this scarcity has led energy companies to consider siting in rural areas, in these two Gulf Coast states the solution to an urban land shortage has been the selection of near-urban sites outside residential growth corridors.

Traditionally, energy facilities have clustered in urban coastal areas which provided access to a variety of transportation modes and other services. Coastal cities, especially along the Gulf of Mexico and in California, are also proximate to the energy production from offshore oil and gas wells.

With an increasing number of facilities and concomitant urban pollution problems, siting of new facilities in urban coastal areas has become less attractive from both an ecological and corporate viewpoint. Siting in these traditionally industrial areas exacerbates air and water quality problems. Since many coastal cities, and particularly their industrial areas, still fail to achieve national standards for air and water quality, energy companies also face an expensive, time-consuming, and sometimes impossible task if they wish to obtain the government permits necessary to construct and operate major facilities in these locations. In some areas, such as Houston, Corpus Christi, and New Orleans, suitable sites within existing port areas are simply unavailable.

Rural sites, an obvious alternative to these urban siting problems, have been considered unsatisfactory by many, both environmentalists and industry.[d] Intrusion of energy facilities into pristine areas is considered ecologically and aesthetically undesirable. On a more practical level, rural sites seldom afford energy companies access to port facilities and transportation networks. Furthermore, the skilled labor required to construct and operate major facilities is not readily available, nor are other important services. Governmental regulations, such as those designed to prevent significant deterioration of air quality,[3] may also pose obstacles to a company seeking a truly rural site.

As demonstrated in the two Gulf Coast case studies, one solution to the problem of availability of suitable land in urban areas and compatibility of land uses in rural areas is to site new facilities in near-urban areas. This alternative is practical along the Gulf Coast where undeveloped land is available close to urban centers. These industrial sites are outside residential growth corridors and away from prime recreational land. Siting in previously agricultural areas on the urban fringe allows industry access to needed services and increases the likelihood that necessary permits can be obtained. This solution has proven an effective means of limiting public protests to siting decisions, especially when combined with a comprehensive buffer zone policy.

Availability of near-urban sites has allowed energy companies to purchase large amounts of acreage, reserving land for future expansion while buffering the surrounding area from the impacts associated with major facilities. Energy companies often have purchased far more land than they actually required for their urban fringe facilities. For example, CCPC acquired three times as much land as it planned to use to operate its petrochemical processing plant, and ECOL purchased approximately four times the amount of land required for its refinery and associated operations. These large land purchases in near-urban areas have been relatively inexpensive. Prime land located in a port area is priced at $10,000 per acre or more, but near-urban land along the Gulf Coast can often be acquired for $2,000 to $3,000 per acre.

These large tracts afford companies two advantages. They allow for expansion that, given current governmental regulations, is generally easier than construction of an entirely new facility. In fact, CCPC has indicated that it may expand in the near future, or allow another company to site on its land.[4]

[d]There are exceptions, however. Nuclear energy facilities, given their safety risks, are required to site in low-population areas, and liquefied natural gas facilities may be similarly regulated.

A large amount of acreage also provides space for a buffer zone around the facility, thereby minimizing impacts on any nearby development. Although these sites are outside residential growth corridors, most near-urban areas are scattered with single-family dwellings. Locating major facility operations in the center of a large tract of land effectively buffers any nearby residents from the noise, odors, and visual impact of a major energy facility.

This new variation on the "out-of-sight, out-of-mind" strategy is not discussed openly by either the companies or government officials, but there is adequate evidence to document its existence. ECOL's environmental impact assessment, for instance, noted plans to maintain fragrant vegetation in certain areas around the refining operations to buffer the surrounding area from odors and noise.[5] CCPC officials reported that one available parcel of land in Corpus Christi, located nearer the port area than their ultimate selection, was quickly dismissed from consideration because it would have placed the facility too close to residential development. To paraphrase one CCPC official, the loud noises associated with periodic flaring at the facility would have affected the peace and quiet—not to mention sleep—of nearby residents. In contrast, facilities provided with buffer zones have minimal impact on nearby residents.[6] Thus the provision of a buffer zone is an effective corporate means of managing impacts and discouraging local opposition to the facility.

PROPONENTS AND OPPONENTS: THE POLITICS OF SITING

Organizations favoring the siting of additional energy facilities in Texas and Louisiana are much more influential than those who express objections. In both states, numerous public and private organizations—chambers of commerce, electric companies, and railroad companies, for example—actively and vocally promote industrial development, including development of energy-related activities. Many of these organizations seek out a company contemplating a new project and encourage it to site in their particular area. Both states also have public industrial commissions created primarily to promote development. At the local level, ports and navigation districts, which are legally defined governmental entities, also offer to assist prospective developers. Some Louisiana parish governments are directly involved in promoting siting within their jurisdiction.

Organizations objecting to industrial development are far fewer and less apparent. The efforts of environmentally oriented groups have been directed toward influencing the policies and rules of government agencies and protecting specific natural resources. These groups often have limited personnel and resources, and therefore they feel they can be more effective by focusing on broader issues. Rarely do they become involved in a particular siting decision.

Although there is evidence of increasing concern over the siting of industrial facilities on the Gulf Coast, past opposition to specific siting decisions has been related to facilities thought to pose severe hazards to health or safety. Explosion of a grain elevator in Louisiana has been responsible for opposition in some parishes to the siting of grain elevators near residential areas. In Texas, there has been opposition to the siting of nuclear power plants. However, the major opposition to the only nuclear plant sited in the coastal region came not from local citizens but from outside groups concerned about the general safety and environmental hazards associated with nuclear energy.

Although public reaction to siting decisions has as yet been limited in the Gulf Coast area, there is evidence of increasing concern over the potential impacts of industrial facilities. In the past, land availability and patterns of land use have effectively insulated residential and recreational development from industrial areas. In places where this pattern of insulation has been disrupted, citizen groups on the Gulf Coast can be expected to become more outspoken and wield greater influence.

A recent case illustrates this pattern. Two corporations sited several major petrochemical facilities in the ETJs of a number of the small cities close to Galveston Bay, near Houston. The sites were in an established industrial area already occupied by energy facilities. Each of the cities had zoned the sites for industrial use, supported the companies' siting plans, or both. However, under the aegis of the Galveston Bay Conservation and Preservation Association (GBCPA), residents of an incorporated area adjacent to the sites strongly opposed the facilities and protested to the Texas Air Control Board (TACB), citing the facilities' impacts on air quality and land use patterns in the area. TACB ruled that the facilities were designed to meet air quality standards (although monitoring of the area had not yet begun) and that land use issues were best decided by local governments. Construction of a multimillion dollar petrochemical plant by the American Hoechst Corporation began. The citizen groups appealed to the courts. In August 1979 the court ruled in favor of the TACB's decision to allow construction. The GBCPA plans to appeal to the Texas Supreme Court.[7] Meanwhile, one of the other firms involved announced plans to relocate its planned chlorine processing facility to an alternative site in Louisiana, along the Mississippi River in St. James Parish.[e]

Although these events near Houston are unusual, they may prove to be a portent of the future as more land along the Gulf Coast is converted to residential use. Currently, however, the siting picture in this region is still overwhelmingly dominated by groups who support further industrial and energy development.

PERCEPTIONS OF ECONOMIC IMPACT

Interests favoring additional energy facilities see economic advantages associated with them, especially the general stimulus to the state and local economies rather than specific impacts such as tax revenues or direct employment opportunities. Extensive industrial development is a relatively new phenomenon along the Gulf Coast. Considering the comparatively late arrival of industry in this region, Gulf Coast states do not yet face the difficult task of revitalizing pre-World War I industrial areas as do many East Coast states. Industrial development, and especially energy activities, brought a new economic prosperity to Texas and Louisiana. Their goal now is to maintain strong state economies through further industrial expansion. Large energy facilities are seen as playing a major role in perpetuating this economic prosperity.

Although major energy facilities offer few direct long-term employment opportunities to local labor, they are considered beneficial for the general economic stimulus they provide. The fear of many New Jersey citizens is the hope of many Gulf Coast residents; that is, a major energy facility will encourage further development in the area. Discussions concerning the number of jobs per acre or the tax dollars paid by a facility are rare along the Texas and

[e]This large chemical plant had been proposed by the B. F. Goodrich Company for a site near residential development along the bay.[8] In its battle to halt further construction of the Hoechst facility, GBCPA has been working with local officials and another organization, People for Parks, to obtain funding for a park with 4,000-foot frontage on Galveston Bay as an alternative to further petrochemical development, which dominates the larger community of nearby Houston. In this regard, these citizens have much in common with citizens in Hudson County, New Jersey, where the creation of Liberty State Park on the Hudson River became the focal point of a land use alternative to further heavy industrialization, including petrochemical development.

Louisiana coasts. In fact, most major facilities in Louisiana that meet certain requirements are exempt from local property tax payments for 10 years. A number of Texas cities, Corpus Christi for example, encourage siting outside the city limits, thus exempting a facility from city taxes (it still must pay school district and county taxes, however).

Low unemployment rates and expanding economies allow the people of Texas and Louisiana to appreciate the general economic benefits of a facility rather than dwell on its specific impacts. Certainly, the abundance of available land and the land use patterns have also contributed to this perspective. In other areas of the country where the environment is approaching its absorptive capacity for further development, thus leading to increasing land use conflicts, residents analyze specific impacts to weigh against the benefits associated with a particular facility. The people of Texas and Louisiana have not reached this point. When, if ever, they do reach it, the time and the difference in development history and needs will probably result in concern over a different set of specific issues.[f]

FEDERAL INTERVENTION AND STATES' RIGHTS

The issue of federal intervention in these states assumes a different character from other regions of the country. On the East Coast, there is apprehension that the federal government will force the siting of unwanted facilities. Conversely, local and state governments in Texas and Louisiana tend to fear that federal regulatory authority will be used to constain energy development.

The issue of federal regulatory power has a direct bearing on the process of siting an industrial facility. The federal government not only has the power to require energy facilities to meet more stringent environmental requirements than those demanded by state or local laws, but it also has the responsibility to consider the national interest. Two direct mechanisms potentially allow federal intercession into state or local siting decisions: the federal government may restrict siting through environmental regulations, or it may require siting to ensure that the national interest is protected.[g]

[f]For example, in parts of Texas where fresh water is limited, the concern may focus on the proposed facility's water requirements.

[g]Under the Energy Mobilization Board proposed in 1979, for example; or perhaps under the "national interest" provisions of the Coastal Zone Management Act.

In many regions of the country, the issue of federal intervention has arisen in cases where communities or states have attempted to restrict energy facility siting. Following the OPEC oil embargo and energy crisis, however, the U.S. government has been deeply concerned with determining future energy requirements and ensuring national self-sufficiency in energy production. Operation of energy facilities increasingly is seen as a matter of national interest, thus permitting intervention should an area or state unreasonably restrict the siting of such facilities.

In Texas and Louisiana, the issue of federal intervention takes on a different cast. Citizens often speak warily of the large number of federal laws enacted to protect the environment, fearing that these laws may restrict or halt the siting in their area of major energy facilities.[h] As discussed previously, energy development and production are not seen as a threat to health or safety. Nor do citizens point to energy facilities as a major source of environmental degradation. In most coastal areas of the two states, energy facilities have been in evidence for over 30 years without severely impacting the lives of nearby residents; they have contributed significantly to the local and state economies. Thus, although based on a different perspective, Gulf Coast residents, like citizens in other regions, are apprehensive about the federal government's power to override local decisions.

THE EAST COAST AND THE GULF COAST IN COMPARATIVE PERSPECTIVE

The energy facility siting experience on the Texas-Louisiana Gulf Coast provides a good contrast with the East Coast situation. On the Gulf Coast, energy development took place gradually over decades. From the beginning, oil and gas were an integral part of this area's basic industrial profile.[9] Thus, communities here did not experience the shock of sudden change that new OCS development

[h]There are certain exceptions. In Texas, opposition has arisen to the federal government's appropriation of salt domes for strategic petroleum storage. This opposition is based not on the use of salt domes for this activity but on the possible impact of brine outfall on shrimp production if brine is discharged in waters near the coast. The federal government's plans to transport nuclear waste across the state and possible storage of these wastes in Texas has also raised the issue of federal intervention in a manner similar to the emergence of this issue in other regions of the country.

areas anticipate, even in places like New Jersey where refineries and petrochemical processing facilities have been firmly established for several decades. The energy industry on the Gulf Coast has been largely unopposed and unexamined by the area's residents. Oil and gas development and associated petrochemical facilities are seen as a natural and indispensable aspect of life, accepted—at least to date—with very little question.

Along with California, the Gulf Coast and Mid-Atlantic are the largest oil refining areas in the nation. New Jersey alone has 5 of its area's 10 oil refineries, accounting for 34 percent of the refining capacity on the East Coast (about 4 percent nationally).[10] The Gulf Coast is a very much larger energy-producing area, with extensive offshore oil development and 82 refineries accounting for almost 40 percent of total U.S. capacity.[11] The Texas Gulf Coast alone has the greatest concentration of chemical plants in the country, producing 80 percent of the nation's synthetic rubber, 60 percent of the sulfur, and more than 40 percent of every basic petrochemical. As of 1978, 58 petrochemical plants were operating in the Texas coastal zone; at least 10 additional plants were proposed or under construction.[12] Texas also has 81 operational natural gas processing facilities[13] (in contrast with New Jersey, where none exist). Like Texas, petrochemicals are New Jersey's largest industry, a $5.6 billion dollar giant (the next largest industries are agriculture and tourism, each generating about $3 billion).

In the Texas siting case, the chemical plant was located just outside the city limits in an area free of higher city taxes. This site is five miles inland, with the facility using a pipeline to transport its raw materials and products to and from the urban harbor. One of the company's major considerations in selecting this Texas site was the ability to obtain local, state, and federal permits with little if any anticipated opposition. In the Louisiana case, the company dropped several alternative sites from further consideration for various reasons, including anticipated opposition from environmental groups, especially in one locale in South Carolina. In contrast, energy companies have continued to propose new facilities in New Jersey even in the face of citizen opposition. Both Gulf Coast locations were outside of large population centers and away from residential areas.

The area chosen for the refinery in Louisiana had actively used a public relations campaign to encourage facilities to locate there. Prevailing policy in this parish is to encourage development along the Mississippi River and constrain siting outside of this corridor, thereby keeping industrialization away from the ecologically sensitive wetlands. Political support for this policy comes from citizens who use the wetlands for recreation, primarily fishing and hunting. According to Louisiana state law, a company must obtain a parish permit before seeking state and federal approval. In New Jersey, by contrast, one of the siting issues involved conflict over the timing of local and state approval, with some state decision makers proposing to pre-empt local authority.

The major distinction between energy facility siting on the East Coast and the Gulf Coast probably emanates from the geography itself. There is generally a feeling of space along the Gulf Coast: space for cropland, recreational and residential areas, and major industrial development. Industrial development has remained discrete from residential and recreational areas, thus lessening its intrusion into the daily lives of local residents. This difference of land availability between the East and Gulf Coasts has produced markedly different political climates for industrial development.

The East Coast is an attractive location for energy production because the region's energy requirements provide a ready market for refined products, eliminating the need for extensive transportation. However, announcement of a company's plans to locate even a small energy facility in certain areas has generated strong public opposition, which on numerous occasions has been quite effective.

In Texas and Louisiana, on the other hand, the political climates strongly support further energy development. There is a widely held belief in these two states that environmental concerns must be tempered with economic considerations. Energy facilities are generally not deemed dangerous to health, safety, or the quality of life, and their positive economic benefits are valued. Until they are seen as a threat to the historically abundant supply of natural resources, it is likely that this attitude favoring energy development will persist along the Gulf Coast, drawing corporate attention to this area rather than to the East Coast.

NOTES

1. An in-depth discussion of these factors is presented in Research and Planning Consultants, Inc., *Siting Industrial Facilities on the Texas Coast*, 1978, pp. 10-20 (produced by RPC for the General Land Office of Texas); also see Chapters 9-11.
2. Personal interview with Robert Becnel, Secretary-Treasurer of the Police Jury of St. John the Baptist Parish, May 30, 1978.
3. Federal Clean Air Act, 42 U.S.C.A., secs. 7470-7491.
4. Personal interview with Alstair Fleming, CCPC Deputy Facilities Project Director, May 1978.

5. ECOL, Ltd., *Environmental Assessment ECOL, Ltd., Energy Refinery, St. John the Baptist Parish* (Baton Rouge: Louisiana State University, School of Environmental Design, 1975).
6. Interview with one CCPC official.
7. "Appeals Judge Upholds Bayport Chemical Plant OK," *Houston Post*, August 23, 1979.
8. *Ibid.*
9. See RPC, *Siting Industrial Facilities. . .* , op. cit., and RPC, *Energy Facility Siting in the Gulf Coast Region* (Austin, Texas: October 1978).
10. Interview with Roy Young, Refining Associate, American Petrochemical Institute, Washington, D.C., May 22, 1979.
11. Ibid.
12. RPC, *Energy Facility Siting. . .* , op. cit.
13. Information provided by Leah Pagan, RPC, Austin, Texas, March 16, 1978.

Part III

The Economics of Energy Facility Siting: A Corporate Perspective

Chapter 9

The Economics of Permitting: An Approach

*Energy and Environmental
Analysis, Inc.*

Different permit processes and locational scenarios have varying kinds of impacts on the economics of energy facility development. This can be seen in the northeastern United States, where
proposed petroleum refineries, petrochemical plants, energy storage
terminals, and similar facilities have encountered strong opposition
from community organizations and environmental groups. In most
cases, these opposition groups have thwarted construction of the
proposed facilities.

The permitting process required for new energy facilities thus has
presented corporate investors with new costs and new dimensions
of uncertainty. Two issues are of principal importance in this
analysis:

The economic impact of the permitting process on the desirability
of an investment in an energy or industrial facility

The possible effects of the location selected for the facility on the
permitting process and investment economics

The overall intent is to determine if the additional costs of innovative
siting can be offset by reduced permitting costs.

This analysis takes the perspective of a firm facing an investment decision in a new energy facility. The dimensions of the permitting process relevent to its investment decision are:

The cost of the process
The length of the process
The probability of failing to receive any of the required permits
The impact of challenges to previously issued permits resulting in midconstruction delays

The proposed facility location can influence the investment decision in two ways:

Directly, through the site's impact on capital, operating, and transportation costs
Indirectly, by the site influencing the length and probability of successful completion of the permitting process

Some key questions are related to these issues. Why do companies persist, as in Hudson County, New Jersey,[a] in seeking coastal sites where they face known strong environmental opposition? Would a firm be willing to locate in a site resulting in somewhat higher costs (e.g., an inland site) if choice of this location were to reduce expected permitting delays? What specific capital or operating costs would a firm be willing to trade for a reduction in permitting delays and uncertainties?

The Northeast is an ideal region in which to explore these issues. There are many competing land use alternatives, and local environmental groups are opposed to further deterioration in an already poor environment; yet new energy facilities of various kinds are needed to meet increasing market demands. Growing demand for oil products has resulted in confrontations between energy companies proposing new refinery capacity and environmental or citizen groups opposing these facilities. Indeed, battles over refinery siting illustrate well the broader questions. In the past 15 years, 23 grass roots refineries[b] have been proposed for East Coast sites. None reached the construction phase, and only two proposals are still under active consideration.

---

[a]See Chapter 2.
[b]A grass roots refinery is a refinery built totally new, as opposed to expansion of an existing refinery.

METHODOLOGY

An investment in a grass roots oil refinery producing 200,000 barrels per day was chosen for economic analysis. The permitting procedures and siting issues for construction of large energy or industrial facilities have many common features. The conclusions drawn from a sensitivity analysis of oil refineries should, therefore, be valid for a wide range of facilities. In addition, distribution of refined products, delivery of crude oil to the refinery, and the facility's general operations present many coastal land use and environmental controversies that highlight coastal-inland and urban-rural locational tradeoffs. Another advantage of an analysis based on a refinery is the availability of information on the required permitting procedures and associated costs.

Data on the permitting process were collected through case studies of recent refinery proposals and through interviews with industry decision makers. Case studies of 16 refineries proposed for East Coast sites that were either rejected or abandoned were used to identify general trends in the permitting process that may influence facility location. Many of these studies involved reviewing decisions made four or five or even more years ago, and the information was often incomplete.

To supplement this material, in-depth interviews were conducted with decision makers at four oil companies that have recently undergone, or are now involved in, the permitting process for a major new oil refinery. These interviews were used to gather specific information about the economics of different facility sites, to determine the costs to the firm of the permitting process, and to gain industry's perspective on permitting problems.

Two pairs of locational alternatives were employed in the analysis, coastal versus inland sites and rural versus urban sites. Within these broad siting categories different crude oil delivery and product distribution systems are available. Three types of transportation systems were examined: a deepwater port (DWP) for offshore delivery of crude oil; a pipeline for crude oil transportation from the coast (or the DWP) to an inland site; and a products pipeline for distribution of refined products to their markets.

To evaluate the impacts of the permitting process and facility location on the investment decision, a scenario-sensitivity analysis was used. Information from the case studies, interviews and an overall analysis of the permitting process was used to construct facility location and permitting scenarios. The economics of each scenario were developed and then used to determine the sensitivity of the investment decision to varying locational and permitting parameters.

After determining the sensitivity of the investment to the permitting process, the investment model was used to calculate the amount of money a firm might be willing to pay in increased capital or operating costs to avoid the delays and uncertainties of the permitting process. This tradeoff price can be viewed as the cost to the firm of the permitting process. The tradeoff price also determines the extent to which a firm will seek a location with higher costs but reduced permitting delays. Figure 9-1 illustrates this overall methodology.

NORTHEAST PETROLEUM CONSUMPTION AND SUPPLY PATTERNS

The Northeast is heavily dependent on petroleum products. New England relies on energy derived from petroleum for more than 80 percent of all its energy; whereas New York, New Jersey, and the Mid-Atlantic states rely on petroleum products for 60 percent of their energy needs. This compares to a national average of 45 percent of all energy derived from petroleum.

The northeastern states consume 26 percent of the nation's petroleum products, but they contain only 9 percent of the nation's refining capacity. The East Coast as a whole has only enough refinery capacity to meet 25 percent of its refined product demand (see Table 9-1); the balance is supplied from foreign imports (25 percent) and shipments from other domestic regions (48 percent), predominantly the Gulf Coast and the Midwest.

Relative transportation costs provide an economic incentive for oil companies to expand their refinery and storage capacity in the Northeast. Crude oil is generally cheaper to transport than refined oil products. This promotes the siting of refineries near the markets for their products. This market orientation of refined products has not developed in the Northeast, however. No new crude oil facilities have been built there since 1958, and the area's share of national refining capacity has declined from 14 percent in 1955 to 9 percent in 1975.

Expansion of refinery capacity in the Northeast poses many land use and environmental problems. However, an increase in local refinery capacity can reduce the environmental hazards related to oil spills by decreasing the distance petroleum products are shipped.

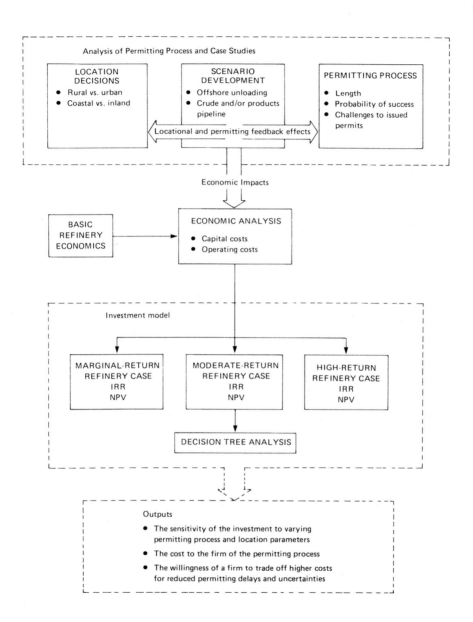

Figure 9-1. Economics of permitting—a methodology.

Table 9-1. Regional Operating Refinery Capacity and Petroleum Demand (1976)
(thousands of barrels per day)

	Petroleum Demand	Refinery Capacity	Capacity Shortfall or Overage (Demand minus Capacity)
PAD I (East Coast)	6,437	1,677	−4,760
PAD II (Midwest)	4,871	4,137	−734
PAD III (Gulf Coast)	3,252	6,197	+2,945
PAD IV (Rocky Mountains)	531	552	+21
PAD V (West Coast)	2,352	2,364	+12
Total United States	17,444	14,927	−2,517

The lighter petroleum products (i.e., gasoline, distillate, and kerosene) are generally more toxic and, historically, have a much higher spill rate than do crude oil shipments. In the Long Island and northern New Jersey waters, 97 percent of all oil spills (by volume) involved refined products.[1] Light refined products account for 52 percent of the Northeast's petroleum products imports. Half of these are transported to the region via the coastal waterways. Expansion of refinery capacity within the area could substantially reduce the number of refined product spills in coastal waters, particularly if pipelines were used to move the products from refineries to the distribution system.

The costs of transporting refined products are expected to increase relative to other refinery costs during the next five years. Although a surplus of tankers in coastal markets has resulted in low coastal shipping rates, this surplus capacity is not expected to continue. New safety and mechanical regulations proposed by the U.S. Coast Guard will probably result in the scrapping of many older vessels. The costs of installing new pipelines have increased tremendously over the past several years, and this trend could continue for several more years. Although transportation costs are only one of many costs to consider when siting a refinery, they are usually very important because of the large volumes of crude oil that will be processed. Thus increasing transportation costs will result in further incentives to locate additional refineries in the Northeast.

PERMITTING TRENDS

Permitting procedures for construction of energy facilities or energy-intensive industrial facilities have many common features.

Although this analysis is based on the permitting process required for siting a grass roots oil refinery, the conclusions should be applicable to a wide range of energy-related investments.

The approval process required for a new refinery involves a series of local, state, and federal permits. Each permit harbors the possibilities of delays (both pre- and midconstruction), outright rejection, and plant modification to reduce environmental impacts.

Local Siting Review: Rejection

The case studies indicate that acquisition of local or state siting approval has been the most difficult hurdle. Twenty-one proposed refineries that have been rejected or abandoned in recent years are listed in Table 9-2. Only one refinery was rejected as the result of a federal law; all of the others were rejected as the result of local or state action. Nine were rejected at the local level through zoning ordinances, referenda, or city council actions; five were rejected at the state level because of opposition from local or regional environmental groups; and six proposals were withdrawn by the firm because of local opposition or unspecified internal management decisions.

Even though local or state action resulted in final rejection of nearly all of the refinery proposals, a number of the proposals did receive popular community support. In these cases the city council either went against popular opinion to reject the facility or, more often, regional environmental groups took their case directly to a state authority. All six of the communities that actively supported refinery projects are rural communities; in contrast, no refinery proposed for an urban site received popular local support.

To increase the probability of success in the local approval process, a rural-inland site seems desirable. An inland location reduces land use conflicts present in the coastal zone and removes the refinery from the environmentally sensitive coastal wetlands. The tax and employment benefits of a refinery have a greater impact in rural areas and can help offset the facility's undesirable environmental effects. Urban tax bases are generally broad, and the reduction in a resident's taxes from revenue generated by the refinery will be small. In a rural community the taxes paid by a large refinery can significantly lower property taxes. An increase of 150 jobs has more effect on a rural work force of 1,000 people than on an urban work force of 150,000 people.

Table 9-2. Refinery Projects Rejected or Abandoned in Recent Years

Location	Company	Size (barrels per day)	Rural or Urban	Comments
Baltimore, Md.	Crown Central Petroleum Co.	200,000	Urban	State and local officials strongly favored this project. However, it was proposed for a somewhat residential area and drew strong citizen and environmental protests. A citizen's lobby exerted enough pressure on the county commissioners to kill the project.
Brunswick, Ga.	Georgia Refining Co.	200,000	Urban	Blocked through actions of the office of the state's environmental director.
Delaware Bay, Del.	Shell Oil Co.	150,000	Rural	Refineries were forbidden by Delaware's Coastal Zone Management Act.
Dracut, Mass.	Saber-Tex Co.	100,000	Urban	Townspeople strongly favored project. However, plan dropped because of internal company decision.
Fort Pierce, Fla.	Ashland Oil Co.	250,000	Rural	Halted by an internal corporate decision.
Hoboken, N.J.	Supermarine, Inc.	100,000	Urban	Proposal withdrawn under pressure from environmental groups.
Jamestown, R.I.	Commerce Oil Co.	50,000	Rural	Townspeople supported project 7 to 1 in local referendum. Zoning changes were granted. Construction blocked in court through actions of the Jamestown Protective Association.
Jersey City, N.J.	JOC Oil Co.	50,000	Urban	Proposal rejected because of citizen and environmental group pressure.
Machiasport, Me.	Occidental Petroleum Co.	300,000	Rural	This project was killed by political opposition at the federal level, not by local referendum or council vote.

Table 9-2 – Continued

Location	Company	Size (barrels per day)	Rural or Urban	Comments
Newington, N.H.	C.H. Sprague and Son, Inc.	50,000	Rural	Not specified.
New London, Conn.	In-O-Ven Co.	400,000	Urban	Proposal abandoned because of opposition from state government and environmental groups.
Paulsboro, N.J.	Mobil Oil Co.	150,000	Urban	Project canceled because of changes in refining capacity and demand.
Piney Point, Md.	Steuart Petroleum Co.	100,000	Rural	Rejected by local referendum on environmental grounds.
Port Manatee, Fla.	Belcher Oil Co.	200,000	Rural	Voted down in nonbinding public referendum. Opposition from retired constituents was a major factor. County commissioners voted 3 to 2 to grant the permit, but Belcher withdrew its proposal, fearing a change in the political climate.
Riverhead, N.Y.	Fuels Desulfurization Co.	200,000	Rural	City council rejected proposal following overwhelming public opposition.
Rochester, N.H.	Granite State Refineries, Inc.	400,000	Rural	Proposing firm dissolved with principal's death.
Sanford, Me.	Gibbs Oil Co.	250,000	Rural	Town voted 7 to 3 in favor of the project. However, coastal protection groups brought pressure to bear at the state level, halting the planning.
Saybrook, Conn.	Pepco Co.	400,000	Urban	Strong opposition at state, county, and local levels prevented project from proceeding past preliminary stages.

Table 9-2 – Continued

Location	Company	Size (barrels per day)	Rural or Urban	Comments
Searsport, Me.	Maine Clean Fuels Co.	200,000	Rural	Local population supported the proposal. Outside environmental groups put pressure on state government to halt project. The Maine Environmental Protection Board eventually rejected proposal.
South Portland, Me.	Maine Clean Fuels Co.	200,000	Urban	Local environmental groups presented substantial public opposition. Proposal was blocked through creation of a fire zone and ordinance that the refinery was incapable of meeting.
Tiverton, R.I.	Northeast Petroleum Co.	65,000	Rural	Public sentiment was strongly in favor of the project. Persistent opposition was able to sway council votes through lengthy hearing process. Council rejected proposal.

State and Federal Permits: Delay

Since the majority of refineries have been rejected at the local level, the impacts of many state and federal laws are still uncertain. The proposed Hampton Roads (Virginia) and Eastport (Maine) refineries have obtained local approval, but they are still engaged in the state and federal permitting processes.

In contrast to local rejection, delays in the permitting process have resulted predominantly from the requirements of federal laws, particularly permits that require preparation of an Environmental Impact Statement (EIS) under the National Environmental Policy Act of 1969 (NEPA). In most instances local approval has not resulted in substantial delays. A favorable or unfavorable decision was usually made at the local level within six months to a year after submission of the proposal.

Though federal permits pose much greater problems of delay, they present a much smaller likelihood of outright rejection than does the local approval process. Federal laws generally specify certain emission levels or conditions that must be met, and if these are met, the permit is granted. Though this is an oversimplification, usually the company will have the opportunity to obtain the permit if it complies with specific standards.[c] Such compliance, however, may be costly to the company, perhaps increasing the costs of the refinery to the point where it no longer represents an economic investment.

State permits do not lend themselves to any generalizations concerning potential delays or possible rejection. Many states administer permits under federal law. A state may also have site selection laws requiring approval by a state environmental board of any development potentially harmful to the environment. For example, Maine requires all oil refinery construction to receive state approval. This site selection law can pose as much difficulty as local approval, since local and regional opinion is usually a major criterion. A state may also have passed its own air and water quality laws that may be more restrictive than the federal standards. Since state-issued permits do not require an EIS under NEPA, the state permits are generally subject to less delay than are federal permits. However, some state laws do require an environmental impact analysis similar to the NEPA process. Key state siting restrictions on the East Coast are listed in Table 9-3.

---

[c]A major exception to this is the U.S. Army Corps of Engineers dredge and fill permit, approval of which is dependent upon a subjective evaluation.

Table 9-3. East Coast Siting Restrictions Affecting Oil Refineries

State	Siting Restrictions
Connecticut	Local referendum required
Delaware	Prohibition of oil refineries along the coastal zone
Maryland and and Maine	In both states, state environmental control boards established with authority over coastal energy facility siting, especially petroleum facility siting
Massachusetts	Has exclusionary zones for pipeline siting Local referendum required
New Hampshire	Explicit final approval up to the state legislature Local referendum required
New Jersey	Oil refineries prohibited on barrier beaches; has exclusionary zones for pipeline siting
Rhode Island	Has exclusionary zones for pipeline siting Explicit final approval up to the state legislature

Summary of Key Federal Permits

The approval process for federal permits for a refinery has been very lengthy, in some cases lasting as long as five years. Permits required by federal law have been responsible for most of the delays encountered by the proposed facilities. The most substantial delays have resulted from permits where an EIS is required. NEPA requires an EIS for any "major Federal action significantly affecting the quality of the human environment."[2] Issuance of a federal permit related to air and water quality can constitute a "major Federal action." Preparation of the EIS often requires public hearings where any interested party can challenge the statement's contents. As an example, the impact statements required of the Eastport and Hampton Roads refinery proposals took approximately three years to complete.

The federal-state permitting process is extremely complex, and the following paragraphs only introduce its many issues.[3]

National Pollution Discharge Elimination System Permits. The National Pollution Discharge Elimination System (NPDES) permit program was established in the Federal Water Pollution Control Act Amendments of 1972. Under the program, it is unlawful for any person to discharge a pollutant from a discrete site into navigable waters without an NPDES permit.

The NPDES program can be administered by a state or by the U.S. Environmental Protection Agency (EPA). If a state chooses to administer this permit program, it must have its permitting system approved by the EPA. A federally issued NPDES permit still requires state certification indicating that the applicant will comply with all state and local effluent limitations. A federally issued NPDES permit falls under the NEPA provisions, and an EIS may be required, preparation of which increases the probability of lengthy delays. A 1978 court decision excluded state-issued NPDES permits from NEPA,[4] thereby reducing the probability of delays in states that administer their own NPDES program. The East Coast states that issue NPDES permits are listed in Table 9-4.

The likelihood of outright rejection of the NPDES permit for a proposed refinery is generally quite low. Effluent standards are set that the facility must meet, and if the requirements are met, the permit is issued. The standards may result in expensive treatment procedures that can increase refinery costs, however.

Air Quality Permits: Nonattainment. All major new facilities require permits to ensure that their air pollution emissions are compatible with the state implementation plan (SIP) for air quality prepared under the Clean Air Act. In those areas (including much of

Table 9-4. State Administration of NPDES Permit Program

East Coast States with State-Issued NPDES Permits:
  Connecticut
  Delaware
  Georgia
  Maryland
  New York
  North Carolina
  South Carolina
  Vermont
  Virginia

East Coast States with Federally Issued NPDES Permits:
  District of Columbia
  Florida
  Maine
  Massachusetts
  New Hampshire
  New Jersey
  Pennsylvania
  Rhode Island

the East Coast) where the air remains dirtier than the national standards (called "nonattainment areas"), further permit review is required. Oil refineries wishing to construct or modify in a non-attainment region before July 1, 1979, were subject to the emissions offset policy[d] and require EPA approval. After July 1, 1979, the states must have an EPA-approved program for issuing permits to new sources in nonattainment areas. If the state does not have such a program by this time, no construction permits are to be issued in these areas.

The probability of rejection depends on the existence of possible emission offsets. A plant wishing to locate in a nonattainment area must purchase or arrange for emission reductions from existing sources such that total emissions from existing and proposed sources will be reduced. Where adequate emission tradeoffs are possible, the permit will be granted; where possible tradeoffs are limited, the source of the pollution is sometimes taken into consideration. Permits are to be granted more leniently if the pollution is from a natural source.[e]

Air Quality Permits: Prevention of Significant Deterioration. The Clean Air Act stipulates that a preconstruction permit is required for an oil refinery (or other major stationary source) wishing to construct or modify in a prevention of significant deterioration (PSD) area. To obtain this permit, the applicant must employ the best available control technology (BACT) for all pollutants covered under the act and ensure that allowable pollutant increments will not be violated in local or neighboring areas.

There are three PSD clean air area classifications:

Class I, in which practically any air quality deterioration would be precluded

Class II, in which deterioration in air quality arising from moderate growth would not be considered significant

Class III, in which intensive and concentrated industrial growth can occur while not departing from the intent of the PSD regulations

The 1977 amendments to the Clean Air Act designated certain areas as mandatory Class I:

---

[d]See Chapter 5 for a detailed review of the offset policy.
[e]This was a consideration in the air quality permit granted to the Pittston refinery in Eastport, Maine.

All international parks

All national wilderness areas that exceed 5,000 acres in size

All national memorial parks that exceed 5,000 acres in size

All national parks that exceed 6,000 acres in size and that are in existence on the date of enactment of the Clean Air Act Amendments of 1977, and all areas that were registered as Class I under regulations promulgated before the date of enactment

All other so-called clean air areas were classified in the 1977 amendments as Class II. Most can be reclassified by the state as Class I or III, except for the following, which are prohibited from redesignation as Class III:

An area that exceeds 10,000 acres in size and is a national monument, a national primitive area, a national preserve, a national recreation area, a national wildlife refuge, a national lakeshore, or seashore

A national park or national wilderness area established after the date of enactment of this act that exceeds 10,000 acres in size

Each classification area is assigned a maximum allowable increment for concentrations of specific pollutants. As long as this increment is not violated by the proposed refinery, the chances of permitting delay are minimal. If Class I areas are threatened by refinery emissions, however, delays can be substantial. In addition, the permittee must agree to conduct monitoring to determine the effects of resulting emissions on area air quality.

To date, the possibility of rejection of a PSD permit has been low. However, as Class I air increments are allocated, a strict no-siting policy might replace the present more lenient policy.

U.S. Army Corps of Engineers Permits. The Federal Water Pollution Control Act and the Rivers and Harbors Act mandate that persons discharging dredged or fill materials into navigable waters, constructing a marine facility, or both, must obtain a permit from the secretary of the army, acting through the chief of engineers, that is, a U.S. Army Corps of Engineers permit. This permit requires preparation of an EIS.

The probability of delay in this permit process is high. Preparation of an EIS is usually prone to delays. In addition, the Clean Air Act (Section 309) requires that EPA approve all EISs. Hence, EPA must approve the U.S. Army Corps' EIS before this permit can be issued. This interagency review process can potentially add further delays. Moreover, the probability of rejection in this permit process is higher than in other federal permit processes. Rather than having set standards that must be met, issuance of this permit depends upon balancing the public and private need for the project against a host of environmental considerations, including the project's effect on coastal wetlands, water quality, animal life, and also the historical, scenic, and recreational values of the site.

The exhaustive nature of these permit criteria almost requires that the corps permit be the last permit granted. The EIS and public hearings required for other permits are needed by the corps for its comprehensive evaluation. In addition, the corps is required to solicit the opinions of other state and federal agencies, notably the EPA, Fish and Wildlife Service, and National Marine Fisheries Service. How competing factors like national energy needs and environmental concerns will be evaluated by the corps is uncertain.

On permits for which set standards are specified, a sponsoring company can more easily determine its odds of approval even though there may be some question about which standards apply. The subjective evaluation required for the U.S. Army Corps permit makes its issuance more uncertain.

Postapproval Period

After all the required permits have been granted, delays are still possible. A legal challenge can be filed on any issued permit. Regardless of the outcome, the challenge can result in a court injunction postponing or halting construction while the litigation is resolved.

Certain federal laws and permits can be administered by state agencies. Among these are the Clean Air Act, the NPDES permit program, the Resource Conservation and Recovery Act, and the Coastal Zone Management Act. A state-issued permit under these laws can be challenged by a federal agency. Most examples of challenges concern NPDES permits or permits required under the Clean Air Act. Challenges usually result in an injunction halting facility construction while the permit conditions are revised. A major cause of federal challenges is the failure of states to revise their permit requirements to comply with amendments to federal laws.

A public interest suit can be filed against a facility or permitting agency claiming that the EIS prepared to obtain a federal permit did not meet NEPA requirements. NEPA requires that an EIS clearly demonstrate the significant environmental impacts expected to result from the proposed action; in this case, issuance of a permit.

The impacts of all reasonable alternatives to the proposed action must also be identified. Suits most frequently claim that an adequate evaluation of impacts was not made, or that alternatives to the action were not fully explored. The start of construction may be delayed if an EIS is returned to the issuing agency for revisions. If construction has already started, the court may issue an injunction halting work pending the filing of an adequate EIS.

Permitting Process Summary

The present permitting process is very cumbersome. This is partially the result of the many acts and amendments. The federal agencies have had little experience administering these new laws, and a stable permitting framework has not yet developed. Several ideas for streamlining the process have been proposed. Among them are the creation of a national dispute service, which would employ professional arbitrators to mediate energy-environmental controversies, and an energy mobilization board, which would have overriding authority. Regardless of the streamlining procedures employed, the present laws and their interpretation call for a permitting process of uncertain length and outcome. A deadline placed on the issuance of permits cannot eliminate the possibility of postapproval federal or NEPA-related challenges to issued permits. Indeed, a time limit on the approval process may make such challenges even more likely.

If given local approval, the proposed facility usually can meet state and federal environmental standards by using additional pollution control equipment or emission offsets. In some cases resulting cost increases may make the project uneconomical, and in other cases the standards may not allow any additional emissions and offsets may not be available. Even though federal laws have not directly resulted in refinery rejections, federal requirements, particularly the EIS, have caused substantial delays. However, few refineries have reached the federal stage of the permitting process.

A time line for an optimal permitting process under existing conditions for an East Coast refinery is presented in Figure 9-2; it is optimal in that no unusual delays occur (e.g., as a result of EIS preparation). The time line is based on recent permitting cases— primarily, the Hampton Roads Energy Company facility in Virginia and the Pittston Company refinery in Eastport, Maine—and discussions with federal regulatory agencies. Table 9-5 presents the permit process chronology for the Pittston refinery.

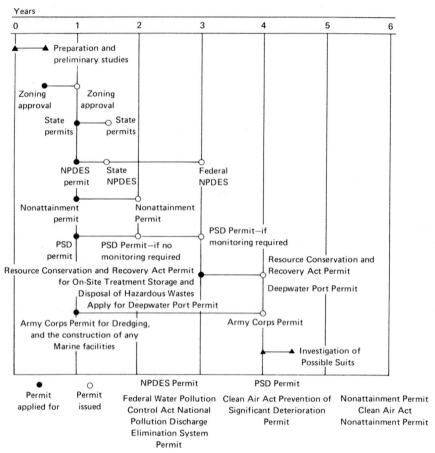

Figure 9-2. Typical permitting schedule.

Table 9-5. Permit Approval Chronology for Eastport (Maine) Refinery

5/73	Refinery proposal announced. Applied for site location permit, state waste water discharge permit, and state air permit. Site location permit is used by Maine Board of Environmental Protection. All three permits were applied for separately.
	Public hearings started 5/73, ended 6/75.
	State attorney general's office stated that no permit-granting body shall entertain applications unless applicant has the title, right, and interest in property in question. Pittston had options on most, but not all of the lands. This resulted in a nine-month delay.
	Hearings convened, Pittston presented a commitment for the land in question. Acceptable as a substitute for title, right, and interest in property.
7/75	Maine Board of Environmental Protection approved site permit.
8/75	Pittston began working with EPA on the EIS.
8/76	NPDES permit applied for.
4/77	PSD permit applied for.
6/77	State air and water permits issued.
8/77	Clean Air Act amendments were passed. Campobello became a Class I area—created PSD permit problems.
1/78	PSD permit revised to consider new PSD restrictions.
6/78	EIS completed, sent to U.S. Army Corps for their use. (The EIS took nearly three years.)
7/78	EIS comment period of 30 days over.
8/78	PSD permit issued. (PSD permit was heavily contested by opponents who claim that the refinery will violate Campobello's increment.) NPDES permit deferred pending consultation concerning endangered species.
8/79	U.S. Army Corps permit decision expected.

Note: The Pittston refinery still faces several substantial obstacles. The Canadian government opposes the use of Head Harbor passage by tankers in route to Eastport. There is also concern over possible detrimental effects on the bald eagle and certain species of whales. Both are classified as endangered species.

A CASE STUDY OF REFINERY SITING: TIVERTON, RHODE ISLAND

Northeast Petroleum Company's attempt to locate a refinery producing 65,000 barrels per day in Tiverton, Rhode Island, was chosen as a case study because it embodies many of the problems common to local siting attempts. When this facility was proposed in August 1970 the company stressed three points:

The economic advantages conferred by the refinery
The provision of environmental safeguards
A concerted public relations campaign

Northeast claimed that its refinery would generate over $1 million in annual tax revenue, allowing Tiverton's tax rate to be lowered from $39 to $22 per $1,000 of assessed value. In addition, the facility would provide 150 jobs with an average salary of $15,000 per year.[f] A great deal of this income would be spent locally, stimulating business.

Northeast also offered environmental safeguards to the community. The company volunteered to provide $500,000 to establish a conservation foundation to guard the environmental quality of Mount Hope and Narragansett Bays, which surround Tiverton. It also pledged to install the best available oil spill containment and cleanup equipment. This, Northeast asserted, would improve the environmental climate in the bay, as it would be available for use throughout the area.

Accompanying these promises was a concerted public relations campaign. Northeast mailed a 24-page color brochure explaining the refinery's benefits to all town residents. The townspeople were also invited to dinner, 100 at a time, to view a promotional film and discuss the project.

Following this effort, public support was clearly behind the refinery. The town was attracted by the environmental guarantees, and most importantly, by the economic benefits. However, a small group of middle- and upper-middle-class citizens opposed the refinery. Nine of them incorporated into a group named Save Our Community (SOC), and they hired an attorney to fight the project. Many of them lived in the residential area where the refinery was to be built, and all questioned Northeast's ability to fulfill its promises.

Local rezoning hearings provided a forum for SOC to confront the proposed facility. Following Northeast's presentation, the group began a well-organized attack on the project. In a series of public hearings they presented expert witnesses to refuse Northeast's claims and criticize elements of the proposal. The choice of a residential

---

[f]In a rural area such as Tiverton this can have a large employment impact; however, in a larger urban area this impact is greatly reduced (see Chapter 11).

site was condemned, and environmental and economic claims were either refuted or seriously questioned. Northeast's credibility and competence were both closely scrutinized. The company's process and engineering studies were as yet incomplete, and the refinery model presented to the town had omitted 19 large storage tanks. Northeast had also suffered a 170,000-gallon oil spill off Falmouth, Massachusetts, in 1969, and the environmental effects of this spill were still being felt. SOC emphasized these points.

Northeast's presentation at the rezoning hearings lasted one evening; SOC's case, on the other hand, occupied 13 sessions and covered 3 months. This time was used for continual lobbying, which gradually swung community support toward SOC. Moreover, several oil-related accidents took place during the hearings:

A refinery in New Jersey exploded, killing several people.

A valve at Northeast's bulk storage facility in Tiverton developed a leak, spilling 50 gallons of No. 2 fuel oil into the Sakonnet River where it left film and heavy odor for three to four miles in each direction.

Two tankers collided in San Francisco Bay, spilling more than 2.5 million barrels of crude oil

These disasters fueled environmental fears about the Tiverton project and greatly aided SOC's case. In a town council vote, the refinery project was defeated 4 to 2.

A review of this case reveals that the economic and tax benefits offered by the refinery served their function of creating widespread public support. However, a lack of proper planning and management, combined with aggressive opposition, weakened public confidence in the firm's ability to handle the project. Oil-related disasters provided the final blow to the project, creating the fear that Tiverton would suffer a similar fate if it were to accept an incompletely conceived and poorly managed oil refinery.

CHOICE OF INVESTMENT PARAMETERS FOR SENSITIVITY ANALYSIS

This section discusses the choice of internal rate of return (IRR) or net present value (NPV) as the investment parameters to be used in the sensitivity analysis. The equations and assumptions used to calculate the IRR and NPV are presented at the end of the section.

Investment Parameters

A number of empirical studies have identified the capital budgeting techniques actually used by industry; five of these studies are referenced in Table 9-6. In 1977, 15 interviews were conducted with energy-intensive industries to obtain more specific information concerning capital budgeting techniques for energy-related investments.[5] The results of the study by J. M. Fremgen, shown in Table 9-7, illustrate two points common to nearly all of the studies. First, the discounted IRR and payback period are the two most widely used techniques for evaluating capital investments. Both the simple rate of return and NPV generally rank fairly far behind the discounted IRR and payback period. Second, use of more than one

Table 9-6. Summary of Published Studies of Capital Evaluation Techniques

Author	Number of Companies Responding to Survey	Sector(s) of Surveyed Companies	Size of Companies
Davey[a]	136	84% manufacturing 16% various nonmanufacturing[f]	Mainly large
Fremgen[b]	177	Various sectors	Varied
Klammer[c]	184	100% manufacturing	Varied
Petry[d]	284	68% manufacturing 32% various nonmanufacturing[f]	Large
Petty[e]	109	100% industrial ("Fortune 500")	Large

[a]Patrick J. Davey, *Capital Investments: Apprasials and Limits* (New York: the Conference Board, 1974).

[b]James M. Fremgen, "Capital Budgeting Practices: A Survey," *Management Accounting* (May 1973), pp. 19-25.

[c]Thomas Klammer, "Empirical Evidence of the Adoption of Sophisticated Capital Budget Techniques," *Journal of Business* 45, no. 3 (July 1972), pp. 387-397.

[d]Glenn H. Petry, "Effective Use of Capital Budgeting Tools," *Business Horizons* 18, no. 5 (October 1975), pp. 57-65.

[e]J. William Petty; David F. Scott, Jr.; and Monroe M. Bird, "The Capital Expenditure Decision-making Process of Large Corporations," *Engineering Economist* 20, no. 3 (1975): pp. 159-172.

[f]Generally includes retail, utilities, transportation, mining, etc.

Table 9-7. Investment Evaluation Techniques ("Methods in Actual Use")

	Methods Used	*Most Important*
Discounted internal rate of return	71%	38%
Payback period	67%	14%
Simple (or "accounting") rate of return	49%	22%
Net present value	20%	4%
Other methods	16%	6%

Source: James M. Fremgen, "Capital Budgeting Practices: A Survey," *Management Accounting* (May 1973), pp. 19-25.

technique is common. Overlap between the discounted IRR and payback period is particularly noticeable.

The 1977 interview survey indicated a heavier reliance on discounted cash flow techniques (both IRR and NPV) by energy-intensive companies. Only one company did not use discounted cash flow analysis, and the simple rate of return was used by only two companies.[6] The prevalent use of discounted cash flow analysis in the energy-intensive industries suggests that the discounted IRR and NPV should be used to measure the impact of the permitting process on investment desirability.

The five studies cited in Table 9-6 indicate that a majority of companies explicitly account for risk in their capital budgeting decisions. The most common techniques include a risk-adjusted hurdle rate, sensitivity or scenario analysis, and probabilistic analysis. A relatively simple technique is to require higher hurdle rates for more risky investments. The published surveys suggest that this hurdle rate adjustment was one of the more common techniques used by large corporations. However, the adjustment was felt to be unsatisfactory when used in isolation because it is difficult to determine exactly how the rate should be adjusted. The 1977 survey showed that sensitivity analysis was a widely used technique, frequently used in conjunction with a risk-adjusted hurdle rate.[7] Sensitivity analysis selects different values for key variables and determines their impact on the rate of return. This allows the company to examine favorable or unfavorable scenarios and at least to estimate the possible up-side benefits and down-side risks associated with the investment.

The probabilistic methods carry sensitivity analysis one step further. Instead of a few different values for key variables, the entire population of outcomes of a key variable is estimated.

Then Monte Carlo techniques are used to develop the entire probability distribution of the investment's return. However, in these techniques there are problems dealing with interdependent variables, and the assessment of an input's probability distribution is difficult to make. Only one energy-intensive industry surveyed currently used probabilistic analysis. Two companies had tried it in the past but no longer used it.[8]

The final investment decision is nearly always made on the basis of both quantitative measures of economic worth and qualitative considerations. Employee morale and safety, corporate image, legal or regulatory requirements, and social concern are all frequently mentioned as qualitative factors, dependent upon the preferences of the person making the investment decision. They will vary by company.[9] The emphasis in the analysis that follows is on the quantitative measures of a project's worth.

In summary, based on previously published studies and a survey of energy-intensive industries, an investment's desirability is assessed through discounted IRR and NPV analysis. The IRR is the most widely used investment criterion. While NPV is not widely used across all industry classifications, it was found to be a significant factor in investment evaluation among energy-intensive companies. In addition, capital budgeting theory demonstrates that the NPV criterion is superior to the IRR when a choice must be made between two mutually exclusive investments. The approach used here to identify the risks or costs of the permitting process is a simple sensitivity analysis of the IRR and NPV, supplemented by a decision-tree framework to capture another dimension of permitting uncertainties.

Derivation of the IRR and NPV Equations for Baseline Refining Cases

All cash flows in this analysis are discounted to reflect the fact that a dollar received in the future is less valuable than one received today. The present value of cash flow over n time periods is:

$$\text{NPV} = \frac{CF_1}{(1+d)} + \frac{CF_2}{(1+d)^2} + \ldots + \frac{CF_n}{(1+d)^n} \qquad (9\text{-}1)$$

The cash flow (*CF*) for each period is the total revenue minus total costs for that period. It can be negative or positive. The discount factor (*d*) is usually taken to be the cost of capital and reflects the opportunity costs between receiving a dollar in the present and receiving a dollar one time period in the future. In calculating the NPV, the cash flows and discount rates are known, and the present value is calculated from Equation 9-1. The IRR is the return that results in a NPV of zero. To calculate this return, the NPV is set equal to zero and Equation 9-1 is solved yielding a value of d.[g]

Both the IRR and NPV will give an accept-reject decision for a project. A project is accepted if the IRR is greater than the cost of capital or another hurdle rate assigned by the company. Under the NPV criterion, a project is accepted if the NPV is greater than zero. Under certain conditions, however, the NPV and IRR methods can rank projects differently. And if mutually exclusive projects are being evaluated or if there is a capital constraint, the choice of the IRR or NPV as the criterion for evaluation can be important. In theory, since the NPV measures the overall contribution of an investment to the value of the firm, the NPV should be used when conflicts arise; however, empirical studies indicate that many firms do not use the NPV. This may be the result of firms whose goal is to maintain a given return on equity. In the context of a refinery, this could mean that as soon as a refinery site is found that meets the corporate IRR criterion, there is no further search for a better site.

The equations used to calculate the refinery IRR and NPV are presented in Table 9-8. The IRR is found by solving for the discount rate that results in a NPV of zero in equation (5) in Table 9-8. The NPV is found by solving equation (5) in Table 9-8 using a discount rate of 15 percent, the hurdle rate commonly assumed in the petroleum industry. Use of a 15-percent discount rate yields consistent accept-reject decisions for investments evaluated by either the IRR or the NPV.

---

[g]If the cash flows are not well behaved, it is possible to have two values of d that satisfy the equation.[10]

NOTES

1. Data obtained from U.S. Coast Guard records.
2. NEPA, 42 USC 431, Sec. 102 (4332).

Table 9-8. IRR and NPV Equations

---

(1)   Before tax cash flow in year i:

$$CF_i = REV_i - OP_i - CAP_i$$

(2)   After tax cash flow in year i:

$$CF_i = (1 - T)(REV_i - OP_i) - CAP_i = .49(REV_i - OP_i) - CAP_i$$

(3)   Depreciation in year i:

$$DEPR_i = DEP_i \times \sum_{i=1}^{j} CAP_j$$

(4)   The incorporation of the 10% investment tax credit:

$$ITC_i = .1 \times Equip$$

(5)   Net present value equation:

$$NPV = \sum_{i=1}^{n} (.49(REV_i - OP_i - DEPR_i) + (DEPR_i - CAP_i + ITC_i)) \frac{1^{i-1}}{(1 + DIS)}$$

Variable Names

CF =	Cash flow	REV =	Total revenue
OP =	Operating costs	CAP =	Capital costs
T =	Tax rate = .51	$DEPR$ =	Depreciation
DEP_i =	Depreciation factor[a]	Total Capital costs = $\sum_{i=1} CAP_j$	
ITC =	Investment tax credit		
NPV =	Net present value	$Equip$ =	Cost of equipment
n =	Investment life	DIS =	Discount factor
		j =	Construction period

---

[a]The depreciation factor will vary depending on the method of depreciation used and the assumed life of the plant.

3. A more comprehensive presentation of the permitting process can be found in Energy and Environmental Analysis, Inc., *Federal Environmental Statutes and Regulations Relating to Resource Application Technologies* (Arlington, Va.: 1978), prepared for the Office of the Assistant Secretary for Resource Applications, U.S. Department of Energy.
4. *Chesapeake Bay Foundation* v. *U.S.*, No. 77-0367-R, U.S. District Court, Eastern Virginia, June 28, 1978.
5. Energy and Environmental Analysis, Inc., *Investment Risk Evaluation Techniques: Use in Energy-Intensive Industries* (Arlington, Va.: EEA,

July 1977), study prepared for the U.S. Energy Research and Development Administration.

6. Ibid.
7. Ibid.
8. Ibid.
9. Ibid.
10. See J. F. Weston and E. F. Brigham, *Managerial Finance* (Hinedale, Ill.: Drydin Press, 1975), 5th ed., p. 296.

Chapter 10

Impacts of Permitting Delays on Investment Desirability

*Energy and Environmental
Analysis, Inc.*

This chapter uses the approach set forth in Chapter 9 to examine the effect of delays resulting from the permitting process on the desirability of a proposed refinery investment. To measure the impacts of delays, cost and revenue data were obtained for a refinery producing 200,000 barrels per day of fuel. Three baseline refinery cases were used. One case incorporates relatively conservative parameters, resulting in a refinery investment of marginal desirability. The second case is optimistic, and thus yields a higher investment return. The third case represents a high expected rate of return, possibly caused by government intervention or regulation resulting in favorable economics for a refinery in a particular location or serving a particular market. This examination of permitting process impacts as a function of project profitability allows for a more general interpretation of the analysis.

The refinery investment depicted in this analysis is intended to highlight the impacts of the permitting process, not to determine if an East Coast refinery is a good investment. The latter would require a much more extensive market analysis, including projections of future raw material costs and product prices and a more detailed analysis of site-specific costs.

BASELINE REFINERY CASES

The cost and revenue data for this investment analysis were obtained from interviews with industrial refiners. Some of the information obtained from these interviews is proprietary; as a result, the costs incorporated in this analysis do not reflect any particular refinery or location, but they are meant to describe a "typical" refinery that produces 200,000 barrels per day of fuel. The primary products of the refinery are gasoline (60 percent) and light fuel oil (25 percent), with a mix of residual oil and heavier products making up the remaining 15 percent.

The refinery costs used to establish the baseline refinery returns are presented in Table 10-1. The refinery product slate along with assumed product prices are presented in Table 10-2. The relevant baseline parameters are:

Plant construction period	3 years
Plant life	20 years
Effective income tax[a]	51 percent
Inflation rate	6 percent for all costs and revenues

These parameters were used to calculate the internal rate of return (IRR) on total capital invested and a net present value (NPV) based on a 15-percent discount rate.

Table 10-1. Baseline Refinery Costs (in millions of 1978 dollars)

Capital Costs		Operating Costs[a]	
Process units	310.00	Feedstocks	10
Support facilities	175.00	Catalysts and chemicals	7
Royalties	8.00	Purchased utilities	7
Parts	7.50	Maintenance	10
Depreciable assets	$500.50	Supplies	1
		Wages	19
Land	4.00	Product transportation	11
Initial catalysts and		Advertising and marketing	10
chemicals	7.00	Taxes and insurance	10
Startup	4.00		
Interest on Construction	45.50		
Working capital	80.00		
Total Investment	$641.00		$85 per year

[a]Operating costs assume 360 operating days per year.

---

[a]Includes state and federal taxes.

Table 10-2. Product Slate and Revenues for Baseline Refinery (1978 dollars)

Product	Price ($ per barrel)	Production (barrels per day)	Revenues ($ per day)
Gasoline	17.72	107,792	1,910,100
No. 2 fuel oil	15.77	48,859	770,500
No. 5 fuel oil	13.19	13,037	172,000
LPG	11.65	11,345	132,100
Bunker oil	10.00	11,326	113,300
Sulfur	73.50 ($/LT)	142 (LT/day)	10,500
Total Revenue: $1,119,000,000 per year			$3,108,500

The three baseline refinery cases have been used to examine the impact of delays on investments with different returns. To isolate the effects of the permitting process, the facility location scenarios are evaluated in Chapter 11. The product transportation costs result from transporting the products by barge to nearby terminals.

Baseline 1—Marginal Return Case: The costs and revenues in Tables 10-1 and 10-2 are applicable. In addition, a crude oil price of $12.80 per barrel is assumed and straight line depreciation is used. The calculated IRR is 15.4 percent and the NPV is $15.2 million.

Baseline 2—Medium Return Case: The costs and revenues in Tables 10-1 and 10-2 are still applicable; however, a more optimistic crude oil price of $12.20 per barrel is assumed and double declining balance depreciation is utilized. The resulting IRR is 19.9 percent and NPV is $204 million. The dramatic increase in IRR and NPV is primarily the result of the decrease in the crude oil price, since the tremendous volumes of crude oil processed each year make the refinery investment very sensitive to its price.

Baseline 3—High Return Case: To increase the generality of the results a scenario with a high rate of return is analyzed. This scenario assumes refined product prices that are 10 percent higher than those presented in Table 10-2. All other parameters are identical to Baseline 1; that is, a crude oil price of $12.80 per barrel is assumed and straight line depreciation is used. This yields an IRR of 25 percent and an NPV of $465 million.

The IRR and NPV for each baseline case are presented in Figure 10-1. Assuming the 15 percent investment hurdle rate required by most major oil companies, the first baseline case is only a marginally profitable investment according to the accept-reject criteria outlined

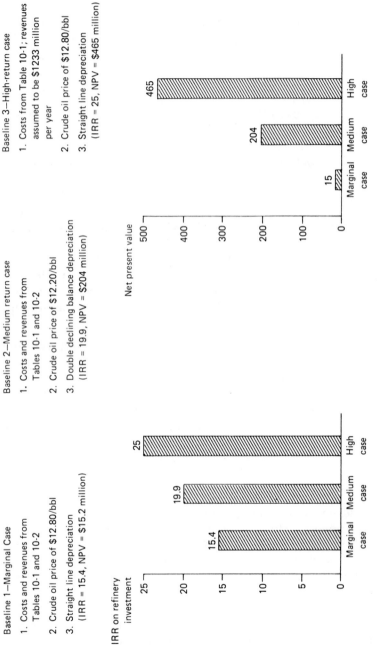

Assumptions

Baseline 1—Marginal Case

1. Costs and revenues from Tables 10-1 and 10-2
2. Crude oil price of $12.80/bbl
3. Straight line depreciation (IRR = 15.4, NPV = $15.2 million)

Baseline 2—Medium return case

1. Costs and revenues from Tables 10-1 and 10-2
2. Crude oil price of $12.20/bbl
3. Double declining balance depreciation (IRR = 19.9, NPV = $204 million)

Baseline 3—High-return case

1. Costs from Table 10-1; revenues assumed to be $1233 million per year
2. Crude oil price of $12.80/bbl
3. Straight line depreciation (IRR = 25, NPV = $465 million)

Figure 10-1. IRR and NPV of baseline cases.

214

in Chapter 9. The other two baseline cases easily satisfy the accept-reject criterion for both the IRR and NPV.

IMPACT OF PERMITTING DELAYS

To determine the impact of environmental and permitting delays on the baseline investment, the effects of permitting processes of 3 years, 5 years and 10 years duration were examined. Five years represents the anticipated "normal" approval process. No unusual delays are experienced, and all permits are granted within the time considered typical or most probable by the relevant regulatory agency. The case studies and interviews with oil companies currently applying for permits indicated that the costs of the five-year permitting process can range from $4 to $7 million. A worst case assumption of $7 million was used to evaluate the impact of this delay. It was not possible to assign costs to individual permits, since the engineering and environmental studies assembled by management and consultants are used in the application procedures for more than one permit. The only meaningful figure is a cost that relates to the overall permitting process. This includes the costs of consultants, legal fees, and corporate resources devoted to the process. Figure 10-2 illustrates the anticipated flow of funds for the five-year permitting process.

The 10-year permitting delay scenario is a worst case situation, and it is assumed to cost $13 million. A three-year permitting scenario provides a significant contrast, in that several reform proposals have advocated limiting the approval process to three years.

The impact of these three delay scenarios on the marginal return refinery (Baseline 1) is presented in Figure 10-3. Here the delays had a rather small impact on the IRR. The worst case scenario, with a delay of 10 years, reduced the IRR by only 0.5 percent. The impact of these delays on the NPV was more pronounced, but it was still small. Even though the refinery is only marginally profitable in the baseline case, the investment still meets the accept criterion[b] using either the IRR or NPV for a 3-year or 5-year permitting process, and it just barely fails to meet the accept criterion even with a 10-year approval process.

In the medium return case (Baseline 2), permitting delays resulted in a greater reduction in the IRR and NPV relative to the baseline values. Still, from the results in Figure 10-4, a 10-year permitting

[b]15-percent hurdle rate for the IRR and a positive value for the NPV.

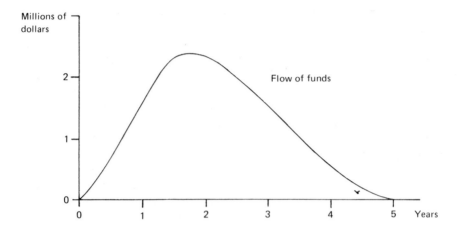

Figure 10-2. Flow of funds.

delay only decreases the IRR from 19.9 to 19.2, less than a 4-percent change in the overall IRR value. The NPV is much more sensitive, however. Here a five-year delay results in a loss of $74 million in the present worth of the investment, a reduction of 36 percent.

The sensitivity of the high return case (Baseline 3) is presented in Figure 10-5. Again the calculated IRR is relatively insensitive, but the NPV of the investment decreases by over $150 million as the result of a five-year permitting process.

The sensitivity analysis in all three baseline refinery scenarios thus showed two common characteristics. One, the refinery investment's IRR was quite insensitive to permitting delays and costs. Two, the NPV of the investment was very sensitive to permitting delays. In addition, the impact of the permitting delays on both the IRR and NPV increased as the profitability of the proposed investment increased. This is particularly noticeable in the NPV results.

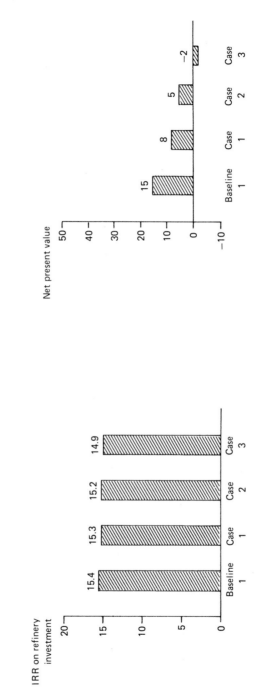

	IRR	NPV
Baseline 1: Marginal Return Case (no delays)	15.4	$15.2 million
Case 1: Permitting delay of 3 years ($5 million cost)	15.3	$ 7.6 million
Case 2: Permitting delay of 5 years ($7 million cost)	15.2	$ 4.7 million
Case 3: Permitting delay of 10 years ($13 million cost)	14.9	$ 1.8 million

Figure 10-3. Impacts of permitting delays—Baseline 1 case.

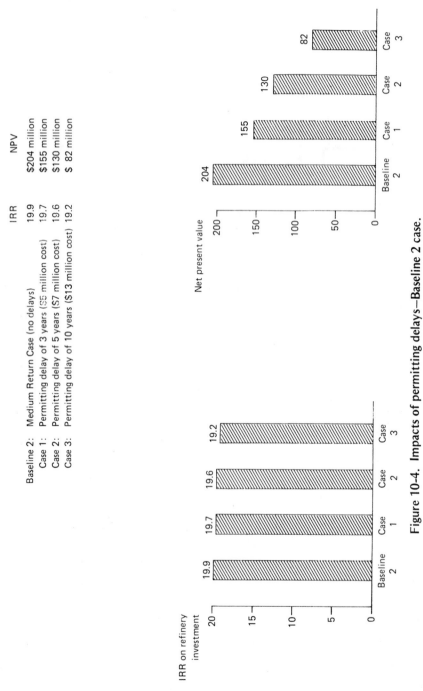

	IRR	NPV
Baseline 2:	Medium Return Case (no delays)	19.9	$204 million
Case 1:	Permitting delay of 3 years ($5 million cost)	19.7	$155 million
Case 2:	Permitting delay of 5 years ($7 million cost)	19.6	$130 million
Case 3:	Permitting delay of 10 years ($13 million cost)	19.2	$ 82 million

Figure 10-4. Impacts of permitting delays—Baseline 2 case.

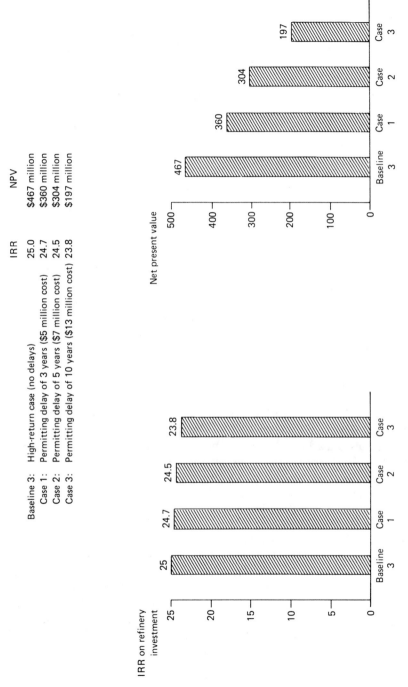

	IRR	NPV
Baseline 3:	High-return case (no delays)	25.0	$467 million
Case 1:	Permitting delay of 3 years ($5 million cost)	24.7	$360 million
Case 2:	Permitting delay of 5 years ($7 million cost)	24.5	$304 million
Case 3:	Permitting delay of 10 years ($13 million cost)	23.8	$197 million

Figure 10-5. Impacts of permitting delays—Baseline 3 case.

Cause of the IRR's Insensitivity
to Permitting Delays

In all of the scenarios examined the IRR was relatively insensitive to the length of the permitting process, due to the reinvestment assumption implicit in the IRR calculation. The assumption required by the IRR formula allows for reinvestment at a rate of return equal to the calculated IRR. This means if a $600-million investment with an expected return of 19 percent is delayed five years, the firm can invest that money elsewhere and still earn 19 percent. Therefore the delay has no penalty, except for the actual cost of the delay itself. In the Baseline 1 example, the IRR declines from a value of 15.4 percent with no delays to 15.2 percent with a five-year permitting delay solely because of the $7 million cost of the permitting process itself.

In contrast, the NPV calculation assumes a different reinvestment rate of return, and was found to be very sensitive to permitting delays. The discount rate is by definition the opportunity cost of capital. In evaluating the impacts of delays, the NPV formulation takes into account the difference between the discount rate and the rate of return that could be earned on the refinery if the refinery were to be built earlier. Thus the NPV more accurately reflects the true costs to the firm of permitting delays.

Costs to the Firm of Permitting Delays

The amount of money that a firm would be willing to pay to avoid permitting delays can be viewed as the cost to the firm of the permitting process. Table 10-3 lists the net change from the baseline IRR to the IRR from each permitting delay case, along with the capital or operating cost increase a refiner would be willing to undergo in order to avoid these delays. For example, a three-year permitting delay for a Baseline 1 refinery would decrease the IRR by 0.1 percent. The next column shows the increase in capital costs[c] that would result in an equivalent IRR if the refinery could have been built immediately. In other words, a refiner using the IRR as the measure of an investment's desirability would be indifferent about a three-year permitting delay before building the refinery as compared to starting construction immediately and paying an additional $3 million in capital costs over the three years of construction. In either case the IRR would be the same. The potential

---

[c]Holding all other costs constant.

Table 10-3. Potential Capital and Operating Cost Tradeoffs[a] Based on Comparative Internal Rates of Return (all costs in millions of dollars)

	Baseline 1			Baseline 2			Baseline 3		
	Net Change in IRR	Potential Capital Cost Tradeoff	Potential Operating Cost Tradeoff	Net Change in IRR	Potential Capital Cost Tradeoff	Potential Operating Cost Tradeoff	Net Change in IRR	Potential Capital Cost Tradeoff	Potential Operating Cost Tradeoff
Case 1 (3 years)	.1%	3	.9	.2%	5.1	1.6	.3%	7.5	2.9
Case 2 (5 years)	.2%	6	1.7	.3%	7.2	2.4	.5%	12	4.6
Case 3 (10 years)	.5%	15	3.8	.7%	18.9	5.5	1.2%	28.8	10.6

[a]A cost tradeoff is the cost increase in either capital or operating costs that would yield the same IRR if there were no delays. This represents the *maximum* amount a refiner would be willing to pay for the right to avoid the delays and start construction immediately provided the IRR were the criterion used to assess the desirability of the investment.

operating cost tradeoff presented in the third column represents the increase in annual operating costs a refinery would be willing to trade for the opportunity to avoid the permitting process and start construction immediately.

Table 10-3 indicates, not surprisingly, that the amount of money a refiner would be willing to pay in either additional capital or annual operating costs increases as the profitability of the investment increases. Note that the increased costs a refiner would be willing to trade off, based on the comparative IRRs, are very small when compared to total capital costs of $650 million, annual operating costs of $85 million, and annual crude oil costs of $920 million.

A similar cost tradeoff analysis for the NPV criterion is presented in Table 10-4. If the NPV is used as the investment criterion, a refiner is willing to make much larger cost tradeoffs to avoid delays. In the medium return case (Baseline 2), for example, a refiner would be willing to incur increased capital costs of close to $100 million or increased operating costs of $18 million annually to avoid a five-year delay in construction. These figures represent a strong incentive for a refinery (or other energy facility) to locate at a site where construction could start quickly, even if the site resulted in increased capital costs, operating costs, or both. This could explain why many oil companies are building or expanding oil refineries in the Gulf Coast and then incurring the additional costs of shipping their refined products to the Northeast.

PERMITTING DELAY IMPACTS: OTHER CONSIDERATIONS

The delays resulting from the permitting process can have certain broader impacts in addition to their effects on the investment's IRR and NPV. These indirect impacts can be significant in some instances, although they often appear to be given too much emphasis. Factors commonly discussed in this regard are:

Effects on overall corporate strategy
Impacts on funding and financing
Increased uncertainty
Increasing construction costs
Changing market conditions

Permitting delays can influence overall corporate strategy. Since a large number of petroleum companies are vertically integrated, a

Table 10-4. Potential Capital and Operating Cost Tradeoffs[a] Based on Comparative Net Present Value (all costs in millions of dollars)

	Baseline 1			Baseline 2			Baseline 3		
	Net Change in NPV	Potential Capital Cost Tradeoff	Potential Operating Cost Tradeoff	Net Change in NPV	Potential Capital Cost Tradeoff	Potential Operating Cost Tradeoff	Net Change in NPV	Potential Capital Cost Tradeoff	Potential Operating Cost Tradeoff
Case 1 (3 years)	7.6	10	1.8	48.5	63.7	11.8	107.2	141	26
Case 2 (5 years)	10.5	13.8	2.5	74	97.2	18	163.5	215	39.7
Case 3 (10 years)	17	22	4.1	122.2	161	29.7	269.8	354	65.5

[a]A cost tradeoff is the cost increase in either capital or operating costs that would yield the same NPV if there were no delays. This represents the *maximum* amount a refiner would pay for the right to avoid the delays and start construction immediately provided NPV were the criterion used to assess the desirability of the investment.

permitting procedure with substantial delays could result in production bottlenecks. Conversations with several petroleum companies indicated that the industry does not view this as a significant risk or cost, however. If a company has crude oil it cannot refine, this oil can be sold to independent refiners or even to other major companies. If its distributors need additional refined products, these can be obtained from other wholesalers until the company's own refinery is completed. Generally, it was felt that unexpected delays in a proposed refinery posed the possibility of undesirable effects on other corporate operations but that these would be of minor consequence. To the extent that each investment is made on its own merits, the effects of permitting delays on a proposed refinery would not significantly impinge on other company operations and overall corporate strategy. For industries other than petroleum, particularly those with more local, segmented markets, these undesirable effects may be greater.

The financing of larger projects can present problems for some companies, and the situation will be more complicated when delays of uncertain length occur prior to construction. Generally, the smaller, independent companies will have greater problems, particularly if a partnership is being sought. However, most companies considering an investment in a major oil refinery are large, and they have enough diverse financing opportunities to obtain the funds at the time needed.

The remaining three factors just listed are all interrelated. The uncertainty of the permitting process can be viewed from two perspectives: (1) the uncertainty inherent in the process itself (i.e., the length and possibility of rejection of a required permit); or (2) the chance that market conditions may change during the permitting process, resulting in the refinery no longer being profitable. There is always the possibility that one of the required permits may not be granted. If the refinery is rejected during the permitting process, the company loses the money invested in the permitting procedures, usually $5 to $10 million. However, this risk would seem acceptable since the *economic* risks associated with a $650-million refinery with annual cash flows of close to a billion dollars present the potential for much greater losses. If all the permits are granted, the refinery investment decision should be reevaluated at the end of the permit process to see if it still makes economic sense. If at this point the economics indicate that it is a poor investment, the project can be terminated with the loss of the money invested in the permitting process, which is a comparatively small sum.

Two particular factors could impinge on the refinery's economics during the permit process. One results from having a competitor enter the market proposed for the new refinery. The new competitor could establish a firm foothold while the proposed refinery was delayed. The prospective economics may have been favorable at the start of the permit process, but the delays allowed another entrant into the market, resulting in a reduction in anticipated market penetration by the new refinery. The second factor results from having construction costs increase during the permit process up to the point where it is no longer economically wise to build the refinery. This assumes that construction costs are rising more rapidly than are revenues from refined products. This has been the situation for the past five years and has led to cancellation of several projects delayed by the permitting process.

To investigate the impacts of rising construction costs during the permitting process, several inflation scenarios were examined. The medium return case (Baseline 2) was used for analysis of inflation-related impacts. The previous analysis of permitting delays assumed a 6-percent rate of inflation for all cost and revenue factors. To look at the impact of construction costs rising more rapidly than other cash flows, the three-year delay scenario and the five-year delay scenario were evaluated with construction costs increasing at 9 percent and 13 percent while all other flows were inflated at 6 percent. The results, presented in Figures 10-6 and 10-7, indicate that:

> Modest increases in the capital cost inflation rate have a large impact on both the IRR and the NPV.
>
> The permitting process and resulting delays will have *much* harsher penalties when capital costs are rising faster than product revenues, even when operating costs are held constant.

The trend over the last four or five years has been for construction costs to increase more rapidly than product revenues.[d] As long as this continues, the impact of delays on energy facility investments will be more significant.

PERMITTING DELAYS: CONCLUSIONS

The general conclusions resulting from this analysis are straightforward:

[d]There is no inherent reason for this phenomenon. If product prices are deregulated, there is also the potential for product revenues to increase more rapidly than capital costs during the delay period.

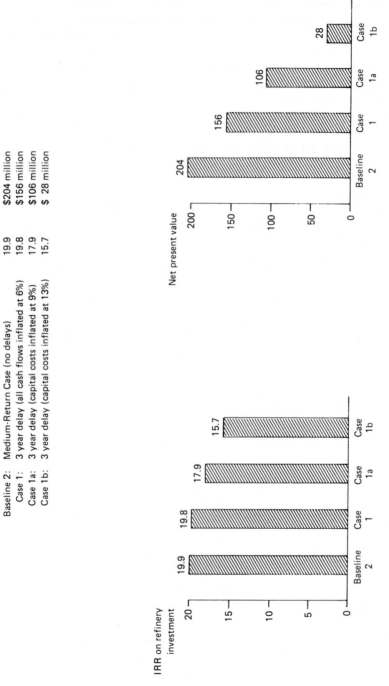

	IRR	NPV
Baseline 2:	Medium-Return Case (no delays)	19.9	$204 million
Case 1:	3 year delay (all cash flows inflated at 6%)	19.8	$156 million
Case 1a:	3 year delay (capital costs inflated at 9%)	17.9	$106 million
Case 1b:	3 year delay (capital costs inflated at 13%)	15.7	$ 28 million

Net present value

IRR on refinery investment

Figure 10-6. Impact of increasing construction costs in a three-year permitting process.

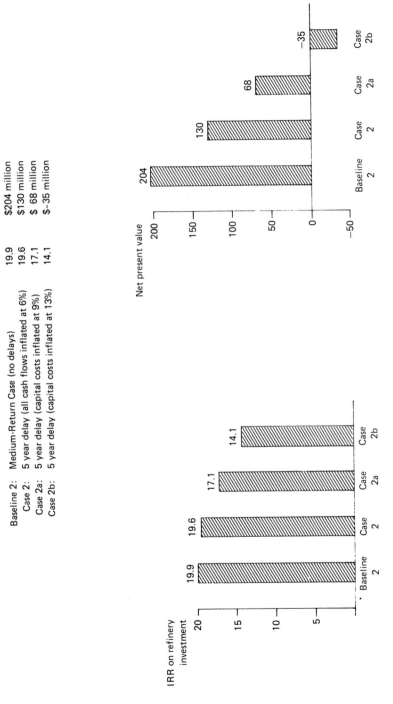

		IRR	NPV
Baseline 2:	Medium-Return Case (no delays)	19.9	$204 million
Case 2:	5 year delay (all cash flows inflated at 6%)	19.6	$130 million
Case 2a:	5 year delay (capital costs inflated at 9%)	17.1	$ 68 million
Case 2b:	5 year delay (capital costs inflated at 13%)	14.1	$–35 million

Figure 10-7. Impact of increasing construction costs in a five-year permitting process.

Permitting delays can have a large impact on an investment's NPV. Using the NPV criterion a refiner would be willing to trade sizeable increases in capital or operating costs, or both, for a reduction in delays. This tradeoff illustrates the large impacts that delays can have on an investment's desirability.

The permitting delays conceivable under present conditions will have only minor impacts on an investment's IRR.

The impact of permitting delays on the IRR and NPV increase as the profitability of the investment increases.

If capital costs are rising more rapidly than are revenues, permitting delays have a much larger impact on both the investment's IRR and NPV.

Up to now, there has been little discussion concerning which investment criterion, the IRR or NPV, is the most appropriate. Finance textbooks and capital budgeting theory point to the use of the NPV over the IRR, since this approach will maximize the overall value of the firm. However, empirical studies indicate that management is more familiar with the IRR concept, and corporate goals are often expressed in terms of earning a given return on equity or capital. This analysis demonstrates that the choice of investment criteria, IRR or NPV, yields very different implications for permitting delay impacts. Use of NPV incorporates more information and should provide management with better guidelines for evaluating investments subject to delays. For this reason, it is felt that the NPV criterion will be more important and will be used more often than the IRR for making the final decision on energy facility investments potentially subject to delays.

IMPACT OF POSTAPPROVAL DELAYS

Once the permitting process is complete and all the required permits have been obtained, substantial delays may still occur. As outlined in Chapter 9, previously issued state permits can be challenged by federal agencies and public interest suits can be filed under the National Environmental Policy Act. Regardless of the outcome, the challenge can result in a court injunction postponing or halting construction.

Delays that halt construction in midstream can be particularly damaging to an investment's profitability. To measure the impact of midconstruction delays on the investment parameters, delays of one, two, and three years were placed two-thirds of the way through plant construction. A cost of $10 million was assumed for each year of delay as an allowance for storage of construction equipment, meeting contracts for receipt of refinery process equipment, and maintaining key personnel on the payroll. This cost estimate is speculative and is believed to be very low.

The results of these midconstruction delays for each refinery baseline case are presented in Table 10-5. To facilitate a comparison of the impacts of permitting and midconstruction delays, the IRR and NPV values calculated from the previous permitting delay scenarios are also included. These results indicate that midconstruction delays have a significant impact on the IRR. This is in sharp contrast to the results of the permitting delay scenarios, where virtually no impact was felt on the IRR. In all three baseline cases a one-year midconstruction delay has a larger impact on the IRR than a ten-year delay during the permitting process. The impact of midconstruction delays on the NPV was also much greater than those produced by permitting delays, although the difference between the NPV values is not as great as that demonstrated for the IRR values.

Recently, interest has been shown in various permit process reform proposals such as "one-stop" approval where one regulatory agency would be responsible for evaluating the environmental impact statement (EIS) and approving all (or most) of the major permits. It is felt that this type of approval process could reduce the duration of the permitting process to three years or less. This type of reform proposal could reduce much redundant bureaucracy. However, a shortened regulatory review of the EIS could lead to more NEPA public interest suits challenging issued permits. Opponents of an energy facility could argue that the shortened permit process did not allow for an adequate evaluation of the EIS. They could file suit against the regulatory agency under the current interpretation of NEPA and ask for an injunction to stop construction of the facility.

To examine this possibility, the IRR and NPV were calculated for a scenario combining a three-year permitting delay with a one-year midconstruction delay. The analysis was performed on the moderate return case (Baseline 2) and yielded the results shown in Table 10-6.

The impact on both the IRR and NPV of the three-year permitting delay with a one-year midconstruction delay is greater than a five-year delay during the permitting process. This indicates that shortening the permit process may not be an advantage to industry if it results in any greater risk of midconstruction delays.

Table 10-5. Comparison of Midconstruction Delays to Permit Process Delays

Baseline 1: Marginal Return Case
(Baseline 1 IRR = 15.4%; NPV = $15.2 million)

	IRR	NPV		IRR	NPV
Permitting delay of 3 years	15.3	7.6	Midconstruction delay of 1 year	14.1	-27
Permitting delay of 5 years	15.2	4.7	Midconstruction delay of 2 years	13.5	-65
Permitting delay of 10 years	14.9	-1.8	Midconstruction delay of 3 years	12.8	-100

Baseline 2: Moderate Return Case
(Baseline 2 IRR = 19.9; NPV = 204)

	IRR	NPV		IRR	NPV
Permitting delay of 3 years	19.7	155	Midconstruction delay of 1 year	18.3	147
Permitting dealy of 5 years	19.6	130	Midconstruction delay of 2 years	18.1	95
Permitting delay of 10 years	19.2	82	Midconstruction delay of 3 years	17.8	47

Baseline 3: High Return Case
(Baseline 3 IRR = 25, NPV = 467)

	IRR	NPV		IRR	NPV
Permitting delay of 3 years	24.7	360	Midconstruction delay of 1 year	22.6	388
Permitting delay of 5 years	24.5	304	Midconstruction delay of 2 years	20.8	317
Permitting delay of 10 years	23.8	197	Midconstruction delay of 3 years	19.4	252

Table 10-6. Impacts of Midconstruction Delays

	IRR	NPV
Baseline 2: Medium return case (no delay)	19.9	$204 million
Permitting delay of 5 years	19.6	$130 million
3-year permitting and 1-year midconstruction delay	18.1	$105 million

Locational Dimensions: The Economics of Coastal vs. Inland and Urban vs. Rural Siting

Energy and Environmental Analysis, Inc.

The location of a proposed refinery or energy facility can affect the investment decision directly through its impacts on the costs of building or operating the facility. The site can also influence the expected length of the permit process, the probability of successfully receiving all the necessary approvals, or both. To develop an insight into the relationships between facility location, refinery economics, and the permit process several visits were made to oil companies currently undergoing permit review. In addition, a series of case studies of recently rejected refineries proposed for sites in the Northeast were conducted. When possible representatives of the sponsoring company, involved state or federal regulatory agencies, and local politicians or concerned citizens were contacted to develop a broader perspective of each permitting process.

COASTAL VS. INLAND SITING

Coastal and inland refinery locations may each offer distinct advantages as well as pose unique complications. The refineries that have been proposed for the Northeast have virtually all been in coastal locations.

Coastal Site Advantages

Two advantages are common to coastal sites:

Easy access to ocean shipping for receipt of crude oil
Easy access to coastal waterways

The most economical means of transporting crude oil is by very large crude carriers. Coastal ports that can accommodate these vessels are the lowest-cost alternative, with lightering[a] currently the next best alternative.

Barges and coastal tankers offer economical means of product distribution to markets at a medium distance from the refinery. Water transportation of products provides the refinery with a more flexible distribution system. A products pipeline ties the refinery to a particular market, whereas water transportation allows products to be shipped to different markets as the need arises.

Coastal Site Disadvantages

While coastal sites are economically attractive, their associated disadvantages can be overwhelming. These are:

Land use conflicts
Potential harm to valuable adjoining coastal property
Size of damaged area resulting from coastal spills

Coastal lands are a limited resource. As such, many uses compete for available property. These areas are quite valuable as residential and resort areas, and they are also attractive as national parks, reserves, and public recreation areas. Although these uses generally do not generate the tax revenue of an oil refinery, they are also free of its attendant unsightliness and environmental problems.

Much of the land along the East Coast is valuable resort and residential property. Owners of this property have a vested interest in its protection, and they have the financial resources to wage a strong campaign, either in the courts or in political circles, to ensure its quality.

The objections from adjoining coastal property holders often center on the dangers of coastal oil spills. Oil, particularly refined products, spreads tremendous distances on surface waters. When combined with the wind and current conditions off the East Coast,

[a]Lightering refers to the transfer of crude oil from larger ships to shallower draft tankers, which are able to enter coastal ports, rivers, and harbors.

enormous areas can be affected, 50 to 100 hundred miles in each direction. It is clear that significant opposition can arise in such a large region. A case in point is Jamestown, Rhode Island, where the main opposition to a proposed refinery project originated in the coastal regions of southern Massachusetts, Rhode Island, and Connecticut rather than in the community itself.

Inland Site Advantages

Many of the advantages of inland sites contrast with coastal site disadvantages:

Lessened land use constraints
Minimizing likelihood of coastal pollution
Avoidance of proximity to valuable coastal property

Inland land is relatively plentiful compared to coastal property. Because a lesser percentage is desirable for recreational and residential areas, constraints from competing uses on its development as industrial property are less significant. Inland sites can also be chosen to avoid the most valuable recreational and residential property, thus lowering the potential for opposition.

Removal of oil facilities from the coast lowers the fears of coastal pollution from effluents and structural failures in the crude oil refining process. The scarcity of coastal land makes this a positive benefit.

Inland Site Disadvantages

Inland sites suffer from their more limited access to navigable waterways and their distance from markets. Some products of the refining process cannot be shipped long distances by pipeline because of their low viscosity. These products are most economically distributed by barge. Therefore, if an inland refinery is not located adjacent to a navigable waterway or to a large consumer of heavy refined products, a separate pipeline must be provided to transport these products to the nearest barging terminal.

Isolation from navigable waterways also restricts the refinery's ability to respond to supply and demand fluctuations. Pipelines run from source to market and do not provide the flexibility necessary to direct products from regions of glut to those of undersupply.

If its major markets are located on the coast, which is frequently the case, an inland refinery may be at a cost disadvantage. The distances required to transport crude oil to the refinery and refined products to the market are both increased. This generates an increase in total operating costs. If, however, the refinery is located between the receiving terminal and an inland market, there may be only a slight cost disadvantage. The oil must cover the same route, whether in the form of crude oil or refined products, and the cost is determined by the differential between crude oil and product transport costs.

Corporate Perspectives on Coastal vs. Inland Siting

Several interviews were conducted with companies that had proposed coastal refineries. Each of the companies stated that they had considered inland refinery sites but felt that there was no particular advantage to them. Whether a coastal or inland site was chosen, they expected the same amount of environmental opposition. The danger of oil spills in coastal waters was a key environmental issue for most of the refineries, a concern which was not reduced by moving the site inland. In either case, crude oil must be delivered by tanker and unloaded at the coast.

The particular companies interviewed did not feel that land use considerations represented a significant constraint on coastal siting. The consensus was that enough rural coastal land is available to meet competing needs. Only a few densely populated areas presented severe land use limitations. The real constraint on coastal refinery siting, they felt, may be the potential damage to the delicate ecosystem of the coast and adjoining wetlands. However, it is not clear that disposal of wastes upstream from the coastal wetlands is better than releasing them more directly into the ocean.

Respondents emphasized that inland refinery locations suffered an economic disadvantage because of the added transportation costs of shipping the crude oil from the coast to the refinery. However, they noted that if the market for the refined products were located inland, an inland refinery site may actually be more economical since it is generally cheaper to transport the crude oil than the refined products.[b]

---

[b]However, the costs of transporting the crude oil and refined products are very close. Whether it is cheaper to transport crude oil or refined products depends on the amount of fuel consumed by the refinery. A complex refinery can use 10 to 15 percent of the crude oil as fuel. By locating the refinery at the coast, the cost of not having to ship the crude oil required to fuel the refinery itself is saved.

RURAL VS. URBAN SITING

Rural communities have been actively sought areas by the petroleum industry for refinery sites. As Table 11-1 indicates, 14 of the 23 East Coast refineries proposed in the past 20 years have been in rural locations.

Rural Siting Advantages

Rural sites offer lower taxes and frequently have plentiful land for development. Moreover, the fact that a community is in a rural setting does not preclude it from being relatively close to its product market. The coastal regions of New Hampshire and southern Maine provide excellent examples, with Boston and northern Connecticut as the relevant product markets. Parts of rural New Jersey are also very near major energy markets.

Obtaining popular local support for a proposed refinery has often

Table 11-1. Proposed East Coast Refinery Sites

Rural[a]	Urban[a]
Delaware Bay, Del.	Baltimore, Md.
Dracut, Mass.	Brunswick, Ga.
Durham, N.H.	Hoboken, N.J.
Fort Pierce, Fla.	Jersey City, N.J.
Jamestown, R.I.	New London, Conn.
Machiasport, Me.	Paulsboro, N.J.
Newington, N.H.	Portsmouth, R.I.
Piney Point, Md.	Saybrook, Conn.
Port Manatee, Fla.	South Portland, Me.
Riverhead, (L.I.) N.Y.	
Rochester, N.H.	
Sanford, Me.	
Searsport, Me.	
Tiverton, R.I.	

Summary

23 communities
14 rural
9 urban

[a]Rural-urban distinctions were made by reference to the map in U.S. Department of Commerce, Bureau of the Census, *Population Distribution, Urban and Rural, in the United States: 1970.* (Also see Chapter 9, Table 9-2.)

been the largest obstacle in the overall site approval process. Rural sites have several distinct advantages over urban locations in their ability to generate this support. While each proposed site has many unique aspects, favorable factors are common to most rural locations:

> The tax revenues generated by refinery operation have a more pronounced effect on rural communities than on urban sites.
> Employment effects are felt much more strongly in rural locations.
> Secondary economic effects have a greater impact in rural locations.
> The population base available from which to draw opposition to the facility is much smaller in rural locations as compared to urban areas

Tax effects generated by a new industrial base have a much greater impact in rural areas than in urban areas, despite the fact that the rural tax rate is usually substantially less. Urban tax bases are generally broad, and the incremental reduction in residents' taxes from the new revenue source will be relatively small. Rural communities, on the other hand, often have a limited tax base, consisting mainly of residential and business property. The industrial tax base provided by a refinery, with its great assessed value, could significantly lower the prevailing tax rate. For example, Northeast Petroleum estimated that their proposed refinery facility in Tiverton, Rhode Island, would allow a reduction in the tax rate from $39 to $22 per $1,000 of assessed value.

The employment generated by a new refining facility has more forceful impact on a rural community than an urban community, for many of the same reasons as the tax effect. Obviously, an increase of 150 jobs is felt more strongly by a work force of 1,000 people than by a work force of 150,000 people. Similarly, the increased expenditure of $15,000 (a starting refinery worker's salary) by 150 families will have a greater impact on the limited number of local merchants than it would on the multitudes of establishments in an urban area.

Very significant is the fact that refineries face more potential local opposition in urban areas than in rural sites. More property owners, nearby residents, and organized environmental groups in urban areas feel the facility's direct negative effects. In addition, since a refinery's positive effects are more diffused over a greater population, the general public is more willing to oppose the facility.

As Table 11-2 shows, rural communities give their support to refinery projects more readily than do urban communities. While clearly not all rural communities actively welcomed the proposed facilities, not a single case of urban community support for a refinery project presented itself.

Rural Siting Disadvantages

Although rural locations offer several advantages, there are certain drawbacks:

Product distribution costs
Lack of municipal services
Need for skilled labor
Community concern over growing too fast

A rural site is likely to be some distance (30 to 100 miles) away from its principal refined product markets or a major product terminal. This factor can increase the costs of product distribution, particularly of the heavier products: residual oil, bunker oil, and asphalt. Pipelines and barges are the two most feasible methods of distribution. However, a pipeline can be costly, and obtaining rights-of-way may be difficult and time-consuming. Product distribution by coastal waterways increases the potential for damaging spills.

Table 11-2. Communities That Actively Supported Refinery Projects

Community	*Classification*[a]	*Comments*
Dracut, Mass.	Rural	Townspeople voted 6 to 1 in favor of the project.
Jamestown, R.I.	Rural	Townspeople voted 7 to 1 in favor of the project.
Machiasport, Me.	Rural	Town sentiment estimated at 50-50; surrounding communities heavily in favor.
Sanford, Me.	Rural	Voted 73 percent in favor of a refinery in a public referendum.
Searsport, Me.	Rural	Local population favored the project.
Tiverton, R.I.	Rural	Citizens heavily in favor of the project prior to zoning hearings.

[a]The rural-urban classification was made by reference to U.S. Department of Commerce, Bureau of the Census, *Population Distribution, Urban and Rural in the United States: 1970.* (Also see Chapter 9, Table 9-2.)

For a rural site to be desirable it should be located close (within 5 miles) to an active railroad line and within 10 miles of a navigable river or inland waterway. Residual oil can only be piped short distances economically. Such a location would allow residual oil to be piped to the waterway and then moved by barge to the final market. Even if a pipeline were used to transport the lighter refined products, it is very desirable to have the option of transporting the products by barge to alternative markets in case of product gluts or shortages.

A rural site can also result in increased construction costs for the refinery. Skilled construction workers may have to be attracted from outside the area, which may require paying premium wages. There may also be a shortage of skilled refinery workers, thus possibly causing higher than usual operating costs for a period after the plant opens. These economic disadvantages can be partially offset by cheaper, nonunion labor being available and by the lower taxes in rural areas.

Refineries require substantial municipal services. Small rural communities often are not capable of meeting this demand, and they are hard pressed financially to expand their facilities. Two to three thousand transient construction workers require housing, schools, and public utilities, and yet they do not represent a long-term planning requirement. Thus, small communities have difficulty accommodating their short-term needs. Rural locations may lack the heavy transportation facilities necessary to deliver the large prefabricated components of a refinery. The refining firm must provide these facilities at an increased expense.

Some rural communities feel that construction of a new refinery will result in subsequent uncontrolled industrial growth. They want to preserve the rural community atmosphere and feel that increased industrial growth will lower the "quality of life" and change the character of their community.

Urban Siting Advantages

As is to be expected, many of the urban advantages are analogous to the rural disadvantages. They are:

Proximity to markets
Existence of large, well-trained work force
Availability of municipal services

A large metropolitan area can provide adequate skilled labor for refinery construction and operation, minimizing the problem of dealing with 2,000 to 3,000 transient workers during the construction period. Availability of this skilled labor force can also lower the training period for the 150 to 300 full-time employees, thus reducing costs. However, strong labor unions prevalent in many metropolitan areas may result in higher labor costs.

The existence of well-developed schools, housing, and transportation systems eliminates many of the municipal problems faced by refineries sited in rural communities. Most urban communities also possess the fiscal strength necessary to expand services as needed.

Urban Siting Disadvantages

In the past, the disadvantages of urban locations have been insurmountable. Their main drawbacks are:

Land acquisition problems
Widely varied and competing land use interests
Large population base for potential opposition

Refinery sites require large contiguous tracts of land to accommodate their processing and storage equipment. In developed urban areas such as the New Jersey side of New York Harbor, such land is often difficult and expensive to obtain, if such large tracts exist at all.

With many urban population densities greatly exceeding 250 people per square mile, an urban refinery will impact heavily on a large population. With urban land, particularly the coastal or riverfront property most suitable for refinery development a relatively scarce commodity, a variety of land use alternatives exist for each piece of property. As many urban communities are already extensively industrialized, a trend is developing to oppose further waterfront industrialization and use the land for public recreation and community development. An example of this trend is New Jersey's Liberty State Park, located amid heavily industrialized areas along New York harbor. There is a strong public movement to prevent further industrialization and increase public land holdings and development wherever possible in this area.[c]

Opponents are generally more vocal in their opposition to a proposal than supporters are in their support. Thus, an organized opposition group that can draw supporters from the large population reservoir of an urban area can present a forceful public display of

[c]See Chapter 2.

protest to local politicians. A petition with 20,000 signatures can be a powerful tool in influencing public officials' actions.

THE ECONOMICS OF COASTAL VS. INLAND AND URBAN VS. RURAL SITES

To evaluate the impact of an inland-urban and an inland-rural site on the refinery's internal rate of return (IRR) and net present value (NPV), the incremental costs associated with transport of the crude oil inland and refined product distribution were emphasized. There are many other potential capital and operating cost differentials between inland and coastal sites and rural and urban sites. However, these cost differentials vary according to the specific site and do not lend themselves to a general analysis. For example, the capital cost differential between a rural-inland and an urban-coastal refinery site would depend on labor costs, labor productivity, equipment freight costs, availability of municipal services, availability of construction equipment, and local taxes. These costs are all site-specific with no common differential between coastal and inland or rural and urban sites. For example, labor costs at a rural site could be higher or lower than those at an urban site. Generally, wages are cheaper at rural sites because of the availability of nonunion labor, and often productivity is higher. However, an adequate supply of labor may not be available in some rural locations, and a premium wage might be required to attract workers from surrounding areas.

To maintain some general validity and avoid detailed site-specific analysis, two potential cost differentials between sites were considered: environmental costs and transportation costs (for both crude oil and refined products). An examination of present environmental standards and the resulting control costs indicated that coastal-inland or urban-rural differences would not cause significant variations in environmental costs. Virtually the entire Northeast is classified as a nonattainment area with respect to oxidants. Northeast areas not at present classified as nonattainment are usually those areas in which the required monitoring has not yet been performed. Thus pollution offsets would be required for any site in the Northeast. Other environmental costs may vary considerably from site to site, but this variation will not be caused by general coastal-inland or rural-urban factors. For example, state environmental laws may cause substantial control cost differentials for sites in different states.

The cost differentials between sites examined in this analysis are the result of different crude oil and refined product transportation requirements. As discussed in Chapter 10, the three baseline refinery cases are all coastal-urban sites. To develop the economics for an inland-urban refinery site, the cost of a crude oil pipeline from the coast to the refinery is required. An inland-rural refinery is assumed to require a products pipeline in addition to the crude oil pipeline.[d]

Inland-Urban Site — The refinery is located 30 miles inland, with a 24-inch pipeline used to move the crude oil from the coast to the refinery

Crude Oil Pipeline Costs[1]

Capital Cost: $270,000 per mile installed ($8.1 million overall)

Annual Fuel and Maintenance Costs: $22,000 per mile ($660,000 per year)

Inland-Rural Site — The refinery is located 30 miles inland, again requiring a 24-inch crude oil pipeline from the coast. In addition, the rural site is not near any existing product distribution systems. A 60-mile, 12-inch product pipeline is used to move the refined products to the nearest common carrier pipeline or product terminal.

Product Pipeline Costs[2]

Capital Cost: $200,000 per mile ($12 million overall)

Annual Fuel and Maintenance Costs: $8,300 per mile ($500,000 per year)

The impact on the IRR and NPV resulting from an inland-urban and an inland-rural refinery location is illustrated in Figure 11-1. The calculated IRR and NPV show that the additional crude oil and product transportation costs associated with the two inland sites have only a moderate impact on the desirability of the refinery investment.

---

[d]From the inland-rural site the refined products could be shipped by barge to the nearest product terminal if it were located on a suitable waterway; however, barges present more environmental problems than a pipeline.

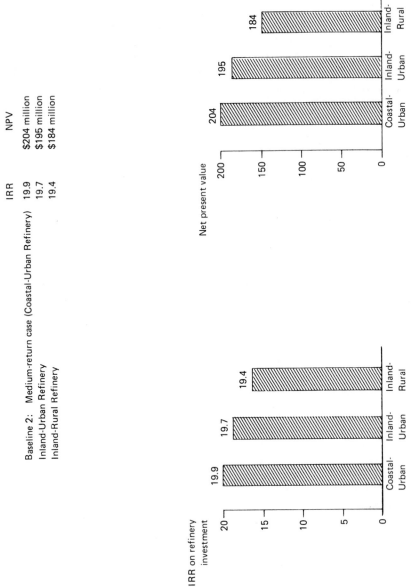

Baseline 2: Medium-return case (Coastal-Urban Refinery)

	IRR	NPV
Baseline 2: Medium-return case (Coastal-Urban Refinery)	19.9	$204 million
Inland-Urban Refinery	19.7	$195 million
Inland-Rural Refinery	19.4	$184 million

Figure 11-1. Impact of an inland-rural or an inland-urban refinery location.

Since the effect of inland locations on the IRR and NPV is quite moderate, a refinery sponsor might consider an inland site if such a site could reduce the length of the permitting process or increase the probability of a successful end result. However, interviews with refinery sponsors on the East Coast indicated that, in their opinion, inland sites provided none of these advantages. The environmental problems associated with the delivery of crude oil and distribution of refined products in coastal waters are not reduced by locating the refinery inland. Therefore, a scenario that could alleviate some of the major objections to refinery siting was explored, using a deepwater port for offshore unloading of crude oil.

USE OF DEEPWATER PORTS

Delivery of crude oil feedstock poses the single greatest environmental hurdle to overcome in refinery siting, and it is independent of whether the refinery is located on the coast or inland. Oil lost during unloading operations accounts for the largest volume of coastal spills. Minimizing this environmental impact may therefore be the key to successful refinery siting.

The development and technological improvement of single point moorings (SPMs) have made deepwater ports using offshore unloading the environmentally preferred method to deliver and unload crude oil. Use of such a facility could reduce some of the environmental effects that have resulted in significant opposition to new refinery construction on the East Coast. The potential effects of oil spills in coastal waters have been one of the major objections to new refinery siting. The additional tanker traffic increases the chances of groundings or collisions, and the emissions from the tankers can cause a deterioration in air quality. These problems are just as important for refineries located inland as they are for proposed coastal refineries.

Since there are no crude oil pipelines to the Northeast at the present time,[e] all the crude oil delivered to the region's refineries must come by tanker. Regardless of the location of the refinery, coastal tanker traffic and crude oil unloading operations will increase the probability of oil spills. The environmental impact statement (EIS) for the Louisiana Offshore Oil Port (LOOP) estimated that onshore oil deliveries using smaller (50,000 deadweight tons) tankers

[e]The one exception is Buffalo, New York, where some crude oil is delivered by pipeline.

would result in a spill rate of 34 barrels per million; the spill rate for the LOOP facility was estimated at 5 barrels per million.

A deepwater port would allow the crude oil to be unloaded about 20 miles out at sea and piped to the coast (or directly inland) via undersea lines. This delivery method could reduce the potential for oil spills. The deepwater port would also reduce congestion in harbor traffic, which is important because the greatest grounding and collision hazards lie in the narrow and busy shipping channels close to the coast. A specific objective of offshore ports is to avoid these hazards.

A spill either at a coastal unloading port or during the lightering operation will have a greater impact on coastal areas than a spill further out at sea. This is important, for the most toxic fractions of crude oil are also the most volatile and will evaporate from the surface given sufficient time at sea. This lessens the environmental damage that results when the oil does come ashore. A deepwater port does present some environmental problems, particularly during construction of the undersea pipeline; however, these are one-time disturbances, and the benefits of the deepwater port would seem to outweigh these disadvantages.

To achieve the water depths required by very large crude carriers with a deadweight tonnage of 250,000 to 380,000 tons, the offshore unloading platform would have to be located 20 to 30 miles from the coast. The deepwater port in this analysis is designed to supply a refinery processing 200,000 to 250,000 barrels per day. Based on standard economic analysis, a deepwater port at this scale has been found to be uneconomical when compared to the costs of lightering.[3] However, using a broader perspective that incorporates into the analysis the potential benefits from a reduction in permitting delays or an increase in the probability of a successful permitting process suggests that a deepwater port of this size may be much more favorable economically.

The offshore unloading system would consist of two single buoy moorings located 8,000 feet from a deepwater platform which would support the pumps, unloading personnel, and flow monitoring equipment. Two 36-inch pipelines would run from the pumping platform to an onshore crude oil storage facility, and a small feeder pipeline would then transport crude oil from this storage area to the refinery. The pipe sizes and pump design could be chosen to facilitate future expansion. A 20-day storage capacity is assumed to provide an adequate supply of crude oil. To supply fuel to the platform, a 6-inch pipeline running parallel to the main crude oil lines is used. In this design, all pipelines are buried in the sea bottom; however, this may not be possible in some locations. Inadequate sand could require blasting trenches through granite and then covering the lines with cement.[f] This could more than double the cost of the pipeline. The estimated costs of a deepwater port are presented in Table 11-3.

AN OPTIMAL SITING STRATEGY
TO OBTAIN LOCAL APPROVAL

Since local approval is generally contingent upon public support, an optimal strategy would minimize opposition based on land use and environmental considerations. This will maximize the chances of obtaining local siting approval.

Table 11-3. Deepwater Port Capital Costs

Two single buoy moorings—$8.5 million each (with hoses and underwater manifold)	$17 million
Pumping platform (includes pumps, monitors, personnel quarters, and fuel storage tank)	$15 million
Pipelines	

Undersea—25 miles from platform to onshore storage
  1 mile from each SBM to platform
  20 miles from platform to shore
  3 miles from shore to storage tanks
  Two parallel 36-inch pipelines and one 6-inch fuel line;
    estimated cost $2.5 million per mile
	$62.5 million

Overland—Where the refinery is placed inland away from the storage tanks, a 24-inch pipeline is used to feed the crude from the storage to the refinery; a site 30 miles inland is assumed; estimated cost $270,000 per mile	($7.3 million)[a]
Engineering and contingencies	$14.2 million
(15 percent of capital costs)	($15.5 million)[a]
Total	$108.7 million
	($117.1 million)[a]

Sources: U.S. Department of Transportation, *Atlantic Coast Deepwater Port Study* (Washington, D.C.: July 1978); and cost estimate presented to U.S. Department of Transportation, Office of Deepwater Ports, for licensing of the Louisiana Offshore Oil Port (LOOP).

[a]For inland sites

[f]This is felt to be necessary for a deepwater port to be placed off the New Hampshire or Maine coasts, for example.

Minimizing Land Use Objections

A rural location provides the greatest opportunity to:

Avoid land with numerous competing uses
Avoid the sources of land use objections
Make full use of positive refinery impacts

Generally, rural areas have plentiful land available for development, whereas new development on urban land is constrained. Urban land is more actively sought, and further industrial development is not a high priority for land use for many urban dwellers.

With a large population seeking to use limited land, plentiful opposition to further industrial development can be found in urban communities. Rural locations, however, offer the opportunity to site away from the general population with an increased probability of acquiring the needed land area (including a sizeable buffer zone).

Some argue that it is desirable to preserve pristine land areas, confining industrial growth to areas where industry now exists. However, it is usually possible to select rural sites that do not have great natural beauty and environmental sensitivity.

Finally, rural communities offer refineries the opportunity to use a fixed number of job opportunities and limited tax payments most effectively for creating local support. These impacts are felt more strongly in rural communities, and they can sway public sentiment in favor of the project.

Minimizing Environmental Objections

The optimal strategy here is to:

Minimize the chance of spills reaching coastal areas
Minimize contact with coastal regions
Minimize impacts of transporting crude oil and refined products

It appears that the most desirable means of fulfilling these criteria is to combine a deepwater offshore unloading terminal, an inland-rural refinery, and a products pipeline distribution system. Offshore unloading reduces tanker traffic, which has been shown to be proportional to the frequency of oil spills. It virtually eliminates the problems of tanker grounding and collision by locating the single point mooring in deep, easily accessible water away from main traffic lanes. It also eliminates the need for multiple crude oil transfers associated with lightering operations. Onshore pipelines remove crude oil and refined products from the heavily traveled waterways. In addition, offshore terminals have the advantage of being located far from the coast, and thus any spill that does occur has less chance of coming ashore.

An inland refinery site can lower environmental objections. A site some distance from the shore lowers the probability that accidents at the refinery site will foul coastal areas. It is also unnecessary to acquire expensive coastal land, and in this way it is possible to avoid confrontation with coastal protection groups.

The optimal system design would result in the refinery being located three to five miles inland. This would allow the crude oil storage tanks to be placed adjacent to the refinery and yet be connected directly to the deepwater port. If the refinery were located further inland, a crude oil tank farm would be placed at a site as close to the coast as possible, thus minimizing the distances covered by the two primary crude oil feeder pipelines from the deepwater port. From the tank farm a 24-inch pipeline would feed crude oil to the refinery at its daily utilization rate.

Based on these considerations, the optimal siting strategy appears to call for a suitable inland rural area along with a deepwater port and pipeline for crude oil delivery. The higher refinery costs may be economical for the firm given its assessment of relative permitting costs at this and other sites.

SCENARIOS DESIGNED TO MINIMIZE PERMITTING UNCERTAINTIES

In devising a refinery location scenario that could reduce the probability of permitting delays or outright rejection, use of a deepwater port for crude oil delivery appears to assume great importance. Conversations with officials at the U.S. Environmental Protection Agency (EPA) and the U.S. Department of Transportation indicated that a deepwater port could significantly reduce environmental opposition to a refinery site.

Three specific scenarios have been examined using a deepwater port for crude oil delivery.

Deepwater Port 1—coastal/urban refinery location: The refinery and onshore crude storage are located together 3 miles from the coast. The unloading platform is located 20 miles offshore.

Two 36-inch pipelines transport the crude oil directly from the platform to storage facilities at the refinery site.

Deepwater Port 2—inland-urban refinery location: The refinery is located 30 miles inland; however, the crude oil storage facility is located 3 miles from the coast, where the two 36-inch pipelines terminate. The refinery is located close to an existing product distribution system, possibly serving an inland market. There are no additional costs associated with product distribution.

Deepwater Port 3—inland-rural refinery location: This scenario is identical to that described for Deepwater Port 2, except that a rural location not near any existing product distribution system is assumed. A 60-mile, 12-inch products pipeline is used to move the refined products to the nearest common carrier line or product terminal. The heavier products, residual and bunker oil, can only be moved short distances by pipeline. The refinery would either have to have a local market for the small amounts of heavy products produced or access to an inland waterway.

The comparative costs of these three deepwater port scenarios are presented in Table 11-4. The case for Deepwater Port 3 is considered to be the most desirable from an environmental standpoint. Use of a deepwater port reduces harbor congestion and lessens the chance of coastal oil spills. Use of a products pipeline also reduces the possibility of damaging product spills, whereas the inland, rural location poses fewer land use conflicts. Even though a products pipeline is used to move the lighter refined products, it is unlikely that a new refinery would be built without access to an inland waterway, which would provide additional distribution options in times of product gluts or shortages. This kind of flexibility may be required before a refinery would be built inland.

The IRR and NPV for these deepwater port scenarios is presented in Table 11-5. For each baseline case, a substantial reduction in the IRR and NPV occurs between the baseline values and first deepwater port scenario. After this initial reduction, moving the refinery from a coastal to an inland location and the additional requirement to build a products pipeline for distribution have only minor effects on the IRR and NPV. Comparing the results of the deepwater port scenarios to the permitting delay scenarios in Chapter 10 shows that using a deepwater port has a considerably greater impact on the IRR than either a 5- or 10-year permitting delay. Based on the IRR,

Table 11-4. Deepwater Port Scenario Costs

	Capital Costs (millions of 1978 dollars)		
	DWP 1	*DWP 2*	*DWP 3*
2 Single point moorings	17	17	17
Platform	15	15	15
Pipeline			
Offshore	62.5	62.5	62.5
Onshore	0	7.3	7.3
Engineering and contingencies[a]	14.2	15.3	15.3
Product pipeline[b]	0	0	12
Total	108.7	117.1	129.1

	Annual Operation and Maintenance Costs (millions of 1978 dollars)		
	DWP 1	*DWP 2*	*DWP 3*
2 Single point moorings	2.5	2.5	2.5
Platform	.7	.7	.7
Pipeline			
Offshore	.6	.6	.6
Onshore	0	.1	.1
Fuel and power	2.4[d]	2.9	2.9
Taxes and insurance	1.3	1.5	1.5
Product pipeline[c]	0	0	.5
Total	7.5	8.3	8.8

[a]Estimated as 15 percent of capital costs.
[b]Includes contingencies.
[c]Complete operating, maintenance, and fuel costs, estimated as 4 percent of capital costs.
[d]Based on $0.25 per ton for the 30 miles from platform to storage.

this indicates that a refiner would be unwilling to install a deepwater port to reduce permitting delays. However, using NPV as the criterion yields mixed results. In the marginal return case (Baseline 1), the NPV for all deepwater port scenarios is negative and the refinery would not be considered. In the moderate return case (Baseline 2), DWP 1 and DWP 2 scenarios without delay would both be preferred to a coastal refinery with a five-year permitting delay. And in the high return case (Baseline 3), the NPVs indicate that all of the deepwater port scenarios without delay are preferable to even a three-year permitting delay.

Table 11-5. Impact of Deepwater Port on the Economics of Permit Processing Delays

Baseline 1: Marginal Return Case
(Baseline 1 IRR = 15.4%, NPV = $15.2 million)

	IRR	NPV		IRR	NPV
Permitting delay of 3 years	15.3	7.6	DWP 1: Deepwater port—coastal location	14.1	$−40
Permitting delay of 5 years	15.2	4.7	DWP 2: Deepwater port—inland location	14.0	−50
Permitting delay of 10 years	14.9	−1.8	DWP 3: Deepwater port—inland-rural location	13.8	−61

Baseline 2: Medium Return Case
(Baseline 2 IRR = 19.9, NPV = $204 million)

	IRR	NPV		IRR	NPV
Permitting delay of 3 years	19.8	156	DWP 1: Deepwater port—coastal location	18.3	$157
Permitting delay of 5 years	19.6	130	DWP 2: Deepwater port—inland location	18.1	147
Permitting delay of 10 years	19.2	82	DWP 3: Deepwater port—inland-rural location	17.8	137

Baseline 3: High Return Case
(Baseline 3 IRR = 25, NPV = $465 million)

	IRR	NPV		IRR	NPV
Permitting delay of 3 years	24.7	350	DWP 1: Deepwater port—coastal location	22.8	$414
Permitting delay of 5 years	24.5	304	DWP 2: Deepwater port—inland location	22.5	404
Permitting delay of 10 years	23.8	197	DWP 3: Deepwater port—inland-rural location	22.2	389

IMPACT OF INCREASING
THE PROBABILITY OF
RECEIVING ALL
NECESSARY PERMITS

The preceeding analysis looked at the possible benefit of reducing the length of the permitting process or increasing the probability of a successful result as a result of facility location. Use of a deepwater port may be more likely to ensure the overall success of the permitting process than to reduce the time required to receive the permit. The present interpretation of the National Environmental Policy Act and the current regulatory environment could easily result in approval processes of nearly equal length for all proposed facilities, regardless of their location and environmental safeguards.

To evaluate the impact of increasing the probability of a successful permitting process, a decision-tree framework has been used. This analysis considers two scenarios: the medium return case (Baseline 2), subject to a five-year permitting delay, and the environmentally "best" case (DWP 3) which also projects a five-year delay. The IRR and NPV for these two scenarios have been calculated as:

	IRR	*NPV*
Baseline 2 refinery with 5-year delay	19.6	$130.3 million
DWP 3 with 5-year delay	17.5	$ 83.2 million

By using either the IRR or NPV as the investment criterion, the baseline refinery thus becomes the better investment. However, utilizing a deepwater port and a pipeline for product distribution could increase the probability of successful permit approval. This is reflected in the decision tree presented in Figure 11-2.

The first event on the tree pertains to local siting approval. It is assumed that a rural-inland site along with a deepwater port can increase the probability of local approval from .2 without the deepwater port to .5 with the deepwater port and an inland refinery site.

The second event on the tree relates to the state and federal permitting process. Applications for state and federal permits may be filed while local approval is still being sought, but approval or rejection at the local level will come before the state and federal decisions. The indications from interviews with federal agencies

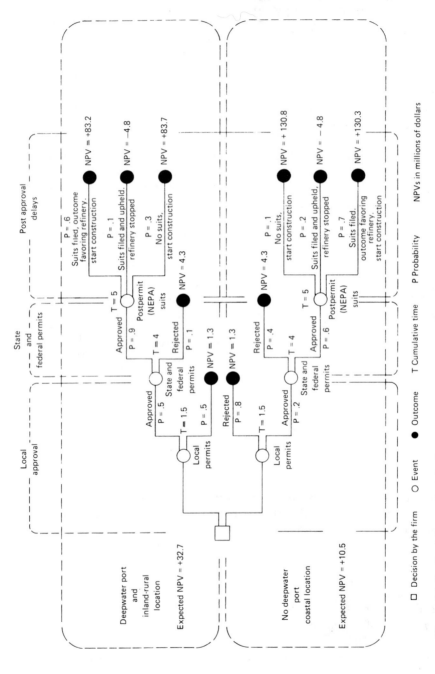

Figure 11-2. Decision-tree analysis—coastal-urban refinery vs. inland-rural refinery with deepwater port.

□ Decision by the firm   ○ Event   ● Outcome   P Probability   T Cumulative time   NPVs in millions of dollars

Deepwater port and inland-rural location

Expected NPV = +32.7

No deepwater port coastal location

Expected NPV = +10.5

Local approval

State and federal permits

Post approval delays

Local permits
T = 1.5
Approved P = .5
Rejected P = .5
NPV = 1.3

State and federal permits
Approved P = .9
Rejected P = .1
NPV = 1.3

T = 4

T = 5
Postpermit (NEPA) suits
NPV = 4.3

P = .6 Suits filed, outcome favoring refinery. start construction
NPV = +83.2

P = .1 Suits filed and upheld, refinery stopped
NPV = −4.8

P = .3 No suits, start construction
NPV = +83.7

Local permits
T = 1.5
Approved P = .2
Rejected P = .8
NPV = 1.3

State and federal permits
Approved P = .6
Rejected P = .4
NPV = 4.3

T = 4

T = 5
Postpermit (NEPA) suits

P = .1 No suits, start construction
NPV = +130.8

P = .2 Suits filed and upheld, refinery stopped
NPV = −4.8

P = .7 Suits filed, outcome favoring refinery, start construction
NPV = +130.3

254

are that a deepwater port could greatly increase the probability of obtaining necessary federal permits. Based on this information, the probability of approval at the state and federal level is increased from .6 without the deepwater port to .9 with the deepwater port. Even though there is an increase in the likelihood of overall success, the length of the permitting process may not be significantly shortened. There will still be opposition to the refinery that has the right to be heard; use of a deepwater port, however, probably would increase the strength of the refinery sponsor's rebuttals.

The last event on the decision tree pertains to the likelihood of suits challenging issued permits. A deepwater port is felt to reduce slightly the likelihood of these suits being filed (.7 to .6), and it will also slightly reduce the likelihood of these suits being successful (.2 to .1).

All the outcomes on the decision tree are cast in terms of the NPV. The losses associated with the failure to obtain any required permit are the cost of the permitting process up to that point, discounted back to the present (t = 0). A $7-million permitting process discounted back to time t = 0 yields a present value of $4.3 million.

To calculate the overall expected NPV for the two alternatives, the expected value at each event is calculated starting from the right side of Figure 11-2. Working across the decision tree, an expected NPV of $10.5 million is calculated for the baseline refinery without the deepwater port; an expected value of $32.7 million is found for the refinery with the deepwater port and inland location. Incorporating the increased likelihood of a successful permitting process from using a deepwater port thus results in this deepwater port scenario being the favored investment. This result is dependent upon the judgmental probabilities used in the decision tree, of course, but the probabilities are based on case studies of proposed refineries and therefore are felt to be plausible.

The decision-tree analysis considered only an increase in the probability of overall success in the permitting process; the length of the process was held constant. If using a deepwater port can be expected to reduce the length of the process as well as increase the likelihood of a successful process, the gains would be even larger.

The conclusion that can be drawn from this analysis is that using a deepwater port for offshore crude oil delivery to a refinery sited at an inland-rural location may be economical if it can increase the likelihood of a successful permitting process. The deepwater port scenario was demonstrated to be the preferred scenario when reasonable increases in the probability of permitting approval were assumed. This analysis demonstrates the importance of viewing energy facility investments in a broad perspective that includes the positive or negative impacts on the permitting process of various alternative siting patterns.

NOTES

1. These costs were obtained from company interviews.
2. Ibid.
3. The most recent cost analysis of this nature is presented in U.S. Department of Transportation, *Atlantic Coast Deepwater Port Study* (Washington, D.C.: U.S. Government Printing Office, July 1978).

Part IV

Looking to the Future: An Alternative Destiny for the Urban Coast

Chapter 12

Alternative Energy Technologies
and the Urban Coastal Zone

Linda Kirschner

Since congested urban areas often have little land area and less environmental latitude within which to site large-scale energy facilities, certain alternative energy technologies might be appropriate instead. Indeed, a strategy focused on use of alternative energy technologies might contribute to reducing urban land use pressures. The answers to such conjecture, however, require that both energy and land use policies be clarified. To do so, the policy implications of three topics—urban coastal areas, facility siting, and alternative energy technologies—have been studied. New Jersey was selected as a representative urban coastal area, and five alternative technologies—cogeneration, modular integrated utility systems (MIUS), integrated community energy systems (ICES), fuel cells, and low-Btu gasification—were examined.

Many smaller-scale energy technologies are environmentally cleaner than existing centralized facilities; and they require less land. However, much must be done at state and national as well as local levels before such technologies can help reduce urban siting pressures. For example, national energy and fuels policies contribute to urban siting pressures, yet lie well beyond the range of local influence alone.

This presentation covers three stages. First, facility siting issues in the mid-Atlantic region are discussed, using New Jersey as an example of an area with intense energy facility development. Emerging plans for Outer Continental Shelf (OCS) oil and gas development off the state's coast provide the opportunity to examine contrasts between national, regional, and state energy policy goals. Second, the five alternative energy technologies are described and related to national and state energy policies. And third, relationships between urban coastal areas, facility siting, and alternative energy technologies are examined.

SCALE AND FACILITY SITING: THE NEW JERSEY LANDSCAPE

The Setting

Facility siting controversy throughout the mid-Atlantic area results from environmental, economic, and political pressures. New Jersey is primarily a coastal state, including a 126-mile strip bordering the Atlantic Ocean. Along the Hudson and Delaware rivers are active harbors of national and international trade: Jersey City, Elizabeth, Perth Amboy, and Newark in the northern region; Camden, Trenton, and smaller cities along the Delaware River to the southwest. All are primary locations for oil facilities, chemical plants, industry, and electricity generating stations. These cities comprise the state's major population centers and are hubs for transportation linking New Jersey with the rest of the eastern seaboard from its central position as a "corridor state" between the New York and Philadelphia metropolitan areas.

Competition for air, water, and land has become intense throughout this urbanized region, with proposed energy facilities often the targets of controversy. Local rejection of energy facilities may suggest a general dissatisfaction with the way in which development historically has occurred in this urban coastal zone. In some New Jersey communities, such as Jersey City, Hoboken, and Bayonne, any mention of a tank farm or a power plant instantly produces a coalition of people ready to do vigorous battle with developers.[a]

New Jersey's energy profile includes the demands of a $5.6 billion petrochemical industry, the state's largest, which relies on oil

[a]See Chapter 2.

and natural gas liquids as its basic feedstocks. In 1972, this industry's demand accounted for 10 percent of the state's total oil consumption.

In the 1950s, availability of cheap oil and clean natural gas led these fuels to become dominant for heating and cooling and electric power production. Use of imported oil still dominates in the region, but this fuel is no longer cheap and both petroleum products and natural gas supplies have encountered periodic shortages in the 1970s. Due to environmental constraints, the state now burns a relatively small amount of coal. Electricity is predominantly generated by oil with increasing reliance on nuclear power. Residential energy demand is met in roughly equal shares by natural gas and fuel oil.

Juxtaposed against this energy-intensive industrial profile is the state's second largest industry, tourism. New Jersey's beaches are heavily used, with summer visitors jamming small seaside towns all along the coast. Significant revenue is derived from seasonal recreational activities. Casino gambling in Atlantic City reinforces the importance of coastal tourism. Availability of gasoline for transport to tourist areas thus is an important concern.

The state's ecological characteristics complicate the ability to site energy facilities. New Jersey has only 250,000 acres of valuable wetlands remaining. They are essential as breeding grounds for ocean and bay marine life and as shelter for migrating birds and water fowl; they also yield a significant harvest of estuarine-dependent fish products that provide the mainstay of the commercial fishing industry. The Pinelands in the south central part of the state cover about 1,500 square miles above an immense freshwater aquifer (17.7 trillion gallons). By state law most of this area is to be preserved from development; federal programs are assisting in this effort to preserve a critical environmental area.

The state's 8 million people use a complex network of heavily traveled highways, especially the New Jersey Turnpike and Garden State Parkway, which link the state to its huge metropolitan neighbors to the northeast and southwest. Automobile and truck traffic contribute to degraded air quality throughout much of the state.

New Jersey's coastal zone management plan calls for any needed new facilities to be located away from sensitive coastal areas, and toward already developed areas. However, urbanized areas are only marginally acceptable as energy facility sites, especially because of their degraded air quality and citizen resistance. Additional refineries, power plants, gas-processing plants, or hydrocarbon storage facilities are thus difficult to locate in this state.

Energy Facilities

Many oil, petrochemical, and electricity-generating facilities are already present in the mid-Atlantic coastal zone. New Jersey's urban coast contains refineries owned by Chevron, Exxon, Hess, Humble, Mobil, and Texaco; on the opposite side of the Delaware River in Pennsylvania are Atlantic Richfield, British Petroleum, Getty, Gulf, and Sun refineries. A typical refinery in the state, with a capacity of approximately 100,000 barrels per day, emits an estimated 5,374 tons of sulfur dioxide and 1,161 tons of particulates per year. In the immediate environs of one northern New Jersey urban coastal city, for example, five power plants (an estimated 2,000 megawatts) and one major oil refinery collectively emit over 26,000 tons of sulfur dioxide and 3,350 tons of particulates per year.[1]

The mid-Atlantic region houses about one-quarter of the nation's total petrochemical industry. Petrochemical facilities normally are located in proximity to their markets. Refinery output is predominantly motor gasoline, home heating oil, lubricants, and jet fuels. Future demand for petrochemical products is expected to increase, and New Jersey might become a more attractive location for gas-processing plants, none of which is now sited in the state. Decreasing domestic supplies and increasing prices of natural gas liquids (NGL) have tied petrochemical manufacturing more closely to heavy oil feedstocks. This is already evident in Gulf Coast refining activities. Since heavy liquids are produced from petroleum, it may become desirable to site new petrochemical complexes nearer to oil refineries in the mid-Atlantic region and elsewhere. As demand for these products has increased, the size of a typical petrochemical facility has grown severalfold. Old plants produced 250 to 750 million pounds per year; newer ones are scaled at 1 to 1.2 billion pounds per year. The very scale of such plants, of course, promotes controversy.

Electric power plants are also found in large numbers in the mid-Atlantic coastal zone. New Jersey has 90 power plants with an installed capacity of 11,404 megawatts (MW).[2] A December 1976 Federal Power Commission (FPC) study, *Factors Affecting the Electric Power Supply 1980-1985*, reviewed the relative size of over 9,000 electric power generating units at approximately 3,500 locations. Sixty percent of the steam-electric plants have an installed capacity of 50 MW or greater. Many of the smaller plants are publicly owned, supplying customers in urban locations where the plants are located. The FPC forecast that by 1990 about 200 new large sites would be required, each with a capacity of more than 500 MW and some as large as 6,000 MW. The FPC report further stated:

> Ideally, it would be preferable to locate these generating plants as near to the load center as possible. However, requirements such as air quality and aesthetics are tending to demand that the plant sites be located rather remotely from the load.[3]

National Energy Policy Impacts: Offshore Drilling as an Example

In the spring of 1978 exploratory drilling for gas and oil in the mid-Atlantic commenced. Roughly 60 to 90 miles off Atlantic City, in the Baltimore Canyon Trough, federal leases for exploration and production had been granted to oil companies. From 1974-1975, when former Secretary of Interior Rogers Morton announced these lease sales, to April 1978, when the first rigs were put in place, the OCS issue produced conflict and tension at regional and national levels. Controversy over the possible onshore facilities that would accompany newly developed resources contributed to the conflict.

Accelerated production of domestic oil and gas supplies was the key to the Nixon-Ford administrations' policies, and it is central to present national energy policy as well. The goal has been to reduce U.S. reliance on unstable foreign imports. For the mid-Atlantic region, the prospect of offshore development was potentially threatening to the environment. Many prominent leaders assessed that without an effective national energy conservation program, imports would probably not be replaced by increased domestic offshore production on a one-for-one basis. Instead, more refineries, tank farms, gas-processing plants, pipeline corridors, and perhaps a deep-water port might be built in environmentally sensitive unspoiled areas or in already crowded urban sites. Other regional concerns included the lack of adequate compensation and protection from oil spills and the adequacy of laws and policies that governed the federal leasing program. Regional efforts to delay development were seen by opponents as "elitist," negating an essential federal program; and delay did occur as a result of litigation under the National Environmental Policy Act.

Political phrases originating within the region, like "full and fair return to the public for resources in the federal domain," were met by opposing phrases from the Gulf Coast and elsewhere, such as "let the bastards freeze in the dark." This rhetoric reflected the political tensions. The Atlantic states, concerned that their substantial economic stake in the coastal zone (recreation, fishing) would be threatened by an oil spill in rough Atlantic seas, saw the issues very differently from areas (such as the Gulf Coast) which have embraced oil development. Producing states, backed by the oil industry, favored the Republican administration's policies of accelerated exploration and production without any statutory changes or reforms (except for deregulation of the price of natural gas). Some northeastern governors (most of them Democrats) and their congressional delegations fought this policy, arguing for energy conservation and continued regulation of natural gas prices.

New Jersey and New York unemployment rates in 1974-1975 reached as high as 12 to 13 percent. Some local spokesmen argued in favor of "oil drilling under any circumstances," suggesting that tens of thousands of permanent jobs would be immediately created onshore as a result of OCS exploration and development. While oil refineries were not new to the region, exploration and production activities were. The lack of expertise in matters related to oil development in state government caused conflict between the oil industry and states. Misinformation was rampant. Democratic governors could not expect much cooperation from a Republican president whose energy program was already the subject of intense congressional debate.

While the overall national energy debate continued in 1974 and 1975, some coastal governors sought to express their own energy and urban policy perspectives through pressure to reform the federal law governing the U.S. Interior Department's oil and gas leasing program. They especially wanted greater state participation in Interior Department decisions. Many coastal states saw the federal coastal zone management program as a potential way to influence the onshore impacts of OCS development.

Amendments to the OCS Lands Act were signed by President Carter in late 1978. By then, the policy of expanding domestic oil and gas production through development of the mid-Atlantic OCS had received general acceptance in the region. However, the extent of the resource remains uncertain. Many dry holes have been drilled for oil, while natural gas discoveries have been encouraging though not definitive. Exploration continues.

Conclusions

Several conclusions may be drawn from the mid-Atlantic-New Jersey perspective:

The region is highly developed.

It represents an intense microcosm of facility siting constraints evident elsewhere.

The siting strategies that have typically been sought are based almost entirely on the size and scale of existing facilities, with little or no attention to smaller alternative technologies.

Some citizens in highly developed urban coastal communities are saying "enough is enough." Energy facilities have not brought sufficient jobs and have violated the integrity of the local landscape.

State agencies responsible for planning land uses must anticipate energy demands to satisfy national goals and the need for industrial sites in an uncertain environment.

As the environmental movement moves from the glamorous stage of advocacy to the tougher stage of implementation, professional environmentalists are often caught in battles among citizens, their local governments, and industry.

The long-term presence of powerful companies and the dichotomy of economic interests (industrial, utility, tourist, and agricultural), especially in a small state, add to the complexities of the environment-energy-economy triad.

As land use pressures grow, rivers and the ocean become targets for future development. Proposed offshore nuclear power plants and the Tocks Island Dam on the Delaware River are illustrative.

With half of the nation's population already located in the coastal zone, people and energy facilities will continue to compete for the right to exist. Space, water and air, privacy, security, and an acceptable economy within which to survive are all competing interests.

New Jersey and most other states have found no satisfactory governmental process for identifying suitable sites for large-scale energy facilities. Industry retains the initiative, and economics rather than environmental impact remains the principal siting criterion. Overall state policy calls for siting away from pristine areas and thus toward developed areas. Air quality standards and safety are constraints in finding urban sites for energy facilities, however.

For much of the twentieth century the availability of cheap energy resources, raw materials, a well-trained labor pool, and a policy of regional growth dominated. Natural harbors and transport networks provided excellent access to markets for business and industry. These advantages still continue to be attractive, and industry economics often favors siting in urban coastal locales. The number of participants in the siting process has increased. Industry site selection has become a negotiated process increasingly thrust into the political and legal arenas, as states, localities, citizens, and the courts play a more active role in determining what will be allowed where.

SELECTED ALTERNATIVE ENERGY TECHNOLOGIES

Sites, fuels, energy efficiency, and energy policy are the underlying issues for alternative technologies. Each of the five technologies examined here presents a different set of energy policy dimensions. For example, industrial cogeneration is hampered by institutional, regulatory, and economic constraints. Yet the enormous potential for recycling the steam capacity available in facilities already located in the urban landscape draws great attention to this proven technology. Jersey City's MIUS and Trenton's ICES are two urban examples of "before and after" national awareness of the energy crisis. MIUS is a housing experiment, a self-sufficient community within a larger urban center; ICES is an integral component of a local innovative effort at downtown redevelopment. Fuel cells illustrate a range of feasible applications to convert fuel to electricity directly, without raising steam in the conventional manner. To the extent that this technology is used in a shopping center, housing development, or industrial park, electricity demand from the existing central system would be reduced. Coal gasification offers an option for urban centers that could otherwise use coal only minimally because of air quality constraints. Here the facility probably would be in a rural area (at the mine), but impacts would be felt in the urban center. Although all five alternative technologies thus are different, each offers the possibility of reduced land use conflicts associated with the urban coastal environment.

Cogeneration

As an energy conservation technology, cogeneration of electricity with industrial process steam maximizes the efficient use of existing steam-producing capability prevalent in urban areas. By producing both electricity and steam at an industrial facility, cogeneration has the potential to reduce the total amount of energy required to accomplish stipulated objectives (although, indeed, more fuel may be burned within the urban center).[4] Conversely, at a power plant cogeneration involves use of the steam, otherwise simply a waste product. A variety of systems, equipment choices and institutional arrangements are involved in each approach to cogeneration.

Considerable steam capacity exists at industrial facilities. Industrial process heat requirements within the United States represent approximately 25 percent of the total demand for combustible fuels (excluding feedstocks). About 50 percent of all industrial fuel is used for steam production via direct combustion of fossil fuels. This is relatively wasteful because the high quality of the energy available from high combustion temperatures is not fully utilized.[5]

Prior to the mid-1960s, it was fairly common to find industries, while producing steam, also generating electricity on site for their own use. However, as the cost of electricity to large industrial users from central station power plants dropped in the late 1950s and early 1960s, it became less economical for industry to generate its own electricity, and the practice declined significantly. Thus, while process steam was still being produced by industry in large amounts, electricity was increasingly purchased from the central utility grid.

When fuel was cheap and perceived to be unlimited in supply, squeezing every Btu possible out of a barrel of oil was less important. The central utility system in the Northeast, historically reliant on oil, has provided reliable electricity at reasonable cost. However, the continued practice of using separate industrial and utility systems to raise steam with valuable oil suggests that a combination of functions would make sense. Also, given constraints on siting large new coal and nuclear power plants, use of industrial plants to produce electricity would seem especially relevant in urban coastal areas, where industrial capacity is greatest and the number of acceptable sites for power plants is so limited.

In this sense, industrial cogeneration may have particular relevance to urban coastal siting. Many industries with the capability to co-generate are found on the urban coast. For example, paper and pulp industries, refineries, and chemical plants—all prime candidates for cogeneration—are amply represented within Northeast, Gulf Coast, and West Coast metropolitan areas. However, the estimated potential for economically produced steam and electricity at industrial sites varies considerably (depending on the source of the analysis). New Jersey utilities have assessed the potential for cogeneration to be minimal, despite the sizeable number of industrial steam producers in their service areas;[6] in contrast, studies by Robert Williams of Princeton University indicate that cogeneration could generate a significant amount of electricity for New Jersey, and that nationally cogeneration could replace 230,000 megawatts of nuclear capacity by the year 2000.[7]

Some problems exist in implementing this potentially useful hybrid system: matching production and demand, pricing, and regulatory issues, among others. Industrial requirements for steam and electricity vary greatly from one plant to the next. To produce electricity most economically, most industrial cogeneration facilities will have to be sized on the basis of steam capacity rather than on-site electricity demand, with the excess electricity then exported to the central utility grid. However, if the industrially produced electricity were available to the grid at off peak hours, its value would be diminished, affecting the economics of cogeneration. Thus most industrial cogeneration facilities would have to act like a small version of a utility's base load power plants rather than peaking units. Such export of electricity from the industrial cogeneration facility to the grid requires a cooperative arrangement between industry and utility, which is not easy to arrange. In fact, institutional, jurisdictional, and regulatory barriers have prevented widespread implementation of industrial cogeneration.

Utility boilers fired by gas, oil, coal, and nuclear fuels also raise large quantities of steam, but only to generate electricity. At a typical central station power plant, only about one-third of the fuel's energy value is used; the rest is discharged to the environment in the form of waste heat.

A large central station utility power plant discards about 10 quads of waste heat every year. A utility-focused cogeneration system involves use of otherwise wasted excess steam by nearby industrial plants for their process needs. One problem associated with sale of steam is that power plants are often located some distance from industrial sites; for such recovery to be efficient, the users should not be more than five miles away. Population proximity concerns make unlikely an industry-nuclear plant cogeneration scenario. Another problem involves matching the time of day of the utility's generation of electricity with the industry's steam requirements.

Clearly both types of cogeneration offer the opportunity for improved energy efficiency, using already existing sites or making a new site do double duty. For industrial cogeneration, land use advantages also are evident. By generating electricity at existing industrial sites, fewer sites for new central station power plants would be needed, in urban coastal areas and elsewhere. Environmental benefits from more efficient production of electricity and steam also include reduced atmospheric and thermal discharges.

Cogeneration in central city locations may pose environmental problems, however, in that more fuel will be burned in these locations than if central station power plants in remote locations were to provide the same electricity for urban consumers (the pattern of most recent power plant siting). With certain technological choices, use of emission offset, and appropriate fuel switching (e.g., oil to natural gas) to meet environmental requirements, cogeneration can contribute measurably to resolution of siting conflicts in urban coastal areas relative to siting large-scale central station power plants. Moreover, the electricity would be generated in close proximity to urban consumers, avoiding long-distance transmission and associated energy losses now characteristic of remotely sited centralized generating systems. (Long distance transmission and distribution account for an energy loss of about 10 percent).

The question of implementing this energy alternative in the urban coast and elsewhere centers on resolution of several institutional, regulatory, and environmental barriers. Most importantly, the concept runs contrary to common utility and regulatory practice. Decisions on ownership of the cogeneration facility, rates for sales of industrially produced electricity, and the price to be charged by the utilities for backup electrical service are among the issues to be resolved. Utilities make their profits based on an ever-expanding rate base related to a capital-intensive construction program. Traditionally they have forecast future demand and then planned and built the capacity (base load, peak load, and reserve) to meet that expected demand. Analyses that suggest (contrary to utility planning) that sizable amounts of industrially cogenerated electricity could be brought on line instead of constructing new power plants have often become the targets of sharp utility criticism.

Recently, nonpromotional rate schedules that reflect customer demand have begun to replace declining block rates, which discount the cost of electricity to large customers (such as industrial facilities). At present, small residential customers pay much more per unit for their small-volume electrical use than do large industrial consumers. This discounting practice stems from the days when electricity prices were declining, oil was inexpensive, and bulk delivery at discounted cost was economical and consistent with a plentiful energy supply base. The argument for adopting a revised rate schedule is stimulated by the higher cost of oil, equity issues, the need for conservation, and the desire to allocate true costs to energy production. Faced with increasing electrical costs, some industries already have turned to on-site electricity production to meet their requirements.

If an industry were to design its cogeneration system to supply electricity beyond its own needs (normally the most economical scale), at certain times it would still need to purchase utility power to cover fluctuations in its own operations. The high price of backup power to the industry set by the utility and the low price set for electricity purchased from the industry have constrained industrial cogeneration. In addition, industries express concern about their status in the regulatory framework if they begin to produce and sell electricity.

In sum, the main barriers to implementing this seemingly advantageous power supply system are institutional and regulatory rather than technological. Widespread use of industrial steam capability to cogenerate electricity is perceived to threaten utility practice and thwart their goal of meeting future demand with centralized nuclear and coal-fired generating capacity. It is not surprising, therefore, that efforts to date to implement cogeneration have encountered difficulty, minimizing this technology's contribution so far to lessening siting problems on the urban coast.

Modular Integrated Utility Systems

MIUS, sometimes known as "total energy systems," seem especially appropriate to an urban setting.[8] Although historically the total energy system concept received little attention, in 1970 the U.S. Department of Housing and Urban Development (HUD) and the National Bureau of Standards (NBS) began pursuing the idea as part of a program of innovation in buildings. As one of their projects, they sponsored a MIUS in Jersey City, New Jersey.[9]

The Jersey City MIUS includes a 300-kilowatt total energy plant providing residential, commercial, and institutional buildings on the site with all of their electricity, lighting, cooling, heating, and hot water. The plant uses four conventional diesel engine generators plus a waste heat recovery system. A pneumatic trash collection system conveys garbage and other trash to the power plant through underground pipes. The 6.35-acre site includes four buildings housing 1,300 people in 484 apartments, plus an elementary school, a swimming pool, a 50,000-square foot commercial building, parking space for tenants, and the energy plant itself.

In July 1977, an analysis of the Jersey City MIUS completed for HUD compared the system's performance favorably with that of a conventional energy plant, while recommending modifications in plant design and increased thermal tightness of the MIUS buildings to achieve even greater fuel savings. The study concluded that "an alternative conventional plant using purchased electrical power, oil fueled boilers and absorption chillers, would annually require 160,000 gallons more fuel oil than the Jersey City total energy plant."[10] The overall benefits also included reduced environmental impact.

For the near term, air quality constraints render direct burning of coal unacceptable in the Jersey City area, as in many other urban coastal regions. It is also reasonable to assume that most of the mid-Atlantic will remain heavily reliant on imported oil for some time. The multiplier effect that would potentially occur if many total energy systems like MIUS were implemented could result in reduced demand for electricity from the central utility system, with fewer new central station power plants required (or some plants now operating in urban areas could be retired). The benefits in energy efficiency and environmental impact are obvious. However, the fuels policy question is paramount. The MIUS uses oil, though rather efficiently. Continued use of such oil in the mid-Atlantic region runs contrary to current national energy policies, which emphasize centralized coal or nuclear electricity generation.

Integrated Community Energy System

The ICES planned for Trenton, New Jersey, is a 10-megawatt diesel cogeneration system originally designed to meet the heating, cooling, and electricity needs of a sizable portion of downtown Trenton. The idea was initiated by the city's Department of Planning and Development, which thereafter worked in conjunction with the federal government and the local utility, Public Service Electric and Gas Co. (PSE&G). This case illustrates many of the problems and opportunities involved in using small-scale energy systems in urban sites.[11]

During the summer of 1976, the city planning agency developed a concept for downtown revitalization based on an efficient, decentralized energy system that would provide both steam heat and electricity. Such a system could reduce the capital costs of new buildings and thereby hopefully provide an incentive to developers to build in the downtown area. Initial funding from the U.S. Energy Research and Development Administration (ERDA) in February 1977 allowed the Trenton group to conduct a feasibility study, with PSE&G responsible for determining costs, institutional arrangements, systems, and distribution and private consulting firms responsible for conceptual engineering and architectural design.

The feasibility study determined that an ICES could serve existing low-income housing plus several new commercial buildings to be built by the Mercer County Improvement Authority and leased to the state of New Jersey. The ICES facility would include a public parking garage and a rooftop tennis court complex heated by waste heat from the plant.

ERDA was especially interested in the institutional arrangements among the many municipal, county, state, private, and utility participants. The federal agency therefore funded a detailed feasibility study and preliminary engineering design for the Trenton ICES project.

Soon thereafter, however, professional differences arose between the utility's engineers and technical members of the Trenton city team concerning equipment choices, methods of storage, costs, and other issues. During the second phase of the study, capital cost estimates provided by the construction company and the city's team were continually rejected by the utility, to be replaced by much higher utility estimates. As a result, estimated costs for the ICES escalated enormously. For example, the construction company projected the cost of the waste heat boiler at roughly $240,000; PSE&G's first figure was over a million dollars, which the utility later reduced to about $638,000.

Interviewees suggest that the approach of the Trenton planning team could be likened to "designing a Volkswagen," while PSE&G's approach was "to build a Cadillac." ERDA, by then the U.S. Department of Energy (DOE), was reportedly displeased with the group's 90-day interim report and requested specific information from the utility concerning choice of fuel, rates, ownership, and economics. In early 1978 partial answers to these DOE requests were submitted. DOE then met with the Trenton group and utility staff at the utility's offices. By then, utility cost estimates had risen even further. In March PSE&G called a meeting with the Trenton group to report that the economics of the ICES were now "uncertain". The actual magnitude of the problem, however, was still not revealed. A series of meetings among the construction firm, architects, engineers, and PSE&G continued until finally the utility revealed a total capital cost figure of $22 million for the plant.

Privately at least, others involved were shocked by this estimate. An item-by-item review revealed that instrument and control costs were an extraordinary $1.3 million, up from the Phase I estimate of $22,000; operations and management costs had escalated as well; and there was a 30-percent increase in design costs. PSE&G also estimated that the ICES facility could first become operative in 1982, while everyone else had predicted 1980. Although subsequent discussion resulted in a reduction of some costs, PSE&G never changed its overall figure of $22 million. It thus came as no surprise to those involved when, in the spring of 1978, PSE&G declared the ICES project "uneconomical" from its perspective.

While the contract required all communications to be sent through the Trenton city group (the project managers), a series of articles quoting PSE&G as declaring the cogeneration plant uneconomical appeared in major state newspapers. The Trenton team was concerned that quotes from a utility vice president might have damaged Trenton's ability to attract customers for the cogeneration facility should the city decide to go ahead with the facility under revised owner-manager arrangements.

The Trenton team began to pursue a different institutional arrangement, whereby a municipal utility would purchase the electricity from ICES; by mid-1979 discussions were taking place with PSE&G concerning wheeling power from the ICES to the municipal utility. Thus the ICES concept was still moving forward, albeit haltingly.

While it cannot be directly proved, it seems apparent to those close to the situation (including this researcher) that the utility, though cooperative, never really made a firm commitment to the ICES concept. The utility's "reluctant debutante" attitude highlighted the mismatch of goals and practices between those whose business is the centralized energy system and those primarily interested in other issues, such as alternative energy technologies or downtown redevelopment.

Several vital questions must be asked. Is it necessary or desirable to involve utilities in such alternative energy applications? Should the initiative be governmental or private? Since utility experience lies in capital intensive, large-scale plants, was it not unavoidable that the utility would estimate high capital costs? Is the economic calculus of investor-owned utilities the proper basis for measuring the feasibility of alternative energy systems like ICES?

The details of the ICES program illustrate the problems of implementing a small-scale urban alternative energy system to service limited demands in the face of continuing utility preference for large centralized systems. Indeed, with rising fuel, environmental, and land costs, as well as the stress associated with finding suitable sites for coal and nuclear power plants, policies to encourage cogeneration and ICES types of systems in urban coastal areas may require major changes in the regulatory framework that presently governs the utilities.

Fuel Cells

The fuel cell directly converts fuel into electricity by controlled oxidation, without going through the intermediate stage of steam production common in today's utility power plant.[12] The first U.S. fuel cell application took place in the space program in the early 1960s, when United Aircraft Corporation's Pratt and Whitney Division developed the fuel cell for NASA's Apollo flights.

Fuel cells have encountered two problems: the need for costly fuels and the use of expensive rare metals (such as platinum) as catalysts for the chemical reaction. The technology's value to the space program was in its light weight, high efficiency, and production of pure water as a by-product. As with many other alternative technologies, the fuel cell will have to be built more inexpensively in order to achieve the economics necessary for conventional use.

One advantage of fuel cells is their potential adaptability to various sizes and scales of electricity production. Utilities are eager to see fuel cells used at typical centralized conventional power plants, especially for peaking units. In contrast, Clark and Thorndike, among others, emphasize that the real advantage of fuel cell application would be at smaller scales: home, community, or industrial park.[13] Here the fuel cell would be environmentally beneficial for use in urban sites, as a result of its high energy-conversion efficiency.

Whether for utility application or in smaller-scale use, fuel cells hold environmental advantages for urban coastal siting. As with cogeneration, extensive use of fuel cell systems in urban sites could substitute for capacity met by nuclear or coal power plants sited in remote areas. Conversely, where small power plants serving rural areas today use diesel engines, Pratt and Whitney estimated in 1974 that by 1980 fuel cell plants in remote power applications would be as much as 50 percent cheaper than conventional diesel engines. Another study, by Hydro-Quebec, Canada's largest public power corporation, estimated that a fuel cell plant would save up to 30 percent over the costs of conventional power systems for isolated villages.[14]

Research on fuel cells is continuing. One application appropriate to the Northeast is indicated in the work of Seymour Baron, who has studied two types of fuel cell installations:

A large-scale minemouth-sited fuel cell power plant using synthetic coal gas

Dispersed fuel cell power plants using natural gas, synthetic gas, or distillates

Based only on the cost of installing the plants using 1972-1973 utility and Atomic Energy Commission forecasts, he predicted the emergence of economical, clean power.[15]

Exxon Enterprises and the French Alsthorn Company in December 1972 together began a $10 million development program to produce a fuel cell for home use, remote power applications, and vehicles. As reported in *Science* magazine in 1973, the French found that methanol made from coal or other fossil fuels could be used as a basic fuel. Work on thin cell concepts (packing 5 to 10 times the electrode surface into the same volume as conventional fuel cells) based on the work of Bernard Warszowski also looks promising for commercialization of fuel cells.[16] The platinum problem remains difficult in terms of supply and cost, although Westinghouse under contract to the Interior Department is researching high-temperature fuel cells that do not require expensive metal catalysts.[17]

The utilities' widespread research and interest in fuel cells is encouraging, on the one hand, and yet discouraging if the goal is to reduce the land use impacts of central station power plants (e.g., urban coastal areas). Since fuel cells have the potential to be applied on a decentralized basis as single-structure units, or in multimegawatt central power plants,[18] other considerations eventually will determine the actual range of applications. As with cogeneration, utility interests may well be at odds with the concept of reducing plant size and scale.

Theoretically, if fuel cells were applied to existing central station utility plants, using synthetic coal gas, then the environment could be improved, investment and land already dedicated to utility infrastructure would remain appropriate, and the life of the central utility system would be extended. Use of fuel cells in single-family homes, in apartment buildings, at community scale, or in industrial parks, in contrast, would obviate the need to build some large central power plants. The traditional practices of the electric utility industry in this context thus appear to be challenged by an emerging new technology.

Fuel cells are among the more flexible energy alternatives. When viewed from the urban perspective, they hold great promise for application in both centralized and decentralized systems, at both small and large scales. Economic and material obstacles need to be overcome, however. Decentralized use of fuel cells probably will encounter the same barriers as total energy systems or steam-reliant combined cycle cogeneration systems. As with cogeneration, the fuel problem remains serious, since use of gas and oil in fuel cell applications may be inconsistent with the desired shift away from these fuels. Use of gas made from coal or solid waste, however, may be the best way to reduce this problem.

Low-Btu Gasification

The low-Btu gasification process, which produces gas by partial combustion of coal (or solid waste) with air, is another widely discussed alternative energy technology.[19] Given environmental conditions, it is unlikely that much more coal can be burned directly in most urban coastal areas, even with advanced pollution abatement equipment. Air quality is a particularly tough constraint; water quality is problematic as well. The pollutants emitted depend on the type of coal burned. Eastern coal has a higher sulfur content than western coal. Consequently, it would seem reasonable to convert high-sulfur eastern coal into a more compatible resource for use in environmentally stressed urban environments.

The types and proportions of burnable gases produced (carbon monoxide, methane, and hydrogen) depend on the design of the process. In particular, a fluidized bed combustion system utilizing coal (or solid waste) appears to hold great potential. Because of its very high temperatures, use of this technology should considerably reduce pollutant emissions.

The Stanford Research Institute (SRI) used a computer model to estimate the economic relationships and supply patterns for alternative scenarios for extracting, converting, and distributing energy for the western United States. This study concluded that low-Btu gasification could account for 140-quadrillion Btu's of energy in the year 2000. The SRI scenario showed coal-based synthetic fuel supplying 11 percent of the nation's energy requirements by the year 2000; by that date, low-sulfur western coal would provide 20 percent of all U.S. energy needs, with 15 percent more coming from eastern high-sulfur coal.[20]

Low-Btu gasification minimizes sulfur oxide emissions for western coal. For Illinois coal, liquefaction produces about 12 percent less sulfur oxide than low-Btu gasification. However, low-Btu gasification with either type of coal appears to be many times better than either liquefaction or high-Btu gasification in terms of hydrocarbon emissions.

Use of pipelines to bring gas from minemouth plants to urban demand centers may be the most appropriate strategy to relate coal to urban coastal areas. Limited coal handling capability, air quality constraints, lack of available water, and overall environmental conditions all limit a direct burning policy, even with today's pollution abatement equipment. A network of gas pipelines already exists, much of which could be used to transport coal gas. A mine-mouth coal gasification strategy would lessen pressures for siting major new energy facilities in the urban coastal zone.

One reason coal rather than solid waste was selected in this research effort as the fuel for a low-Btu gasification system is that solid waste recovery facilities are as difficult to site in an urban setting as are power plants and refineries. In addition, it is considered less efficient to convert solid waste to electricity than to liquid and gaseous fuels.[21] The nation will be linked for a long time to expensive oil and gas, the portable fuels, and will continue to need oil, especially in the transportation system. It may pay to wait for developing technologies that convert solid waste into portable fuels rather than committing this potential resource to electricity generation. Indeed, masses of biodegradable wastes beneath the earth's surface in time yield fossil fuels; the harder the substance (such as coal), the less the ease of energy extraction. To take coal that has already had most of its energy properties destroyed by the time it reaches the hardened state and convert it to gas or liquid fuels is like reversing the natural process. However, biomass (solid waste) is at a much earlier stage, and therefore converting it directly to gas is more consistent with natural processes.[22]

If the nation persists in its coal conversion policy, perhaps the best strategy for urban coastal zones involves a combination of electricity generated by cogeneration systems in urban areas coupled with low-Btu gasification at (distant) minemouth plants, with accompanying pipelines to the urban centers. The critical issue is portable fuels, not electricity. Yet electricity appears to be prevalent in today's thinking (even for solar energy).

Summary

Cogeneration, total and integrated energy systems and fuel cell applications may all be quite appropriate for urban siting. Moreover, their implementation could, over time, reduce the number of new power plant sites that would otherwise be needed, in urban areas and elsewhere. Each of these technologies can produce electricity directly; some can also be a source of steam. Each uses fossil fuels efficiently and provides the opportunity for reduced scale. All provide new opportunities for energy conservation. In the case of a facility designed to gasify coal, minemouth sited plants can offer this clean fuel to urban regions striving toward improved air quality.

None of these technologies is free from constraints, and certainly none is easy to implement. However, each could be a part of a larger alternative siting strategy designed to enhance the future prospects for urban coastal areas. The energy future is likely to be diverse in terms of technologies and systems. No single solution is apparent. More importantly, problems need to be defined more carefully before solutions can be sought that are compatible with both the national energy situation and the urban environment.

CONCLUSIONS: NATIONAL ENERGY POLICY AND ALTERNATIVE ENERGY TECHNOLOGIES

The conflicting energy facility siting strategies currently receiving the most attention—urban vs. rural, inland vs. coastal, dispersed vs. clustered, offshore vs. onshore—all relate almost exclusively to existing facility scale and present patterns of fuel use. If our nation's energy system is to stay basically the same, with only the fuels switched (the principal change being a switch from gas and oil to coal and nuclear electrification), these siting options will remain relevant.

Today's siting configurations have emerged as a result of the historical environmental, land use, and economic complexities endemic to urban coastal areas. However, adding more of the same to meet future demands for energy in urban areas may be unacceptable, given the impacts of such facilities on the highly industrialized, energy-intensive urban landscape. While alternative energy systems and fuels certainly are not free from constraints, they may represent an opportunity to reduce the kinds of impacts that result from the scale of development in existence and contemplated for an electrified future in the urban coastal zone.

In contrast to the large-scale facilities commonly in current use, cogeneration and total energy systems require new perspectives on energy siting and land use issues. If a portion of today's electricity demand were met by industrial cogeneration, for example, or if some residential heating and cooling requirements were met by district steam systems, the tensions associated with siting increased central system electricity capacity could be reduced.

Electricity production and oil and gas facilities increasingly compete for limited locations in the mid-Atlantic region. If offshore resources require natural gas processing plants onshore, overall siting constraints may make it imperative that new electricity generating capacity rely on cogeneration systems rather than on additional fossil fuel or nuclear power plants in the same area.

The increased pressure to find suitable sites for various traditional oil, gas, and coal-related energy facilities in the mid-Atlantic occurs as a result of the national policy to develop domestic resources. If accelerated domestic fossil fuel development is in the national interest, and if economic revitalization efforts in urban centers are also to be encouraged, alternative energy technologies may very well offer the best near-term flexibility for reducing siting tensions in these densely populated areas.

Utilities may have to be treated differently in certain parts of the country from others, since industrial steam capability is not uniformly distributed geographically. Institutionally, this may suggest further study of deregulated electricity generation along with distribution by the regional equivalent of a state public service board. To reduce siting problems consistent with energy needs, a clearer electricity policy may become necessary.

At present, there is no policy commitment to take advantage of the opportunities uniquely available through application of alternative energy technologies to relieve the siting burdens in urban coastal zones. An energy future responsive to local differences and reliant on a mixture of systems of various scales, technologies and fuels is relatively disorderly, when compared to the uniformity that exists today through use of gas and oil across the country. From this perspective, present fuel-switching concepts only address a small part of the energy problem. Heterogeneity in energy supply, as suggested here, perhaps would lead to the need to make even more decisions in the political arena. However, the significant lack of progress in national energy policy during the past six years suggests that a multifaceted and sophisticated response to the energy crisis is not being achieved. Instead, the national political process appears to be moving toward a firmly uniform approach: centralized electrification.

A more sophisticated energy policy capability is being built on state, regional, and local levels than is often recognized at the federal level. In this regard, attempts to implement an alternative energy future on a state basis demonstrate an overall disenchantment with the manner and content of emerging national supply and demand policies in Washington. The research report, *Distributed Energy Systems in California's Future*, concludes that alternative energy modes and reliance on indigenous resources are indeed potential major components of California's energy future, allowing the state to discard at least some of its reliance on large-scale traditional energy facilities.[23] New Jersey's Department of Energy has sought authority to make "need determination" for gas, oil, and electricity facilities, and to examine the possibility of implementing alternative technologies as well.[24] The Maryland legislature wants to assess the wisdom of granting variances to industry to burn refuse-derived fuels.[25] Following California's lead, New York's Governor Carey has said he will cease licensing any new nuclear power plants until nuclear waste issues are resolved satisfactorily; this concern is growing in many states.[26]

All in all, there is increasing interest and motivation (if diverse) to reject proposed large new energy facilities. In planning their energy futures, some states are looking elsewhere: to other energy systems, other energy resources, and other institutions to achieve local compatibility with an altered resource base. If such innovative planning is not accommodated at the federal level, federal-state conflict is likely to increase.

While examining the potential for development of their own special capabilities to devise a secure energy future, however, all states must participate (happily or unhappily) in the national scheme. This may constrain their options immensely, depending on their specific legislative authority and the extent of federal preemption. For example, the national policy to develop and utilize domestic OCS energy resources has an impact on the mid-Atlantic region. While New Jersey may be trying to reduce the future impacts of the intense industrial and energy development that for so long has been a feature of this densely populated state, the national interest is being pursued 60 to 90 miles off that state's coast. Federal leasing for exploration of the Baltimore Canyon Trough will undoubtedly give the refineries, gas processing plants and pipelines associated with possible oil and gas production an ability to claim "national interest" in any siting disputes. If commercial finds are made, serious questions may arise when development and environmental protection policies related to New Jersey's own needs conflict with demands for sites in the state for facilities related to the national interest. In addition, whenever pipeline corridors and sites for gas-processing plants are identified, the federal and industry relationship may be forced into an adversary position with state and local governments. (Then again, there may be no oil worth developing in the Baltimore Canyon Trough.)

Single, narrow energy policies tend to be less and less effective and more suspect by localities. President Carter and the governors of several urban states have expressed an imperative need to redevelop the cities. New investment by the private sector in the urban coastal zone would require not only extensive venture capital but would also stimulate public investment in housing, schools, hospitals, transportation, and general municipal services. Energy conservation applications are costly, as are solar energy applications. A major public policy thus involves the extent of available capital and its priority uses in the public interest: urban redevelopment, energy conservation, traditional energy supply technologies, new alternative energy technologies, or other industrial and consumer uses.

While it is hoped that conservation and increased domestic supplies of gas and oil will reduce the foreign exchange drain on the U.S. economy by reducing the amount of crude oil imports, ostensibly making increased capital available for domestic purposes (such as urban revitalization and investments in a renewable energy resource base), decisions left unmade or institutions not redirected to achieve these ends will stand squarely as obstacles. Unmade decisions reflect institutions in conflict and do not bode well for the future of the American economy or the health of our nation's urban centers. Constructive choices and decisions regarding alternative energy technologies can help to brighten the future.

NOTES

1. Calculated by the New Jersey Department of Environmental Protection, Bureau of Air Pollution Control, 1978.
2. J. S. Munson and R. Stern, *Regional Energy-Environmental Data Book* (Upton, N.Y.: Brookhaven National Laboratory, Regional Energy Studies Program, October 1978), pp. 103-108.
3. Federal Power Commission, *Factors Affecting the Electric Power Supply 1980-1985* (Washington, D.C.: FPC), special study by the Bureau of Power, December 1, 1976, p. 228.
4. R. H. Williams, "Industrial Cogeneration," *Annual Reviews of Energy: 1978*, 1979, 3:313-356.
5. S. Nydick et. al., *A Study of Inplant Electric Power Generation in the Chemical, Petroleum Refining and Paper and Pulp Industries* (Waltham, Mass.: Report to the Federal Energy Administration by Thermo-Electron Corporation, 1976).
6. R. F. Dittrich and K. Allon, *PSE&G Cogeneration Evaluation*, Report No. 36.76.12 (Newark, N.J.: Public Service Electric and Gas Co., 1977).
7. Williams, op. cit.
8. "Modular Integrated Utility System," U.S. Department of Housing and Urban Development, Office of Policy Development and Research

(Washington, D.C., 1975). Also see Wilson Clark, *Energy for Survival: The Alternative to Extinction* (Garden City, N.Y.: Anchor Books, 1975), pp. 238-241.

9. See U.S. Department of Housing and Urban Development, *Performance Analysis of the Jersey City Total Energy Site: Interim Report* (Washington, D.C.: HUD, HUD Utilities Demonstration Series, July 1977), vol. 7; *Feasibility Analyses for the Integration of an Incinerator with Waste Heat Recovery at the HUD Jersey City Total Energy Demonstration Site*, vol. 16, September 1977; Final Report, *Design and Installation Total Energy Plant—Central Equipment Building Summit Plaza Apartments "Operation Breakthrough Site," Jersey City, N.J.*, vol. 12, Utilities Demonstration Series, prepared for U.S. HUD Office of Policy and Research, Division of Energy Buildings Technology and Standards (Washington, D.C.: February 1977).

10. HUD, *Performance Analysis*, ibid.

11. The material contained in this section was received through special interviews with individuals involved in the planning of the Trenton ICES project. No one from the utility was interviewed. However, the researcher believes the facts concerning the economic assessment of the project by the utility speak for themselves. The researcher was also involved in the ICES program when she was in state government. She accompanied the Trenton PSE&G group to several presentations in Washington and in Chicago and was part of the governor's Cogeneration Task Force.

12. See Clark, op. cit., pp. 207-252; and E. Thorndike, *Energy and Environment: A Primer for Scientists and Engineers* (Reading, Mass.: Addison Wesley, 1976), p. 92.

13. Ibid.

14. Resources for the Future, Inc., in cooperation with MIT Environmental Laboratories, *Energy Research Needs: A Report to the National Science Foundation* (Washington, D.C.: RFF, October 1971), pp. 84-90.

15. A. L. Hamond; W. D. Metz; and T. H. Maugh II, *Energy and the Future* (Washington, D.C.: American Association for the Advancement of Science, 1973), pp. 47-87, 97-126; S. Baron, "Fuel Cell Power Generation and Gasification," paper presented at the American Public Power Association Annual Conference, San Francisco, June 26-28, 1972.

16. Clark, op. cit.

17. Westinghouse Electric Corporation, *Final Report on Project Fuel Cell*, Research and Development Report 57, prepared for the Office of Coal Research, U.S. Department of Interior, Washington, D.C., 1970.

18. U.S. Department of Energy, Deputy Under Secretary for Commercialization, *Overview of Technology Commercialization Assessment* (Washington, D.C.: USDOE, Report DOE/US-003, Dist. Category UC-13, 1978).

19. Resources for the Future, op. cit., pp. v and 29-48. Also see Council on Environmental Quality, *Sixth Annual Report* (Washington, D.C.: U.S. Government Printing Office, December 1975), pp. 427-436.

20. Stanford Research Institute, *A Western Regional Energy Development Study: Economics*, prepared for CEQ et al., Contracts EQ5AC007 and EQ5AC008; Stanford Research Institute, *Synthetic Fuels Commercialization Program*, prepared for Synfuels Interagency Task Force under Contracts EQ5AC007 and EQ5AC008.

21. D. L. Urban; M. J. Antal; and M. F. Fels, *The Biomass Energy Resource of*

New Jersey: A County-by-County Inventory (Princeton: Princeton University, Center for Energy and Environmental Studies, Report no. 86, May 1979, revised September 1979.)

22. This concept was suggested by Professor M. Antal of Princeton University's School of Engineering and Applied Science.

23. A joint project of LBL/LLL/University of California, Berkeley and Davis, *Distributed Technologies in California's Energy Future*, sponsored by USDOE, Office of Environment, Office of Technology Impacts, March 1978.

24. New Jersey Department of Energy, *New Jersey Energy Masterplan* (Newark: NJDOE, October 1978).

25. W. C. Metz; J. Shyer; and K. Edgecomb, *A Preliminary Assessment of the Prospects For Use of Refuse-Derived Fuel in Maryland* (Upton: N.Y.: Brookhaven National Laboratory, BNL 51065, February 1979).

26. "Atom-Waste Disposal Stirs Debate; 11 States Already Bar the Dumps," *Wall Street Journal*, August 29, 1978.

Chapter 13

Policies for Energy Facility Siting on the Urban Coast

David Morell

The nation's energy facility siting strategies could support, rather than contradict, the innovative redevelopment efforts now underway in many urban waterfronts. The recommendations presented in this chapter, based on research into this policy question, are designed to alter the existing situation in which proposed new energy facilities often directly contradict urban coastal revitalization.

ALTERNATIVE SITING STRATEGIES FOR THE URBAN WATERFRONT

In general, only water-dependent energy facilities should be located at the water's edge. All others should be located at a reasonable distance inland, removed from the immediate coastal land-water interface. Government coastal zone and other regulations should enforce such a preference for inland siting.

This policy is designed to protect valuable ecosystems in the coastal zone, reserving them for amenity, recreational, and residential use where feasible. Too often in the past, energy facilities have been located on rural or urban waterfronts simply because of traditional inertia—"that's the way we always have sited such facilities"—or to achieve modest economic advantages to the firm from choosing a waterfront location. Now, however, available technologies—deepwater ports for offloading at an offshore location, pipelines for transfer of crude oil, natural gas, petroleum products, or other liquids from a coastal transfer station to an inland site for processing and storage, and so on—offer opportunities for environmentally and socially preferable siting of needed energy facilities, without any undue economic penalty to the energy company or the broader economy.

Agencies of federal and state government already have available a wide range of planning and regulatory mechanisms to encourage inland siting: "208" and other water planning programs, plans under the Resource Conservation and Recovery Act and the Toxic Substances Control Act, wetlands statutes, riparian laws, and so on. Coordinated use of such controls in support of inland siting could contribute markedly to environmental protection and urban waterfront redevelopment, while ensuring that all energy facilities actually needed by American society are indeed constructed, and in a timely manner.

In considering the suitability of locales for siting of energy facilities—particularly in complex urban communities with competing needs and land use patterns—it is essential to disaggregate both facility types and community characteristics. Enormous differences exist in the impacts of energy facilities. A gas-processing plant is not a tank farm, and an offshore oil and gas support base is not a power plant. Similarly, cities present highly diverse needs and opportunities. Thus while generalized concepts of energy facility siting in the urban coastal zone certainly are useful as guiding principles, sensitivity to the differing features, plans, and requirements of a community and of proposed facilities are essential planning tools, especially in urban locales already under great environmental and economic stress.

Examples of this phenomenon abound in the New Jersey case study, for example. Because of its heavily industrial nature and the absence of a distinctive aesthetic setting, Perth Amboy could well be a reasonable site for a major storage terminal (air quality concerns aside) or large Outer Continental Shelf (OCS) support base.[1] In contrast, such facilities would be fundamentally unacceptable in Jersey City, with its view of New York City's skyline and the Statue of Liberty and its new 800-acre state park on the waterfront. A smaller environmentally benign OCS service base that did not become a dominant feature in conflict with amenity use on the

Hudson River waterfront might be acceptable in Jersey City, however, especially if this facility were to provide a significant number of new jobs in this area of high unemployment.

The existence today of energy facilities along the urban waterfront in many cities is an insufficient reason to intensify this pattern of development. Such facilities should be restricted to sites that clearly require immediate urban proximity and that contribute to sizable employment creation. Tax payments alone are insufficient justification for introducing additional incompatible land uses into the urban waterfront, often now the nucleus of citywide revitalization efforts.

In order to contribute to solving the serious problem of unemployment in many urban areas, any energy facilities approved for waterfront siting should meet specific tests of employment generation. A minimum figure for jobs per acre could be established for certain areas, so that a labor-intensive offshore oil service base might be acceptable but a fuel storage installation would not. The proposed New Jersey facilities with 80 jobs on 40 prime acres, and 50 jobs on 50 acres, are illustrative of the problem.

Where explicit community efforts at urban waterfront revitalization are already underway—as in Jersey City, Baltimore, Boston, Philadelphia, San Francisco, and similar locations—extraordinary justification must exist to override a normal presumption against allowing new energy facilities. These waterfront areas may be more suited to compatible land uses: residential, commercial, or recreational. Energy companies and government site planners should be cautious about proposing any new energy facilities in these urban areas.

Such incompatible land uses could upset the delicate balance of environmentally responsible development already initiated. Polluting new energy facilities of the type proposed in the New Jersey waterfront area, for example, could preempt decisions to locate new commercial, residential, or employment-intensive light industrial facilities along the urban coast.

Clustered siting of energy facilities in new areas offers a preferred technique to balance society's needs for new or additional technological capacity with the equally important objectives of coastal zone preservation and enviromental protection.[2] In general, sites for such energy clusters can be found on the outer fringe of metropolitan areas (as in the Texas site near Corpus Christi), thereby achieving market proximity while avoiding both the urban waterfront and rural areas of special environmental sensitivity. Further clustering in urban coastal areas is to be avoided.

Energy companies tend to resist the clustering concept, primarily because it implies a greater degree of land use and siting control by government agencies and a shift of siting initiative from private to governmental hands. In some cases, pollution concentrations from a single complex may threaten air or water quality. Nevertheless, the overall advantages of the cluster in alleviating pressures on areas of greater environmental value make this approach worthy of detailed scrutiny. Moreover, labor, infrastructure cost, and other economic advantages may accrue through clustering of several energy (and related petrochemical) facilities at the same site.

Sites for potential energy clusters could be selected in advance of their need, perhaps by the states as part of a national energy facility siting effort. This could accelerate the overall permit review and siting process, although difficult issues of ensuring adequate public participation require careful resolution. Maryland's power plant siting program is suggestive of the kind of approach that could be useful for other types of energy facilities as well,[3] especially in states where environmental values in urban and rural coastal regions are in jeopardy.

Conscious government planning and regulatory action can ensure creation of sizable buffer zones around major energy facilities, and especially around energy clusters, thereby separating conflicting land uses and keeping noxious but necessary facilities at arm's length from the society they are designed to serve.

A buffer zone concept is gaining increasing attention for areas surrounding nuclear power plants. In New Jersey, a ban on extensive residential development for four to six miles around the state's operating reactors was in force for three years under the state's coastal zone management statute. California's law on siting of liquified natural gas (LNG) facilities includes provisions for enforcement of specific land use controls in an extensive surrounding area. Even in the absence of governmental requirements, a number of private energy companies typically include buffer zones around their new facilities; this was done in the Corpus Christi plant analyzed in the Texas case study (see Chapter 7).

Characteristics of buffer zones may vary from one type of energy facility to another, and they may involve restrictions on some or all of the following: residential housing at selected densities, industrial facilities, commercial complexes, or highway access. Inclusion of buffer zones in any broader energy facility siting strategy makes rural (or at least urban fringe) siting imperative. Creation of a reasonable buffer zone would simply be impossible around a tank farm in Jersey City, an oil refinery in Long Beach, California, or an LNG terminal in Boston or New York harbor.

Where safety issues are the dominant concern, as with LNG terminals and facilities for storage or processing of certain toxic or carcinogenic materials, strict prohibitions against urban siting appear warranted. For such energy facilities, remote siting and enforcement of defined buffer zones are imperative.

Safety issues are a dominant concern of citizens. Lengthy, essentially unproductive delays in the permit approval process can be anticipated every time a dangerous facility is proposed for urban coastal siting. Such proposals constitute a "no-win" situation for the energy companies, government agencies, citizen or environmental groups, and the public at large.

The continuing controversies over LNG facility siting in Boston Harbor, Staten Island, New York, on the Delaware River in New Jersey, and along the California coast are illustrative in this regard. The California Coastal Commission's analysis of several alternate sites for an LNG terminal provides a good working model for dealing with the safety issue.

Unless more than compensatory pollution abatement can be achieved through techniques like the U.S. Environmental Protection Agency's (EPA) emission offset regulations, additional polluting energy facilities should not be located in areas where environmental standards have not been met.

In many urban coastal areas, attainment of national ambient air quality standards poses particularly difficult siting constraints. This is one of the principal environmental issues in the rural-urban siting confrontation.

In the attempt to escape from damaging fragile rural coastlines, energy facilities have been proposed for urban waterfronts where air quality—especially for hydrocarbons and photochemical oxidant—fails to meet the national standards: Long Beach, California; Jersey City, New Jersey; Portsmouth, Virginia; and so on. Effective energy facility site planning, combined with strict enforcement of the provisions of the Clean Air Act, can allow achievement of mutual national objectives, rather than gaining one at the expense of another. The emission offset concept has the potential to allow balanced achievement of several national objectives. Used as "creative maneuvering," however, the idea can simply allow unconscionable delay in attaining air quality standards.

Innovative siting approaches should receive attention in governmental and corporate circles. Of particular interest is the combina-

tion of a major energy facility located some distance inland from the coast, along with either a small unloading or pumping station on the coast or an offshore deepwater port. Either of these offloading terminals could be linked by pipeline to the inland facility. A version of this siting mode was used in the Corpus Christi case. Those proposing to construct major energy facilities in coastal locations, particularly on the urban waterfront, should be required to present an innovative alternative scheme along with their traditional siting proposal.

There is simply no technological nor economic reason why all new oil refineries, gas-processing plants, storage terminals, or tank farms have to be located on the water's edge, rather than 3, 5, even 10 or more miles inland. Traditionally, tankers or barges have docked right at the energy facility to unload their products. With modern technology, however, deepwater ports or small coastal unloading stations could serve this need, with the main facility kept away from the coastal edge.

This requirement to consider innovative siting could be enforced through state coastal zone management plans and through state energy facility siting regulations where these are in existence. The national coastal zone management program and the U.S. Department of Energy (DOE) could encourage states to adopt this siting procedure.

California already requires utilities proposing to construct a plant in its coastal zone to propose an inland alternative as well, and thus both sites can be assessed for their environmental and other impacts during the permit review process. Other proposed coastal energy facilities, in California and elsewhere, could be brought under the same type of scrutiny.

URBAN WATERFRONT REVITALIZATION AND ENERGY FACILITY SITING

In many economically depressed American urban centers, efforts at innovative redevelopment of vacant or poorly utilized land on or near the waterfront are the principal positive signs in a rather bleak overall situation.

Commercial and residential development along the urban waterfront in Baltimore, Boston, San Francisco, Seattle, Washington, D.C., and several other cities have brought new life to these areas. In place of vacant lots, rotting piers, and decrepit warehouses, restaurants, boutiques, artist shops, and high-rise apartment buildings now evidence dynamic activity, night and day. Such development has elitist implications, to be sure. Yet it is bringing some of the middle class back into center cities from the suburbs, and it is offering at least the potential for a growing multiplier effect on redevelopment of adjacent neighborhoods.

Examination of waterfront redevelopment efforts in several cities shows that government can regulate growth on the waterfront but that it does not often initiate development, leaving that to private interests. Such a reactive stance is still the rule in energy facility siting as well as in other development.

In urban coastal areas where efforts at redevelopment are underway, many involved citizens fear that petrochemical facilities and other energy-related structures will come to dominate the waterfront in the last decades of the twentieth century as the railroads and other heavy industry did in the second half of the nineteenth century. This citizen concern translates rapidly into intense activism whenever a major energy facility is proposed for their changing waterfront.

In the nineteenth century, many urban waterfronts became dominated by railroads and heavy industry, as well as shipping piers. With the decline of the railroads, the transition to containerized shipping, and the move of many industries to suburban locations served by trucks on the interstate highway system, these areas are now in a depressed, underused condition. Proposals for major energy facilities, as in the areas examined in the New Jersey case study, stimulate citizen opposition.

New urban waterfront development should include provision for public access to the water's edge. Federal coastal zone management regulations should give added emphasis to this policy.

Too often in the past, urban waterfront development has walled off the public from the shore, in the very areas where dense populations require access to such recreational amenities. The railroads did this along most of northern New Jersey's Hudson River shoreline, for example. Popular demand for waterfront access is evident in the numbers of people, particularly in warm weather, who jump the fences and illegally cross the tracks to reach the water's edge.

Compatibility of new facilities with existing and planned land uses in urban waterfront areas is essential if nascent revitalization efforts are to succeed. If any new energy facilities are indeed introduced into such areas, their scale, design, and adjacent land use

*patterns become crucial so that they do not come to dominate the
urban coastal landscape.*

The Providence, Rhode Island, waterfront on Narragansett Bay
offers one example of balanced, mixed use of an urban waterfront.
This area includes the Narragansett power plant, an oil storage
terminal with about 25 tanks visible from the water, a small marina
for pleasure boats, a linear waterfront park of about 50 acres, and a
highly prestigious residential area of larger, older homes only two
or three blocks from the waterfront. All of these facilities are of a
generally compatible scale, so that the industrial and energy development does not dominate the landscape. As a result, the area's overall
land use pattern accommodates a range of different uses needed by
the broader community. Similar situations exist on the Toronto
waterfront and along much of San Francisco Bay.

In contrast, the 242-tank petrochemical storage complex proposed
for the Jersey City waterfront, examined in the New Jersey case
study, was an affront in terms of scale, visual impact, pollution
volume, and land use compatibility. As a result, citizen opposition
to this facility was intense, and it was ultimately successful. In retro-
spect, at least, the facility's proponents had been insensitive to local
realities to have expected otherwise.

ALTERNATIVE ENERGY
TECHNOLOGIES AND
THE URBAN COAST

*Alternative energy technologies examined in Chapter 12—
cogeneration, total energy systems, low-BTU gasification, and fuel
cells—raise a variety of new siting considerations. To a large extent,
the rationale for traditional siting strategies appears to become
irrelevant with respect to these technologies.*

Various siting techniques—inland, coastal, offshore, clustered,
dispersed, and so on—apply primarily to an existing set of energy
facilities. Because of their size, scale, water requirements, air pollution, and other characteristics, power generation plants, refineries,
gas-processing facilities and attendant storage facilities have been
the subject of locational disputes, and thus the targets for strategies
designed to reduce their impacts on the landscape.

For the alternate technologies, new considerations arise. How
many industrial cogeneration facilities of what capacity are needed
to preclude construction of a central station power plant, for example? What percentage of baseload electricity cogenerated at

decentalized urban sites would be sufficient to assure an appropriate level of system reliability? Will the utilities own and operate industrial cogeneration facilities that provide electricity for the grid as well as onsite power? Or should industry be the owner and operator? Since more fuel is actually burned at the cogenerating plant than in a normal industry because steam and electricity are simultaneously being produced, are there appropriate environmental offset measures to mediate any potential increases in hydrocarbons or other emissions from this fossil fuel use in urban locations? Siting considerations are quite different from traditional energy facilities. Cogeneration takes place at existing industrial plants; that is where this new generating capacity would be located. Thus, the need to site new plants solely for the purpose of producing electricity would be reduced if cogeneration technologies were adopted.

Some alternative energy technologies provide the opportunity to reduce siting tensions in urban areas by incorporating development and energy systems in tandem efforts at the same location.

Fuel cells can be used at the scale of a typical central power plant. More interesting, however, is the possibility of developing housing or an industrial park in tandem with a fuel cell energy system. Here suitable sites must be selected. In the total energy system concept, again, the decision is not how to site the energy plant appropriately but where to locate a development that will house the self-contained energy system.

Although many opportunities exist to reduce siting tensions through use of alternative energy systems, one obstacle appears to confound the plant siting issue: the absence of an electrification policy. A national policy should be developed to take into account the various technological options available for electricity generation. In contrast, national policy should recognize that equivalent technological options are not available in the processing and handling of fossil fuels, thereby requiring different siting strategies.

There is no apparent technological alternative to a refinery or a natural gas processing facility, an LNG plant, or a synthetic fuels facility. All these facilities are large in scale and capital-intensive. Some may require coastal locations to achieve economies that are no longer necessarily achieved by large-scale electrical generation. Here technological alternatives on a smaller scale are applicable, especially in urban locations. In addition, none of these fossil fuel options brings the United States closer to reliance on a renewable resource base.

Regional energy policies may be needed to take into account explicit regional characteristics such as the availability of process steam as well as the variables of environmental quality, economic condition, and overall development patterns. Because of the uneven geographic distribution of industrial steam production throughout the United States, regional policies for cogeneration may be especially important.

Any combined cycle system that produces process steam and electricity simultaneously can achieve fuel efficiency that cannot be achieved at separate plants for production of steam and electricity. However, large chemical plants, paper plants, refineries, steel plants, and other steam producers that provide the best opportunity to cogenerate are absent in many states and subregions. Thus any changes made in utility regulation to encourage cogeneration may have little meaning or produce an undesirable result in areas where little or no industrial steam capacity exists.

Use of the total energy system concept may contribute to redevelopment in urban centers.

Through this concept, redevelopment opportunities in urban centers become a reality as sites for job-producing centers and housing are found. The energy plant itself becomes a supplemental consideration to the overall impact of locating the industrial park or housing units in a particular urban area. Energy becomes directly linked to the building structure and type of development or process it services. Investment in housing and industrial development can more easily address life-cycle costing concepts necessary to produce the economies that will make the urban environment more attractive.

THE ECONOMICS OF ENERGY FACILITY SITING

Delays that may be encountered in obtaining the necessary permits under existing regulatory conditions appear to have a significant impact on corporate evaluations of potential energy facility investments. In order to avoid such permitting delays, or reduce their length and seriousness, an energy facility sponsor may be willing to accept sizable increases in capital or operating costs, or both. Changes in government regulatory procedures that encouraged— or even just allowed—such a tradeoff between greater facility cost and lessened permitting delay could be expected to receive substantial support from the energy industry.

Based on case studies of 16 oil refineries proposed in recent years for East Coast sites, but either rejected in the permitting process or abandoned by their corporate sponsors after lengthy delays, and on in-depth interviews with decision makers at four oil companies, sizable costs indeed appear to be associated with regulatory delays. On the basis of the net present value (NPV) calculations used by most of the companies to assess their investment decisions, a firm proposing to build a refinery producing 200,000 barrels per day would be willing to invest $100 million in additional capital, or to assume incremental operating costs of $18 million for 20 years, in order to avoid a five-year permitting delay.

These additional costs could be applied to selection of an environmentally preferred but more expensive site: one inland from the coast, for example. An offshore unloading facility might be installed as well. Alternatively, they could cover the expense of installing and operating more sophisticated pollution abatement equipment. Similarly, the value of reduced permitting delays could be applied to the purchase of an extensive land area, that would provide a buffer zone around an especially dangerous energy facility (e.g., an LNG terminal).

Midconstruction delays are far more costly to the firm than are permitting delays prior to commencement of construction. As a result, governmental actions to lessen the chance of such interventions once a facility has received its necessary permits and actual construction has begun could conceivably be balanced against major additional siting costs or pollution abatement improvements by the firm.

For a typical oil refinery, a one-year delay after construction has begun can have a greater impact on the profitability of the investment than would a permit review process that lasted 10 years prior to commencement of construction. This enormous difference results from the fact that capital is actually tied up in a project once it has reached the construction stage. External financing has been arranged; equipment has been purchased and brought to the site; and labor force commitments have been made. In contrast, expenditures are modest and commitments flexible while final permit approval is still pending. Actual corporate expenditures while the permit process is underway (perhaps $5 to $10 million), though a large sum of money, represent a very small percentage of the total capital costs of a major energy facility like an oil refinery (today perhaps $650 million).

Because of their overwhelming impact, midconstruction delays deserve special attention in any reform of the permitting process. Proposals that could increase the probability of such delays would, in the end, not contribute to energy development; proposals to make such interventions less likely could contribute to energy development (and perhaps to environmental protection at the same time).

As just noted, midconstruction delays can have a devastating financial impact, far greater than permitting delays. If government regulatory procedures could be altered to lessen the likelihood of such delays, major siting or pollution abatement concessions could be exacted from the energy companies in exchange.

Proposals such as "one-stop permitting," while perhaps decreasing the time required for permit issuance, should be viewed with extreme caution if they provide added opportunity for opponents to challenge the project in the courts at a later date, thereby causing a midconstruction delay. Present interpretations of the National Environmental Policy Act and the Endangered Species Act could result in this situation.

Rapid inflation causes difficulties for long-range corporate investment decisions on facilities of the scale of an oil refinery. In this situation, permitting delays can have a much larger impact on the investment's desirability.

Even a modest increase in the inflation rate will have a large impact on the investment's NPV; this is true whenever capital costs are rising more rapidly than anticipated revenues. In this case, government actions to lessen the likelihood of permit delays become particularly crucial.

In addition to the implications of permitting delays, the regulatory process increases the investment's uncertainty. Perhaps after months or even years of study and argument, the siting proposal will be rejected, or abandoned by the company as unworthy of further attention. However, this issue pales in comparison to the costs of midconstruction delay once commitments have actually been made. Thus changes in the regulatory process should focus more on midconstruction interventions than on early announcement of permit approval.

If the project is canceled or rejected during the permitting process, the company loses the money it has invested up to that point ($5 to $10 million for an oil refinery). This sum must be viewed in the context of the entire project ($650 million). For a facility of this scale, which when operating will have annual cash flows of close to a billion dollars, even a slight variation in expected product prices would overwhelm the initial risk of permitting rejection.

It is crucial that the energy corporations' overall investment evaluations for new facilities include the probable impacts of various siting alternatives on the length and uncertainty of the permitting process. Federal guidelines and informational activities could encourage adoption of such new siting evaluation techniques by energy companies.

The economic calculus for assessing the profitability of an investment in an oil refinery, or another major energy facility, will be affected by assumptions about the permitting process. Adoption by energy corporations of analytical techniques to compare permit process changes with higher site costs could allow balanced pursuit of otherwise contradictory national goals.

One alternative siting strategy calls for maximum feasible location of energy facilities away from the water's edge. Economic analysis indicates that the cost differential between coastal and inland locations for a new oil refinery would be relatively small, even when a pipeline is used to deliver the crude oil from a coastal unloading facility to the inland refinery.

Two inland refinery locations were selected for comparison with the coastal-urban base case: an inland-urban site and an inland-rural site. Basically, the economic disadvantage of locating a refinery inland occurs from the added transportation costs of shipping the crude oil from the coast to the refinery. In addition, many other potential capital and operating cost differentials exist between inland and coastal sites. These distinctions, however, are very site-specific and do not lend themselves to a general analysis. For example, the capital cost differential between a coastal-urban and an inland-rural refinery site would depend on such site-specific factors as: labor costs, labor productivity, equipment freight costs, availability of construction equipment, local taxes, and land costs. Based on modeling calculations, analysis showed that the additional crude oil and product transportation costs associated with the two types of inland sites had only a moderate impact on the economic desirability of the refinery investment.

Use of a deepwater port for offshore unloading of crude oil, in combination with an inland refinery location and a products pipeline for distribution of the lighter refinery products, appears to have distinct environmental advantages at modest economic costs. If "reasonable" increases in the probability of a successful permitting process are attributed to use of a deepwater port, the economic viability of such an offshore unloading and transfer facility improves greatly.

Incorporating a deepwater port could significantly reduce environmental opposition to an oil refinery proposal, especially if the refinery were located in a rural area three to five miles or more inland from the coast. Use of an offshore unloading facility could reduce harbor congestion and lessen the chance of coastal oil spills;

use of a products pipeline would reduce the probability of damaging product spills; and the inland, rural location would pose fewer land use conflicts. Using NPV calculations, the additional costs of including a deepwater port in the refinery proposal would be preferable to a permitting delay of three to five years.

However, two possible "secondary" impacts of a deepwater port deserve attention. By allowing use of very large crude carrier oil tankers, the offshore port could reduce the statistical probability of oil spills but increase the consequences should an accident occur to one of the huge ships. Second, existence of a deepwater port might stimulate other energy facilities to locate in its proximity, thereby threatening air quality or other coastal values in the area.

GOVERNMENT INSTITUTIONS AND PUBLIC PARTICIPATION IN ENERGY FACILITY SITING

If balanced pursuit of coastal zone protection, urban development, and energy facility siting is to be accomplished, the fundamental siting initiative must be wrested in large measure from the energy companies and placed instead in the hands of government decision makers at local, state, or federal levels.

To date, government initiative is the exception to the pattern of corporate site selection followed by government review through the permit process. Maryland's program for power plant siting and California's efforts to designate LNG sites stand out as exceptions in this regard.

The energy companies, whether regulated utilities (electricity and gas) or private corporations (oil and coal), cannot be expected to select sites consistently in society's interest. Their own criteria for efficiency, cost minimization, and profit maximization seldom correlate perfectly with optimal siting, as defined in statewide plans, for example. Too many environmental, social, and economic externalities apply. Given the enormous impact of major energy facilities, government-siting initiative seems essential, preferably statewide but at a minimum with respect to the urban coastal zone.

A viable energy facility siting process requires effective procedures for authoritative participation by federal, state, and local levels of government, and by the public. A balance of efficiency, equity, and participation must be devised. Often this will involve a structured sequence of decision making by various levels of government, in turn, rather than centralization of authority in the hands of a single government agency. This generally applicable principle is of special importance along the urban coastal zone, where competing land use pressures and citizen interest run so high.

Too often in the past, and continuing today, siting reform proposals have emphasized administrative efficiency at the expense of equity and citizen participation. Proposals for federal preemption over states' rights, for state override of municipal home rule, for technological decisions by "experts," and for similar authoritative actions all threaten traditional political values in the American federal system of governance. Formal public hearings and public comment on environmental impact statements constitute an inadequate approach to effective popular participation. As a result, the legitimacy of the overall decision-making process has been increasingly called into question.

Energy facility siting plans and strategies clearly are required at national, state, and regional levels. Energy, environmental, coastal zone, and economic development agencies all must be involved. These plans and studies alone are not enough, however. Authority must exist to allow resistance to siting by smaller levels of government to be overriden in the interest of the broader state or national polity. Yet exercise of this authority must be balanced and constrained; it cannot justify exclusion from the decision-making process of the public and its legally constituted units of government at local and state levels. An external override of a formal local decision, when required, is far different from a total shift of authority to a centralized agency, whatever provisions are made for public hearings. The political burden of proof regarding the necessity for a major new energy facility in a specific locale—where it is not wanted—must rest with the agency desiring to exercise such positive authority.

Local authority over energy facility siting decisions increasingly is being constrained by external interventions based on federal and state legislation. Tensions over the balance of authority and over effective public participation threaten the legitimacy of the facility siting process.

Most of the oil refineries planned but not constructed on the East Coast in the last decade were blocked by citizen groups or local governments. Local communities were often the last to know about these siting plans and were informed only when their formal action was required. This occurred only "after substantial corporate commitment had been made to the location in prior consultation with state and federal officials."[4] This was a particularly virulent issue in Durham, New Hampshire, when local citizens learned of secret plans to build an oil refinery in their town.

In recognition of this lack of early involvement by the local unit of government and its citizens, who are most directly affected by an energy facility, several states in New England, including New Hampshire, now have laws calling for local referenda prior to siting of oil refineries.[5] Louisiana law mandates local permit approval (when appropriate) prior to state and federal authorization. In the New Jersey case study, citizens forced their involvement in the energy facility decision process via public hearings and by various other means. This was, however, primarily at the end of the process to get around unresponsive governmental mechanisms, and it did not include early citizen involvement. The citizens' official role in public hearings, sometimes with inadequate notice, occurred late in the planning process. Citizens in Hudson County were ultimately effective in dealing with the local political process, as mayors, city council members, and other local authority figures eventually responded to political pressures. Proposed changes to the siting process designed to centralize authority in state administrative agencies or at the federal level would remove this critical basis for citizen participation.

Most federal programs do not appear to offer sufficient basis for local governments and citizens to participate in planning, management, and decision making. Although "208" formally calls for such participation, results have been less than adequate. Problems are even more evident in various air quality programs (although recent institutional changes are encouraging in this regard). State decisions on energy facility siting, coastal zone management, and exercise of riparian lands authority formally rely on public hearings for public and municipal participation, often with desultory results. Many of the proposals for "one-stop shopping" on energy facility siting decisions need close scrutiny from this perspective.

Local permit approval should be considered first, or at least simultaneously with state and federal agency approval, in order to ascertain local sentiment and preclude lengthy state and federal procedures that may be unnecessary.

Results of the permitting process vary greatly between local governments, on the one hand, and federal regulatory requirements, on the other. In general, acquisition of local siting approval has been the most difficult hurdle. Local governments tend to act fairly rapidly on permit requests (usually within a year), but they may decide to reject the facility. In contrast, the federal review process has a much greater risk of delay (the federal permitting process for refineries typically has lasted from five to eight years), but the risk of outright rejection of a federal permit is significantly less than the risks associated with local siting approval. To the degree that delay rather than uncertainty is the primary cause of additional costs for energy facility investors, therefore, special attention needs to be paid to reform of the federal review process.

Approval of federal permits frequently has been received because environmental laws and regulations stipulate certain emission levels or pollution control technologies, which the proposed refineries have been able to meet, albeit sometimes at a high cost. The major federal hurdle has been the U.S. Army Corps of Engineers dredge and fill permit. Rather than having set standards to meet, issuance of this permit depends on balancing the public and private need for the facility against a host of environmental considerations. The subjective assessment of national energy needs versus environmental concerns required of this permit makes its issuance uncertain in each case. The implications of this problem for facility sponsors and for environmental quality are compounded since decision on this permit comes at the end of the federal review process. Outright federal denial of the permit is unlikely, since by that point so much money has been spent and great corporate ego and interest group pressure have been amassed in favor of the project's construction; further delay often ensues at this final permit stage, however.

Statewide facility siting plans are essential to achieving an effective balance of societal objectives along the urban waterfront and to ensure implementation of optimal siting strategies within that state. These plans should encompass all types of energy (including petrochemical) facilities. In larger states such as California or Texas, a statewide plan may be sufficient; in similar states like New Jersey or Rhode Island, state formulations must be supplemented by explicit interstate planning. DOE and the Office of Coastal Zone Management (OCZM) in the U.S. Department of Commerce should implement special programs to encourage states to develop comprehensive siting plans, with emphasis on the urban coast. Federal funding of such a planning effort appears warranted.

These plans need to meld together statewide objectives for energy development, environmental protection, and urban revitalization within the multitude of regulatory constraints on urban coastal siting. Existing planning efforts in water and air quality, coastal zone management, urban redevelopment, and local zoning and land use regulation all most be taken in account. Use of renewable energy resources and alternate energy technologies deserve special attention for their statewide siting implications.

Plans, once developed, should be made available to the public and various affected agencies of government for their early review and open comment. Although overall site planning should consider all types of energy facilities, specific siting policies should be sensitive to the vital differences between them. Each major type of energy facility has its own intrinsic siting parameters that must be taken into account.

Regional planning for new energy facilities is essential to incorporate environmental suitability and "fair share" considerations into the decision-making process. In some areas, county governments may be the best vehicle for such supramunicipal planning; in others, alternative institutional structures will have to be devised (both intrastate and interstate).

Preferable locations often can be determined only on a regional basis; certainly implementation of the energy cluster concept will require a regional perspective. Nine of eleven cities surveyed on the question of regional land use authority were open-minded or in favor of such a mechanism (see Chapter 3). It is notable that in Jersey City, the largest municipality in Hudson County and the scene of three of the five energy controversies, antipathy toward regionalism was expressed. This reflects the powerful role such a large city already plays in regional affairs and the fear of losing veto power over unwanted development represented in the thwarted energy proposals.

The record of existing regional agencies, however, is spotty. Some, such as the Tri-State Regional Planning Commission covering metropolitan New York, New Jersey, and Connecticut, organized primarily for planning of highway construction, are too narrow in scope. Others, like the Delaware Valley Regional Planning Commission, are so broad that concentration on a specialized aspect of areawide planning is difficult. In addition, most existing regional planning agencies lack effective authority to implement their plans. Their "carrots" and "sticks" rest on their comment ability in the A-95 federal review process for funding local projects such as highway construction. As a result of Tri-State's designation of Hoboken, on the Hudson River waterfront, as a "Primary Urban Economic Cluster,"[6] a category that in effect sanctions almost any type of development, the city has been the target of one heavy industrial proposal after another. Two of the energy proposals rejected in Hoboken because of citizen opposition (a deepwater fuel storage terminal and a desulfurization and storage terminal) resulted in part from this regional zoning designation. This plan lacked sensitivity to waterfront revitalization aspirations expressed by citizens and to the identification by another regional planning entity, the Regional Plan Association based in New York (as is Tri-State), of Hoboken as a "special place."[7]

Proposals for an appropriately scaled and focused regional agency prompted New Jersey Governor Brendan Byrne in early 1979 to create the Hudson River Waterfront Study, Planning, and Development Commission, made up of state and municipal officials and other citizens. This is an example of a regional body specifically dedicated to planning for the urban waterfront. Given the history of siting proposals in this area, decisions on energy facility siting will be near the top of its agenda.

New Jersey's Hackensack Meadowlands Development Commission (HMDC) provides one example of an ongoing focused regional institution. This state agency, a part of the New Jersey Department of Community Affairs, incorporates part or all of 14 municipalities and has authority to make land use decisions, including siting of energy (and resource recovery) facilities. Regional models from "208" areawide water management, air quality maintenance, "701" community development and solid waste planning may also be appropriate.

The "fair share" concept deserves special attention from the perspective of regional planning. Certain municipalities, regions, and even entire states may already have their fair share of energy facilities. Environmental quality constraints and pressures to devise alternative land use patterns mitigate against further reliance on these areas for storage, processing, or generation of energy in its various forms. Whatever the intrinsic merits of this conceptual argument, on which reasonable people can—and do—differ, two implications are clear. First, citizens in an area of intensive energy (or industrial) development see the concept of fair share as a strong motivating force, especially when alternative patterns of development have been initiated. Second, adopting a regional rather than a local perspective provides a better basis for an objective evaluation of "how much is enough."

Regional approaches to siting, while justified on their own, typically encounter resistance from local governments jealous of their fiscal and land use prerogatives. Home rule is an historical tradition in many states (though not all); therefore, the allocation of tax accruals from a new ratable provides the financial justification for strenuous intermunicipal competition.

Systems of tax sharing across municipal boundaries in an urban coastal region may be essential to achieving a balanced strategy of energy facility siting, coastal zone management, and urban development. DOE and OCZM could play a role in devising model statutes for regional sharing of the tax benefits of new energy facilities (sharing of coastal energy impact funds deserves special attention).

Pursuit of tax ratables by each municipality, competing with all the others, contributes to fragmentation of planning, leaves siting initiatives primarily in the hands of the private energy companies (which can play off one municipal competitor against another), and reinforces the tendency to emphasize a proposed facility's fiscal benefits rather than its environmental or social costs to the individual community, let alone to the broader region. Revenue sharing may be essential to foster regional planning since there is little incentive for localities to surrender their planning and development prerogatives without a stake in new growth in the region. HMDC gives an example of procedures for tax sharing from new ratables; Minnesota's Twin Cities Regional Council is another example.

THE RELATIONSHIP OF FEDERAL REGULATORY AND PLANNING EFFORTS TO URBAN COASTAL REGIONS

Specific federal planning programs should address urban coastal siting issues as a unique challenge within the larger urban revitalization and land use framework. In the absence of coherent federal action, planning for better development of these vital areas will remain sporadic and uncoordinated. OCZM should assume primary responsibility for this effort, effecting coordination as required with DOE, EPA, HUD, Departments of the Interior, Commerce, Transportation, and other relevant federal agencies.

To date, urban coastal issues have not received much attention from the federal government. In fact, this issue is conspicuously absent in many plans, programs, and environmental impact statements. Urban areas are either ignored, or it is assumed that energy facilities could easily be accommodated there. For example, the original environmental impact statement for offshore oil and gas leasing off the mid-Atlantic coast paid little note to urban issues. Both the opportunities and potential problems for coastal cities in New Jersey, Delaware, New York, and Rhode Island were neglected, with most attention paid to potential impacts on rural areas. New Jersey's Coastal Area Facility Review Act (CAFRA), as another example, specifically excludes the state's urban coastal areas. Only the rural coastline is incorporated under this regulatory and planning mechanism.

Beginning in 1978, OCZM began to show greater interest in

urban waterfront issues. This was a good beginning; but much more remains to be accomplished in the way of a federal approach to urban coastal zone management.

Innovative federal incentive grants from HUD or the Commerce Department's Economic Development Administration could stimulate further urban waterfront redevelopment. Such grant programs should be an integral component of a larger national urban development policy.

The traditional role of the federal government in urban coastal communities has been to support physical improvements in port and harbor operations. More than 50 federal agencies have ownership and regulatory interests in some aspect of the coastal zone. Very few federal programs, however, are focused directly on developing urban waterfronts, despite the evident fact that these areas can be the nucleus of citywide urban renewal efforts because of available land in these unique and now underused areas.

Beyond the overall effort to improve planning for the urban coastal zone, OCZM should provide modest amounts of federal financial assistance for states that wish to devise special waterfront revitalization plans. Such development planning activities should be closely coordinated with federal and state energy facility siting programs so that the two efforts move in tandem rather than contradicting one another.

As noted above, most of these efforts to date have witnessed very little federal involvement. Expansion of federal interest and financial support could accelerate ongoing redevelopment efforts in several cities and also provide the impetus for their initiation elsewhere.

In addition to special comprehensive plans for the urban coastal zone as a new component of the OCZM effort, federal incentives are warranted to encourage the states to devise energy facility siting plans. It seems appropriate for DOE to take the lead responsibility in this regard, acting in conjunction with OCZM, EPA, and other interested federal agencies.

The importance of such statewide siting plans has been highlighted as several points in this book. A number of states have carried out such planning on their own without extensive federal support. DOE assistance might induce others to do so.

Total federal override (preemption) on energy facility siting will not be tolerable politically in our decentralized federal system, even in an era of continuing energy crises.

Legal authority for federal preemption already exists for natural gas facilities and nuclear power plants. The Federal Energy

Regulatory Commission (FERC) and the Nuclear Regulatory Commission (NRC) have the statutory power to override state and local wishes where they determine that the national interest so requires. Though this federal preemptive power has not yet been applied explicitly to a nuclear power plant siting controversy, it was upheld for radiation standards in the case of *Northern States Power Co. v. Minnesota.* For natural gas siting, the judicial ruling in the case of *Transcontinental Pipeline Co.* v. *Hackensack Meadowlands Development Commission* was a definitive statement of federal preemptive siting authority.[8]

These federal authorities must be used with caution, however. Case study research and other evidence indicate that the American political system has a low tolerance for exercise of such positive siting authority. From the Gulf Coast to New Jersey, and from Maine to California, citizens and local governments argue for their right to determine their own energy destiny; or at least to have a major role in doing so. Ceding all energy siting powers to a preemptive federal establishment would run directly counter to this philosophy.

Availability of a deep channel obviously is vital to successful operation of many major facilities. Dredging of such channels normally is the responsibility of the U.S. Army Corps of Engineers. Because of the difficulty and duration involved in getting the corps to dredge in other areas, corporate site planners often opt to locate their new facilities in areas where channels already exist, despite other deterimental features of the site. Realignment of corps' priorities to accord more closely with federal and state energy siting strategies, while not an easy task, could contribute to a better overall siting pattern.

It would make sense to balance the additional costs of dredging in new areas (or of siting the facility at an offshore location) against the detrimental effects of locating the facility along the urban waterfront, where channel depth may already be adequate. Corporate decision makers cannot be expected to take such externalities into account in their site selection processes; instead, state and national interests must be balanced by the appropriate level of government.

EPA's "208" areawide water quality planning program could contribute far more than it has to date to improved planning for energy facility siting in urban coastal areas.

One of the most innovative features of the concept is the requirement that all EPA permits and grants be consistent with a "208" plan, once it is formally approved by the EPA administrator. Since permits are required for all major energy facilities under the National Pollutant Discharge Elimination System (NPDES) and under state implementation plans (SIPs) for air quality, "208" planning could effectively designate areas where energy facilities are to be either prohibited or encouraged. And in distinction to most plans, such designations would be authoritatively binding.

IN CONCLUSION

It is inconceivable that the United States does not have enough geographic space to accommodate necessary new energy facilities without effacing development initiatives on the urban waterfront and also without endangering fragile rural coastlines. Yet while we have the room, do we have the political will and the institutional flexibility necessary to accomplish an effective balance among these potentially contradictory values? This remains to be seen. Surely the traditional patterns of decision making, with siting initiatives monopolized by the energy companies and externalities displaced onto others in pursuit of narrowly defined least-cost solutions, leave much to be desired. Alternative siting strategies are essential for the urban coast and beyond.

As with any decisions on controversial issues, adoption of alternative energy facility siting strategies would imply discrete costs and benefits for various key interest groups, as well as for society as a whole. Who would be the principal winners and losers associated with the approach suggested here?

The energy companies, and especially the nonutility oil firms, would feel constrained by these policies, their siting options limited (new facilities shifted away from the urban waterfront, for example), their costs (to use alternate sites) possibly higher, and their decision makers responsive to new governmental siting initiatives. The companies would see themselves losing power and autonomy, and their verbal and political resistance could be enormous. On the other hand, the companies could gain if government agencies adopted the recommended permit process changes. Reduction or elimination of major processing delays and introduction of procedures to limit mid-construction interventions could improve the profitability of their energy investments.

The interests of environmental and citizen groups would, in general, be favored by adoption of these siting policies and procedures. Their pursuit of urban waterfront redevelopment goals would be enhanced, without sacrificing preservation of the rural shore. However, procedures to limit opportunities for midconstruction interventions might be seen as antithetical, given the extent to which these groups have relied in the past on litigation and judicial injunction. Groups with a particular concern for the offshore environment, like the American Littoral Society and the Cousteau Society, might be upset at the prospect of using deepwater ports to service inland facilities.

Organized labor, especially in the construction trades, would seem to be a beneficiary of the permit system modifications being suggested. Unions with particular access to urban coastal locations, however, might be disadvantaged by inland siting.

If sequential decision-making procedures were adopted, as proposed, local and state government agencies need not be threatened by the possibility of state and federal siting preemption. Opportunity for initial decision making by local governments should ensure that vertical shifts in authority are not overwhelming, even though final external override power would be introduced.

Society as a whole should be a clear net beneficiary of these alternate siting strategies, for they have been designed to effect a balance among various social objectives.

Conflicting values in our society are articulated by different institutions and individuals. This is natural. Some argue passionately for preservation of remote, pristine rural areas; other advance, with equal fervor, the need to redevelop urban centers. Beaches and dunes along with shore require protection from the ravages of uncontrolled land development; but so do inland wetlands and forests. Economic improvement is essential, especially in an era of apparently unstoppable inflation. Politicians and government policymakers clamor incessantly for investments and jobs in depressed urban areas. However, improved environmental quality may well be a prerequisite to economic revitalization of such communities. If environmental degradation continues to characterize urban areas, desired redevelopment may well not emerge. Thus these goals, so often seen as contradictory, are instead inherently interwined. Neither can be accomplished by sacrificing the other.

Alternative energy facility siting approaches can contribute to such urban redevelopment. Indeed, a clear strategy toward siting of such high-impact activities is imperative. This strategy should designate appropriate land uses for urban and rural areas and also for coastal and inland regions. Clear roles need to be defined for local, state, and federal governments. Public participation is essential to ensuring the continuing legitimacy of the decision-making system. The fundamental locus of initiative for planning new sites needs to be shifted from the energy companies to government at various levels so that the wide range of relevant externalities can be taken into account.

Obviously this discussion of energy facility siting has come rather far afield. This inescapable digression into broader conceptual and institutional issues was the result of the complexity and importance of the many concerns affected by decisions to site such facilities. Three critical national priorities need to be made compatible rather than contradictory in a siting strategy:

Greater energy self-sufficiency
Urban revitalization
Protection of fragile rural coastlines

An energy facility siting strategy must meld all three of these social goals together. Yet this alone is not enough, for what is really required is the creation of a system of governance adequate to meet the challenges of the last decades of the twentieth century. Focus on a single problem like energy facility siting simply points toward this more cosmic political imperative.

NOTES

1. Perth Amboy, in the New York-New Jersey Port Authority district, was suggested as a possible location for an OCS service base in a study by Rutgers University. See *Onshore Support Bases for OCS Oil and Gas Development: Implications for New Jersey* (New Brunswick, N.J.: Rutgers University, Center for Coastal and Marine Studies, September 1977), p. 183.
2. See Peter Meier; David Morell; and Philip Palmedo, "Political Implications of Clustered Nuclear Siting," *Energy Systems and Policy*, 3, no. 1 (Spring 1979), pp. 17-36.
3. See David Morell and Grace Singer, *State Legislatures and Energy Policy in the Northeast; Energy Facility Siting and Legislative Action* (Upton, N.Y.: Brookhaven National Laboratory, National Center for Analysis of Energy Systems, BNL 50679, June 1977), pp. 79-108.
4. Robert Warren, *A Local Perspective in National Energy Policy*, paper prepared for a conference, "The Urban Coast and Energy Alternatives," Princeton University, May 18-19, 1978, p. 2.
5. See Morell and Singer, op. cit., passim.
6. See Helen Manogue, *Waterfront Redevelopment Project—Report 1: Existing Conditions* (Hoboken: Stevens Institute of Technology, Center for Municipal Studies and Services, January 1976).
7. Regional Plan Association, *The Lower Hudson*, 1966, p. 69.
8. See Hannah Shostack, *Federal Preemption and Energy Facility Siting: The Power of State Riparian Statutes* (Princeton: Princeton University, Center for Energy and Environmental Studies, August 1979).

Appendix

Selected Energy Facilities:
Land Requirements,
Environmental Impacts, and
Direct Employment

Facility Type	Land Requirements	Coastal Dependent	Air Pollutants	Waste Water Pollutants	Direct Employment	Jobs per Acre (approximate range)
OCS Related:						
Temporary service bases	5-10 acres	Yes	Hydrocarbons, carbon monoxide, nitrogen oxides	Hydrocarbons and heavy metals	45 jobs per rig; 75% local	4.50-9.00 per rig
Permanent service bases	25-75 acres	Yes	Hydrocarbons, carbon monoxide, nitrogen oxides	Hydrocarbons and heavy metals	50-60 jobs per platform; 50-80% local	0.67-2.40 per platform
Repair and maintenance yards	Varies	No	Not specified—but related to transportation and machinery operation	Not specified	Varies—but labor-intensive	Varies—but labor-intensive
Steel platform fabrication yards	200-1,000 acres	Yes	Sand and metal dust, hydrocarbons, carbon monoxide, etc., from vehicles	Heavy metals, particulates, chemicals	250-550 jobs per steel platform; 80% local	0.25-4.75 per platform
Concrete platform fabrication yards	50 acres per platform	Yes	Sand, cement, and metal dust; hydrocarbons, carbon monoxide, etc., from vehicles	Particulates, heavy metals, chemicals	350-450 average; 600-1,200 peak; 85-90% local	7.00-9.00 (average) per platform
Steel platform installation service bases	5 acres approximately	Yes	Hydrocarbons, carbon monoxide, nitrogen oxides	Hydrocarbons and heavy metals	Onshore: 25 jobs per installation spread; 50% local. Offshore: 100 jobs per installation spread; 25% local	5.00 onshore; 20.00 offshore per installation spread

Facility	Acreage		Air Emissions	Water Effluents	Employment	Ratio
Pipelines and landfalls	50-100 foot right-of-way; 40 acres for pumping station, if required; 60 acres for terminal, if required	Yes	Minimal; primarily hydrocarbons, nitrogen oxides, and sulfur oxides	Chronic low-level leakages of petroleum	Onshore: 0-20 jobs; 15 local to operate terminal or pumping station Offshore: 250-300 jobs per lay barge spread	Varies
Pipeline installation service bases	5 acres approximately	Yes	Similar to temporary service bases		Approximately 25 onshore jobs; 50% local	5.00
Pipe coating yards	100-150 acres	Yes	Carbon monoxide, sulfur oxides, nitrogen oxides, hydrocarbons, particulates	Thermal effluents, chemicals, alkaline substances, metal fragments, etc.	100-200 jobs during season (March-September); 80% local	0.67-2.00
Marine terminals (storage only—no processing)	30 acres	Yes	Hydrocarbons, exhaust emissions	Biological Oxygen Demand, Chemical Oxygen Demand, suspended solids, oil and grease, chronic small spills with potential for large spills	Construction: 560 jobs; 20% local; Operating: 10-90 jobs; 70% local	18.67 construction; 0.33-3.00 operating
Petrochemical Processing:						
Partial processing facilities	15 acres per 100,000 barrels processed	No	Hydrocarbons, hydrogen sulfide, sulfur oxides, nitrogen oxides	Suspended solids, oil and grease, heavy metals, phenols, halogens, chromium	Construction: 150 jobs Operating: 10 jobs	10.00 construction; 0.67 operating

313

Facility Type	Land Requirements	Coastal Dependent	Air Pollutants	Waste Water Pollutants	Direct Employment	Jobs per Acre (approximate range)
Gas-processing and treatment plants	50–75 acres per 400 to 700 million cubic feet per day	No	Hydrogen sulfide, sulfur oxides, hydrocarbons, particulates, carbon monoxide, nitrogen oxides	Dissolved hydrocarbons, sulfuric acid, chronium, zinc, phosphates, bases, sulfite	Construction: 500 jobs; Operating: 45–55 jobs; 60% local	6.67–10.00 construction; 0.60–1.10 operating
Refineries	1,000–1,500 acres (250,000 barrels per day)	No	Particulates, nitrogen oxides, sulfur oxides, carbon monoxide, hydrocarbons	Hydrocarbons, alkaline substances, particulates, metal fragments	Construction: 2,000 jobs; 70% local Operating: 425 jobs; 80% local	1.3–2.00 construction; 0.28–0.43 operating
Petrochemical complexes	200–350 acres minimum (some larger than 2,000 acres)	No	Particulates, hydrocarbons, carbon monoxide, nitrogen oxides, sulfur oxides	Organic compounds, phenols, heavy metals, chromate, zinc, chlorine, ammonia, sulfides	Construction: 2,000 jobs per year for four years Operating: 420 jobs	5.71–10.00 construction; 1.20–2.10 operating
Power Plants:						
Fossil fuel	145 to 2,500 acres for a 1,000-MWe coal-fired plant depending on storage, waste, etc.	*a*	Sulfur dioxide, nitrogen oxide, particulates; low-level radioactive emissions, especially from older coal-fired plants	Thermal pollution, chemical wastes	Actual examples: Construction: 1,000 peak employment for a 816-MWe plant Operation: 159 jobs for an 1162-MWe plant	0.40–6.90 construction; 0.06–1.10 operating

| Nuclear | 1,500 to 3,000 acres average (in addition, a buffer zone of several miles may be required) | b | Regular low-level radioactive emissions (with possibility of large radioactive emissions in event of an accident) | Discharge of radionuclides in liquid effluents; thermal pollution, chemical wastes | Actual examples: Construction: 1,338 peak employment for a 855-MWe plant Operation: 80 jobs for an 855-MWe plant (Nuclear plants require fewer employees of higher skill; they are less likely to draw from the local labor pool) | 0.45–0.89 construction; 0.03–0.05 operating |

[a] For cooling, the plant must be near a body of water, including ponds or canals.

[b] Nuclear plants require twice as much cooling water as do fossil fuel plants.

Sources: (For OCS and Petrochemical facilities): The Conservation Foundation, *Source Book: Onshore Impacts of Outer Continental Shelf Oil and Gas Development* (Washington, D.C.: Conservation Foundation, May 1977).

New England River Basins Commission (NERBC), *Factbook: Onshore Facilities Related to Offshore Oil and Gas Development* (Boston: November 1976).

New England River Basins Commission (NERBC), *Estimates for New England* (Boston: November 1976).

Hudson County Office of Planning, *Hudson County Offshore Oil and Coastal Energy Facilities Study* (Jersey City, N.J.: December 1977).

(For Power Plants): Berkshire County Regional Planning Commission, *Evaluation of Power Facilities* (Pittsfield, Mass.: April 1974).

Great Lakes Basin Commission, *Energy Facility Siting in the Great Lakes Coastal Zone: Analysis and Policy Options*, January 14, 1977.

U.S. Department of Commerce (NOAA), *Coastal Facility Guidelines* (Washington, D.C.: US Govt Printing Office; August 1976).

The Mitre Corporation, *Environmental Data for Energy Technology Policy Analysis* (McLean, Va.: 1978).

Bibliography

Advisory Council on Intergovernmental Relations. *Trends in Metropolitan America*. Washington, D.C.: U.S. Government Printing Office, February 1977.

Ahern, William R. *Oil and the Outer Coastal Shelf: The Georges Bank Case*. Cambridge, Mass: Ballinger Publishing Co., 1973.

American Society of Planning Officials, ASPO Training Project. Devon M. Schneider, ed. *Onshore Impacts of Outer-continental Shelf Oil and Gas Development*, vols. 1 and 2. Chicago, Ill.: American Society of Planning Officials, May 1977.

Atlantic County, N.J. *Offshore Oil and Atlantic County*. Atlantic County, N.J., January 1978.

Backstrom, Timothy D., and Michael Baram. *Artificial Islands for Cluster Siting of Offshore Energy Facilities: An Assessment of the Legal and Regulatory Framework*. Upton, N.Y.: Brookhaven National Laboratory, BNL 50566, June 1976.

Baram, Michael. *Environmental Law and the Siting of Facilities: Issues in Land Use and Coastal Zone Management*. Cambridge, Mass.: Ballinger Publishing Co., 1976.

Berger, Louis, and Associates et al. *Section 303(c) Water Quality Management Basin Plan—Northeast New Jersey Urban Area*, prepared for New Jersey Department of Environmental Protection. East Orange, N.J.: Louis Berger and Associates, December 1976.

Bergsman, Joel, and H.L. Weiner, eds. *Urban Problems and Public Policy Choices*. New York: Praeger Publishing Co., 1975.

Berkshire County Regional Planning Commission. *Evaluation of Power Facilities: A Reviewer's Handbook*. Pittsfield, Mass., April 1974.

Bolan, Richard S., et al. *Urban Planning and Politics*. Lexington, Mass.: Lexington Books, 1975.

Booz, Allen, and Hamilton, Inc. *Design of a Tracking System for Federal Regulatory Energy Facility Siting Actions*, vol. 1. Washington, D.C.: December 1975.

Brookhaven National Laboratory, Energy Policy Analysis Group. *Preliminary Assessment of a Hypothetical Nuclear Energy Center in New Jersey*. Upton, N.Y.: Brookhaven National Laboratory, BNL 50465, November 1975.

Brown, Steven R., and James G. Coke. *Public Opinion on Land Use Regulation*, Urban and Regional Development Series No. 1. Columbus, Ohio: Academy for Contemporary Problems, January 1977.

Bruhne, Cazzola, and Wiatr, eds. *Local Politics, Development and Participation*. Pittsburgh: University of Pittsburgh, 1974.

Burchell, Robert, and David Listokin. *Future Land Use: Energy, Environmental and Legal Constraints*. New Brunswick, N.J.: Rutgers University Press, 1975.

Burlington County Planning Board et al. *Burlington County Outer-Continental Shelf and Energy Facility Planning Program*, final report. Mount Holly, N.J.: January 1978.

California Office of Planning and Research. *Urban Development Strategy for California—Review Draft*. Sacramento, May 1977.

Camp, Coleen. *The Supply and Demand for Small Boats and Associated Services in Northeastern New Jersey*. Hoboken, N.J.: Stevens Institute of Technology, Center for Municipal Studies and Services, December 1977.

Center for the Environment and Man, Inc. *Connecticut River Basin: A Framework for Environmental Impact Evaluation*, prepared for the Federal Power Commission. Hartford, Conn.: Center for the Environment and Man, Inc. December 1975.

Cirillo, Richard R., et al. *An Evaluation of Regional Trends in Power Plant Siting and Energy Transport*, draft. Argonne National Laboratory, December 1976.

Clark, John, and William Brownell. *Electric Power Plants in the Coastal Zone: Environmental Issues*, special publication no. 7. Highlands, N.J.: American Littoral Society, October 1973.

Commoner, Barry. "A Reporter-at-Large—Energy." *The New Yorker Magazine*, February 2, 9, and 16, 1976.

Continental Oil Company. *Offshore Oil Development on the Georges Bank*, proceedings of a symposium held July 1, 1976, at Phillipsburg, Maine. Stamford, Conn.: Continental Oil Company, 1976.

Cowey, Ann Breen. "The Urban Coast from a National Perspective." *Coastal Zone Management Journal* 6, no. 2-3 (1979): 135-165.

———. "The Urban Coastal Zone: Its Definition and a Suggested Role for the Office of Coastal Zone Management." Master's thesis, School of Government and Business Administration, George Washington University, Washington, D.C., 1976.

_____ . "Shorefront Access and Island Preservation Study." *Urban Waterfronts.* Washington, D.C.: National Oceanic and Atmospheric Administration, the Office of Coastal Zone Management, November 1978.

Crenson, Matthew A. *The Un-politics of Air Pollution: A Study of Non-decision-making in the Cities.* Baltimore: Johns Hopkins University Press, 1971.

Cumberland County Planning Board. *Cumberland County Onshore Development Alternatives.* Bridgeton, N.J., January 1978.

Davis, David Howard. *Energy Politics.* New York: St. Martins Press, 1974.

Dawson, Grace. *No Little Plans.* Washington, D.C.: The Urban Institute, 1977.

Delaware River Basin Commission. *Major Electric Generating Projects 1975-1989.* Trenton, N.J., June 1975.

Delaware, University of, College of Marine Studies. *A Comprehensive Marine Transportation System for the Delaware Valley Region,* report prepared under the Delaware Sea Grant Program. Newark, Del.: College of Marine Studies, May 1977.

_____ . *An Evaluation of Multi-Purpose Offshore Industrial-Port Islands,* report prepared under the Delaware Sea Grant Program. Newark, Del.: College of Marine Studies, May 1975.

_____ . *Offshore Oil and Coastal Recreation: Cohabitation or Conflict?* report prepared under the Delaware Sea Grant Program. Newark, Del.: College of Marine Studies, June 1976.

Delaware Valley Regional Planning Commission. *Alternative Future for the Delaware Valley—Year 2000,* report no. 4. Philadelphia: September 1976.

Drennan, Matthew P., et al. *Utilization of Public Resources: New York City's Waterfront.* New York, April 1976.

Duga, Jules, et al. *Energy: The Policy Planning Framework in State Governments,* vol. 1, *Summary Report.* Columbus, Ohio: Columbus Laboratories, September 1975.

Engler, Robert. "The Oil Industry, the Department of the Interior and Public Policy for Energy," unpublished paper prepared for the Nassau-Suffolk Regional Planning Board, n.d.

Environmental Policy Institute. *The Need for Energy Facility Sites in the United States—1985 through 2000,* report prepared for the Council on Environmental Quality. Springfield, Va.: National Technical Information Service, June 1975.

Environmentalists for Full Employment. *Jobs and Energy.* Washington, D.C., Spring 1977.

Falk, Nicholas. "Conservation and Redevelopment Policy for British Urban Dock Areas." *Coastal Zone Management Journal* 6, no. 2-3 (1979): 187-213.

Federal Energy Administration. *Inventory of Power Plants in the United States.* Washington, D.C.: Federal Energy Administration, June 1977.

Federal Interagency Council on Citizen Participation. *At Square One,* proceedings of the conference, Citizen Participation in Government Decision-making, Washington, D.C., 1976. Washington, D.C.: Federal Interagency Council on Citizen Participation, March 1977.

Federal Power Commission, Office of Energy Systems. *Connecticut River Basin: Office of Energy Systems Report.* Washington, D.C.: Federal Power Commission, December 1976.

Ferrar, Terry A., and Frank Clemente. *Energy Centers—A Report on Pennsylvania's Experience,* working paper 34. University Park, Pa.: Center for the Study of Environmental Policy, Pennsylvania State University, n.d.

Field, Ralph M., and Associates, et al. *Northeast New Jersey Water Quality Management Study,* report for the New Jersey Department of Environmental Protection. Westport, Conn., October 1976.

Finkler, Earl, et al. *Urban Nongrowth: City Planning for People.* New York: Praeger Publishing Co., 1976.

Ford Foundation, Energy Policy Project. David S. Freeman, ed. *A Time to Choose: America's Energy Future. Final Report.* Cambridge, Mass.: Ballinger Publishing Co., 1974.

_____. *Exploring Energy Choices: A Preliminary Report.* Washington, D.C.: Ford Foundation, 1974.

Freeman, David S. *Energy: The New Era.* New York: Walker, 1974.

Friendly, Phillip H. *National Policy Responses to Urban Growth.* Lexington, Mass.: Lexington Books, 1974.

Garvey, Gerald S. *Energy, Ecology, Economy.* New York: Norton, 1972.

Gillman, Katherine, Council on Environmental Quality. *Oil and Gas in Coastal Lands and Waters.* Washington, D.C.: U.S. Government Printing Office, 1977.

Goldshore, Lewis. "A Flood of Environmental Legislation: An Analysis of the New Jersey Experience, *1970-1975.*" *Seton Hall Legislative Journal* 1, no. 2 (Summer 1976): 1-19.

Great Lakes Basin Commission. *Energy Facility Siting in the Great Lakes Coastal Zone: Analysis and Policy Options—Final Report for the National Oceanic and Atmospheric Administration.* Washington, D.C.: National Oceanic and Atmospheric Administration, January 1977.

Harrison, Peter. "The Land Water Interface in an Urban Region: A Spatial and Temporal Analysis of the Nature and Significances of Conflicts Between Coastal Uses." Ph.D. dissertation, Washington University, St. Louis, 1973.

Healy, Robert G. *Land Use and the States.* Baltimore: Johns Hopkins University Press, 1976.

_____, ed., et al. *Protecting the Golden Shore: Lessons from the California Coastal Commissions.* Washington, D.C.: Conservation Foundation, 1978.

Hill, Gladwin. *Madman in a Lifeboat: Issues of the Environmental Crisis.* New York: John Day Co., 1973.

Hirst, Eric. *Energy Implications of Several Environmental Quality Strategies,* prepared for the U.S. Atomic Energy Commission. Oak Ridge, Tenn.: Oak Ridge National Laboratories, July 1973.

Hudson County (N.J.) Economic Development Committee. *Hudson County's Overall Economic Development Program.* Jersey City, N.J.: Hudson County Department of Planning and Economic Development, n.d.

_____, Office of Planning. *Hudson County Offshore Oil and Coastal Energy Facilities Study.* Jersey City, N.J.: Hudson County Office of Planning, December 1977.

_____ , Office of Planning and the Jersey City Office of Planning. *Hudson County: Annual Transportation Report—1975*. Jersey City, N.J.: Hudson County Office of Planning, the Jersey City Office of Planning, and the New Jersey Department of Transportation, 1975.

Hudson County (N.J.) Planning Board. *Hudson County Economic Base Study*. Jersey City, N.J.: Hudson County Planning Board, October 1974.

_____ . *Land Use Study and Plan—Hudson County*. Jersey City, N.J.: Hudson County Office of Planning, December 1974.

Jersey City Department of Community Development, Division of Economic Development. *Hudson County Combined Employment and Training Administration—Data*. Jersey City, N.J.: Department of Community Development, Division of Economic Development, 1976.

Jersey City Division of Planning, Mayor's Development Staff. *The City: A Time for Change*. Jersey City, N.J.: Jersey City Division of Planning, Mayor's Development Staff, 1966.

Jersey City Division of Planning. *Jersey City: Comprehensive Waterfront Plan— Technical Reports*. Jersey City, N.J.: Jersey City Division of Planning, November 1971, January 1972, April 1972.

Kalter, Robert J., and Wallace E. Tyner. *Atlantic Outer Continental Shelf Energy Resources: Economic Implications for Long Island*. Ithaca, N.Y.: Department of Agricultural Economics, Cornell University, April 1975.

Kanouse, Randele, and Jens Sorensen. *Balancing Energy Production and Environmental Protection: State Coastal Management Programs and the Federal Department of Energy*. Berkeley: University of California, Summer 1978.

Kneese, Allen V. *Pollution, Prices and Public Policy*. Washington, D.C.: Brookings Institution, 1975.

Koppelman, Lee. *Coastal Zone Management: Long Island*. New York: Praeger Publishing Co., 1974.

Landsberg, Hans H., et al. *Energy and the Social Sciences: An Examination of Research Needs*. Washington, D.C.: Resources for the Future, 1974.

League of Women Voters Education Fund. *Coastal Area Project: Final Report and Evaluation*. Hartford, Conn.: League of Women Voters Education Fund, December 1976.

_____ . *Coastal Zone Management Program*, pamphlet no. 572. Washington, D.C.: League of Women Voters Education Fund, 1976.

_____ . *Energy and Our Coasts: The 1976 CZM Amendments*, pamphlet. Washington, D.C.: League of Women Voters Education Fund, 1976.

_____ . *The Hudson River Basin*. Washington, D.C.: League of Women Voters Education Fund, February 1969.

_____ . *Supercity/Hometown, U.S.A*. New York: Praeger Publishing Co., 1974.

Lee, John. *Energy Supply and Demand in the Northeastern United States*. Upton, N.Y.: Brookhaven National Laboratory, BNL 20427, September 1975.

Linky, Edward J. *Cultural Resources*, staff working paper. Trenton: Office of Coastal Management, N.J. Department of Environmental Protection, November 1976.

Lovins, Amory. *World Energy Strategies: Facts, Issues and Options*. Cambridge, Mass.: Ballinger Publishing Co., 1975.

Maine, Governor's Task Force. *Energy, Heavy Industry, and the Maine Coast.* Washington, D.C.: Resources for the Future, Inc., September 1972.

Maine State Planning Office. *Maine's Coastal Program,* a draft 306 application. Augusta: Maine State Planning Office, October 1977.

Mann, Roy, and Associates. *Aesthetic Resources of the Coastal Zone.* Cambridge, Mass.: Roy Mann and Associates, July 1975.

Manogue, Helen. *Waterfront Redevelopment Project: Reports 1 and 2.* Hoboken, N.J.: Center for Municipal Studies and Services, Stevens Institute of Technology, January 1976 and March 1977.

Massachusetts Executive Office of Environmental Affairs et al. *Massachusetts Coastal Zone Management Program and Environmental Impact Statement,* revised. Boston: Office of Coastal Zone Management, Department of Commerce, March 1978.

Massachusetts Institute of Technology. *A Report on the National Interest in the Coastal Zone,* for the Office of Coastal Zone Management, Department of Commerce. Cambridge, Mass.: Office of Coastal Zone Management, Department of Commerce, n.d.

Massachusetts Office of State Planning. *City and Town Centers—A Program for Growth,* Massachusetts Growth Policy Report (newsprint). Boston: Massachusetts Office of State Planning, September 1977.

_____. *Offshore Oil Development—Implications for Massachusetts Communities.* Boston: Massachusetts Office of State Planning, November 1976.

Mejer, Peter M. *Energy Facility Location: A Regional Viewpoint.* Upton, N.Y.: Department of Applied Science, Brookhaven National Laboratory, BNL 20435, August 1975.

Middlesex County (N.J.) Planning Board. *Policies for Handling Impacts of Offshore Oil and Energy Facilities in Middlesex County.* New Brunswick, N.J.: Middlesex County Planning Board, 1978.

Mid-Hudson Pattern, Inc. *Hudson Basin Project: Final Report.* New York: Rockefeller Foundation, June 1976.

_____. *Hudson Basin Project: (1) Land Use/Human Settlement; (2) Transportation; (3) Environmental Services Systems: (4) Energy Systems: (5) Land Use/Natural Resource Management; (6) Water Resources; (7) Air Resources; (8) Biological Communities; (9) Human Health; (10) Leisure Time and Recreation, Task Group Reports of the Rockefeller Foundation.* New York: Rockefeller Foundation, June 1976.

Mitchell, James K. "Onshore Impacts of Scottish Offshore Oil: Planning Implications for the Middle Atlantic States," unpublished. New Brunswick, N.J., October 1976.

Mogulof, Melvin B. *Saving the Coast: California's Experiment in Intergovernmental Land Use Control.* Lexington, Mass.: Lexington Books, 1975.

Moore, Arthur Cotton, et al. *Bright Breathing Edges of City Life: Planning for Amenity Benefits of Urban Water Resources.* Washington, D.C.: Arthur Cotton Moore Associates, 1971.

Morell, David. "Critical Onshore Siting Decision." *Environmental Comment* (February 1978): 16-17.

_____. *Who's in Charge?—Governmental Capabilities to Make Energy Facility*

Siting Decisions in New Jersey, report 48. Prepared for the New Jersey Department of Environmental Protection and the United States Federal Energy Administration. Princeton, N.J.: Center for Environmental Studies, Princeton University, July 1977.

_____ and Grace Singer. "Energy Facility Siting in the Urban Coastal Zone: Compatible or Not?" *Coastal Zone Management Journal* 6, no. 2-3 (1979): 215-232.

_____ . *State Legislatures and Energy Policy in the Northeast: Energy Facility Siting and Legislative Action.* Upton, N.Y.: Brookhaven National Laboratory, BNL 50679, June 1977.

_____ . "The Urban Coastal Zone: Challenge of Redevelopment." *Coastal Zone '78*, vol. 1. New York: American Society of Civil Engineers, 1978, pp. 66-80.

Moss, Mitchell L. "The Lost Waterfront of New York." *Coastal Zone Management Journal* 6, no. 2-3 (1979): 167-185.

_____ . "The Management of Urban Coastal Resources." Paper presented to the Marine Technological Society, Washington, D.C., September 1976.

_____ . "The Urban Port: A Hidden Resource for the City and the Coastal Zone." *Coastal Zone Management Journal* 2, no. 3 (1976): 223-245.

Narkus-Kramer, Marc, et al. *Environmental Consequences of On-Shore Activity in Four New Jersey Coastal Counties Resulting from Offshore Development.* Springfield, Va.: National Technical Information Service, September 1975.

Nash, Hugh. *Cry Crisis: Rehearsal in Alaska*, edited by Harvey Manning. San Francisco: Friends of the Earth, 1974.

Nassau-Suffolk (N.Y.) Regional Planning Board. *Integration of Regional Land Use Planning and Coastal Zone Science.* New York: Office of Policy Development and Research, Department of Housing and Urban Development, June 1976.

National Association of Counties. *Serving the Offshore Oil Industry: Planning for Onshore Growth.* Washington, D.C.: National Association of Counties, n.d.

National Science Foundation-National Aeronautics and Space Administration, Solar Energy Panel. *Solar Energy as a National Energy Resource.* College Park: Department of Mechanical Engineering, University of Maryland, December 1972.

National Science Foundation, Division of Policy Research and Analysis. *Proceedings of Meeting of Advisory Committee on Energy Facility Siting Held on February 12-13, 1976.* Washington, D.C.: The Mitre Corporation, 1976.

National Urban Coalition. *Community Energy Workbook.* Washington, D.C.: National Urban Coalition, 1974.

Natural Resources Defense Council, Inc. "Treading the Thin Edge—Threats to the Coast." *Newsletter* 7, issue 6 (December/January 1978-79): 8, 9.

_____ . *Who's Minding the Shore?* Washington, D.C.: National Oceanographic and Atmospheric Administration, August 1976.

New Bedford (Massachusetts) Mayor's Committee on Offshore Oil. *Port of New Bedford—Offshore Oil and Gas.* New Bedford, Mass.: Mayor's Committee on Offshore Oil, 1977.

New England River Basins Commission. *Estimates for New England,* Resource and Land Investigations report. Boston: New England River Basins Commission, November 1976.

_____ . *Factbook,* Resource and Land Investigations report. Boston: New England River Basins Commission, November 1976.

_____ . *Methodologies for OCS Related Facilities Planning,* Resource and Land Investigations report. Boston: New England River Basins Commission, March 1978.

New Jersey County & Municipal Government Study Commission. *County Government, Challenge and Change.* Trenton: New Jersey County and Municipal Government Study Commission, April 1969.

New Jersey Department of Community Affairs, Division of State and Regional Planning. *Unified Development Plan: Jersey City Waterfront.* Trenton: Prepared for HUD by the Division of State and Regional Planning, December 1975.

_____ . *Weehawken Yards Report: A Case Study of State Involvement in Proposed Waterfront Development.* Trenton: New Jersey Department of Community Affairs, May 1973.

New Jersey Department of Environmental Protection. *Alternatives for the Coast—1976,* a staff report. Trenton: New Jersey Department of Environmental Protection, Office of Coastal Zone Management, October 1976.

_____ . Decision paper by the Commissioner conditionally approving a CAFRA permit for Public Service Electric and Gas Co. Hope Creek Generating Station, Opinion 20. Trenton: New Jersey Department of Environmental Protection, September 3, 1975.

New Jersey Department of Labor and Industry, Division of Planning and Research. *Statistical Source Directory for New Jersey State Government.* Trenton: New Jersey Department of Labor and Industry, April 1977.

New Jersey Department of the Treasury, Economic Planning Council. *1978 Economic Outlook for New Jersey.* Trenton: New Jersey Department of the Treasury, 1978.

New Jersey Division of Water Resources. *New Jersey Water Resources Program for Fiscal Year 1977-78,* an annual report. Trenton: New Jersey Department of Environmental Protection, July 1977.

New Jersey Office of Coastal Zone Management. *The "Call for Information" on Coastal Facility Siting: An Analysis of Responses.* Trenton: New Jersey Department of Environmental Protection, March 1977.

_____ . *Coastal Zone Management Strategy for New Jersey—CAFRA Area.* Trenton: New Jersey Department of Environmental Protection, September 1977.

_____ . *Interim Land Use and Density Guidelines for the Coastal Area of New Jersey.* Trenton: New Jersey Department of Environmental Protection, May 1976.

_____ . *Nominated Areas of Public Concern in the New Jersey Coastal Zone.* Trenton: New Jersey Department of Environmental Protection, December 1977.

_____ . *Options for New Jersey's Developed Coast.* Trenton: New Jersey Department of Environmental Protection, March 1979.

_____ . *Public Access to Oceanfront Beaches: A Report to the Governor and Legislature of New Jersey.* Trenton: New Jersey Department of Environmental Protection, April 1977.

_____ . *State of New Jersey Coastal Zone Management Program—Bay and Ocean Shore Segment.* Trenton: New Jersey Department of Environmental Protection, May 1978.

New York City Department of City Planning. *Coastal Zone Management— Outer Continental Shelf Program,* study conducted April 1976 to June 1977. New York: New York City Department of City Planning, June 1977.

New York Department of State, Coastal Management Program. "Analysis of Authorities/Organization Energy Facilities Planning," preliminary technical report. Albany, October 1977.

New York State Department of Environmental Conservation, Outer Continental Shelf Study Program. *New York State and Outer Continental Shelf Development.* Albany: New York State Department of Environmental Conservation, October 1977.

Nieswand, George H., and Peter J. Pizor. *Current Planning Capacity: A Practical Carrying-Capacity Approach to Land Use Planning.* New Brunswick, N.J.: Cooperative Extension Service, Cook College, Rutgers University, June 1977.

Norman, Thomas P., ed. *New Jersey Trends.* New Brunswick, N.J.: Institute for Environmental Studies, Rutgers University, September 1974.

Ocean County (N.J.) Planning Board. *Outer Continental Shelf and Energy Facility Planning Study in Ocean County, New Jersey.* Toms River, N.J.: Ocean County Planning Board, April 1978.

O'Hare, Michael. *"Not on My Block You Don't": Facilities Siting and the Strategic Importance of Compensation,* MIT Energy Impacts Project. Cambridge, Mass.: Laboratory of Architecture and Planning, MIT, April 1977.

Polayes, Joanne R. *State Environmental Policy Acts and the Public,* working paper 6. New Haven: School of Forestry and Environmental Studies, Yale University, June 1977.

Port Authority of New York and New Jersey, Outer Continental Shelf Study Program. *Support Bases for Offshore Drilling: The Port of New York Potential.* New York: New York State Department of Environmental Conservation, May 1977.

Princeton University, Center for New Jersey Affairs. *Older Cities Seminar— February 24, 1976,* proceedings. Princeton, N.J., 1976.

Public Service Electric & Gas Co. *Atlantic Generating Station: Units One and Two: Plant and Site Descriptions.* Newark, N.J.: Public Service Electric & Gas Company, August 1972.

Real Estate Research Corporation. *The Costs of Sprawl,* detailed cost analysis and executive summary, prepared for the Council on Environmental Quality, the U.S. Department of Housing and Urban Development, and the U.S. Environmental Protection Agency. Washington, D.C.: U.S. Government Printing Office, April 1974.

_____ . *Guidelines for Urban Renewal Land Disposition*, for the Department of Housing and Urban Development. Washington, D.C.: U.S. Government Printing Office, 1975.

Regional Plan Association. *The Lower Hudson*. New York: Regional Plan Association, December 1966.

_____ . *The State of the Region—1977*. New York: Regional Plan Association, November 1977.

Research and Planning Consultants, Inc. *Inland Canals—An Alternative for Industry*, prepared for the Texas Coastal Management Program, General Land Office of Texas. Austin: The Texas Coastal Management Program, July 1977.

_____ . *Offshore Oil: Its Impact on Texas Communities*, vols. 3 and 4, prepared for the Texas Coastal Management Program, General Land Office of Texas. Austin: The Texas Coastal Management Program, June 1977.

_____ . *Siting Industrial Facilities on the Texas Coast*, prepared for the Texas Coastal Management Program General Land Office of Texas. Austin: The Texas Coastal Management Program, September 1978.

Resource Planning Associates, Inc. *Identification and Analysis of Mid-Atlantic Onshore OCS Impacts*, prepared for the Middle Atlantic Governors' Coastal Resources Council. Cambridge, Mass.: The Middle Atlantic Governors' Coastal Resources Council, September 1973.

Rhode Island, University of, and Coastal Resources Management Council, Coastal Resources Center. *State of Rhode Island Coastal Resources Management Program*, draft. Providence: Coastal Resources Center, Summer 1977.

Ricci, Rocco D., New Jersey Department of Environmental Protection. *A Statement on the New Jersey State Energy Plan*. Paper presented September 26, 1977, before the New Jersey Department of Energy, Atlantic City, N.J.

Richardson, Dan K. *The Cost of Environmental Protection*. New Brunswick, N.J.: Center for Urban Policy Research, Rutgers University, 1976.

Rivkin Associates, Inc. *Guiding the Coastal Area of New Jersey*, prepared for the New Jersey Department of Environmental Protection, Office of Coastal Zone Management. Washington, D.C.: New Jersey Department of Environmental Protection, May 1976.

Ruedisili, Lon C., and Morris W. Firebaugh, eds. *Perspectives on Energy: Issues, Ideas, and Environmental Dilemmas*. New York: Oxford University Press, 1975.

Rutgers University, Center for Coastal and Environmental Studies. *Onshore Support Bases for OCS and Gas Development: Implications for New Jersey*. New Brunswick, N.J.: Center for Coastal and Environmental Studies, Rutgers University, September 1977.

Sanderson, Debra R. *Social and Economic Consequences of Energy Facility Siting in New England: First Summary Report*, for the MIT Energy Impacts Project. Cambridge, Mass.: Laboratory of Architecture and Planning, MIT, January 1978.

Schnidman, Frank. *Awareness and Perception of the States to Local and Regional Needs Created by Energy Production or Extraction Facilities*, prepared for the U.S. Department of Housing and Urban Development,

Office of Community Planning and Program Coordination. Washington, D.C.: Urban Land Institute, March 1977.

Seton, Johnson & Odell, Inc., and Cogan Associates. *Environmental Management and Energy Facility Siting in the Coastal Zone,* technical proposal submitted to the U.S. Environmental Protection Agency. Portland, Ore.: Seton, Johnson & Odell, Inc., July 1977.

Simon, Anne W. *The Thin Edge: Coast and Man in Crisis.* New York: Harper & Row, 1978.

Singer, Grace. "Citizens Defend the Urban Coast." *Bulletin of the Atomic Scientists* 35, no. 6 (June 1979): 47-52.

Singer, Richard, and Thomas C. Roberts. *Land Use Requirements for Five Energy Alternatives,* prepared for the American Nuclear Society. Hinsdale, Ill.: American Nuclear Society, Public Information Committee, n.d.

Smith, Richard A., et al. *An Oilspill Risk Analysis for the Mid-Atlantic Outer Continental Shelf Lease Area,* U.S. Geological Survey, Open File Report 76-451. Washington, D.C.: U.S. Department of the Interior, June 1976.

Stang, Paul R., et al. *Coastal Management Aspects of OCS Oil and Gas Developments.* Rockville, Md.: National Oceanic and Atmospheric Administration, Office of Coastal Zone Management, January 1975.

Train, Russell E. "The EPA Programs and Land Use Planning." *Columbia Journal of Environmental Law* 2, no. 2 (Spring 1976): 255-289.

Treadway, Ralph S. "Industrial Land Use: A Look into Industrial Land Use Efficiency in New Jersey," project of the New Jersey Department of Labor and Industry and the New Jersey State College Research Consortium (unpublished), n.d.

Tribe, Laurence H.; Corinne S. Schelling; and John Voss, eds. *When Values Conflict: Essays on Environmental Analysis, Discourse and Decision.* Cambridge, Mass.: Ballinger Publishing Co., 1976.

Tri-State Regional Planning Commission. *The Economics of Energy.* New York: Tri-State Regional Planning Commission, February 1974.

_____ . *The Tri-State Coastal Zone.* New York: Tri-State Regional Planning Commission, April 1975.

_____ . Transportation Committee. *The Changing Harborfront.* New York: Tri-State Regional Planning Commission, March 1976.

U.S. Congress, Office of Technology Assessment. *An Analysis of the Feasibility of Separating Exploration from Production of Oil and Gas on the Outer Continental Shelf.* Washington, D.C.: U.S. Government Printing Office, May 1975.

_____ . *Coastal Effects of Offshore Energy Systems.* Washington, D.C.: U.S. Government Printing Office, November 1976.

_____ . *Oil Transportation by Tankers: An Analysis of Marine Pollution and Safety Measures.* Washington, D.C.: U.S. Government Printing Office, July 1975.

U.S. Congress, 94th Session. *Energy Facility Siting in Coastal Areas,* Committee Report, 60-762-0. Washington, D.C.: U.S. Government Printing Office, December 1975.

U.S. Department of Commerce, National Oceanic and Atmospheric Administration, Office of Coastal Zone Management. *Coastal Facility Guidelines.* Washington, D.C., August 1975.

_____ . *State Information Needs Related to Onshore and Nearshore Effects of OCS Petroleum Development.* Washington, D.C.: U.S. Department of Commerce, January 1977.

U.S. Department of Housing and Urban Development, Office of Community Planning and Development. *Rapid Growth from Energy Projects.* Washington, D.C.: U.S. Department of Housing and Urban Development, April 1976.

U.S. Department of the Interior, Bureau of Land Management. *Environmental Statement, Proposed 1976 OCS Oil and Gas Lease Sale Offshore the Mid-Atlantic States—OCS Sale Number 40,* vol. 1, draft. New York: U.S. Department of the Interior, December 1975.

U.S. Environmental Protection Agency, Office of Air and Waste Management. *Air Program Strategy for Attainment and Maintenance of Ambient Air Quality Standards and Control of Other Pollutants,* draft. Washington, D.C., October 1976.

_____ . *Air Quality Data—1975 Annual Statistics,* EPA-450/2-77-002. Research Triangle Park, N.C.: Office of Air Quality Planning and Standards of the Office of Air, Noise and Radiation, May 1977.

U.S. Environmental Protection Agency, Office of Research and Development. *Promoting Environmental Quality Through Urban Planning and Controls.* Socioeconomic Environmental Studies Series, EPA 600/5-73-015. Washington, D.C., February 1974.

U.S. Nuclear Regulatory Commission. *Nuclear Energy Center Site Survey—1975,* parts I, IV, and V (NECSS-75) (NUREG-0001). Washington, D.C.: U.S. Nuclear Regulatory Commission, 1976.

Urban Land Institute. *Liberty State Park: An Evaluation of Development Potential in and around the Liberty State Park Site,* prepared for the Liberty State Park Study and Planning Commission. Washington, D.C.: Urban Land Institute, December 1977.

Wachs, Melvin W. "Planning for Energy Needs—701 Helps Meet the New Challenge." *HUD Challenge,* June 1976.

Warren, Robert. *A Local Perspective in National Energy Policy.* Paper prepared for the Conference on the Urban Coast and Energy Alternatives, Princeton University, May 18-19, 1978.

_____ . "The Role of Cities in Managing the Urban Coast." *Coastal Zone Management Journal* 6, no. 2-3 (1979): 125-133.

Weschler, Louis F. "Environmental Quality within an Interorganizational Matrix: A Case Study of the SOHIO Project." *Coastal Zone Management Journal* 6, no. 2-3 (1979): 233-252.

Williams, David, Consultant, and William E. Nothdurff, New England River Basins Commission. *Offshore Activities and Onshore Facilities,* summary report by the New England River Basins Commission for the American Society of Planning Officials. Boston, 1977.

Wohlwill, Joachin F. *Perceptual and Attitudinal Aspects of Land Use: The Case of the California Coastal Zone.* Paper delivered in Denver. University

Park, Pa.: Center for the Study of Environmental Policy, Pennsylvania State University, February 1977.

Woodward-Clyde Consultants. *Mid-Atlantic Regional Study: An Assessment of the Onshore Effects of Offshore Oil and Gas Development.* 1975.

Index

About the Editors
and Contributors

David Morell is a research political scientist and a member of the Center for Energy and Environmental Studies at Princeton; he is also a lecturer in the Department of Politics. Morell received an M.P.A. in public and international affairs and a Ph.D. in political science and public policy from Princeton. Since 1974, he has been directing the center's research program on energy facility siting. Previously, he was with the U.S. Environmental Protection Agency in Washington, D.C., where he was Acting Director, Office of Transportation and Land Use Policy, Air Programs; Director of the Coordination Office for Air Programs; and National Coordinator for municipal water permit programs. His principal interests have focused on land use and energy policy. He is the author of many publications, and is the coauthor of *Centralized Power* (Oelge-schlager, Gunn & Hain, 1979).

Grace Singer has been a research staff member of Princeton University's Center for Energy and Environmental Studies since January 1976. In that capacity, she has conducted studies on various issues, including state legislatures and energy policy in the Northeast; attitudes toward nuclear energy; and citizen opposition to energy facilites in Hudson County, New Jersey. In 1978, Singer directed a conference on "The Urban Coast and Energy Alternatives" at Princeton's Woodrow Wilson School for Public and International Affairs. In 1979 she was appointed by New Jersey's Governor Brendan Byrne as a member of the Hudson River Waterfront Study, Planning and Development Commission to plan for the eighteen-mile waterfront in New York Harbor. Before coming to Princeton, Singer was Director of Air Quality Analysis and lobbyist at the state Legislature for the New Jersey League of Women Voters, and chairman of a municipal Board of Health.

Thomas Ash is a Ph.D. candidate in urban planning at Princeton University's School of Architecture and Urban Planning, from where he received an M.A. in urban planning. He received an M.S. in engineering from Princeton's School of Engineering and Applied Science. Ash has conducted research on transportation policies, air quality, and government regulations.

Peter Denitz received an M.A. in urban planning from Princeton University's School of Architecture and Urban Planning in 1978. His special interests include neighborhood and central area revitalization and housing policy. Denitz has worked as a research assistant in the School of Architecture and Urban Planning at Princeton and as a staff planner for the City of Allentown, Pennsylvania. He is at present a staff planner for Bucks County, Pennsylvania.

Energy and Environmental Analysis, Inc., founded in 1974 by Dr. Robert Sansom, performs environmental consulting and policy and engineering studies in energy-environment interaction. Sansom was the project manager for the research reported in Chapters 9, 10, and 11 in this book. From 1972 to 1974, he served as Assistant Administrator for Air and Water Programs at the U.S. Environmental Protection Agency. Before then, he was Deputy Assistant Administrator for Planning and Evaluation at EPA and a member of the National Security Council staff. Sansom received an M.A. in economics from Georgetown University and a Ph.D. in economics from Oxford University.

The principal investigator for the research was Dan Violette, employed by EEA as a consultant specializing in industrial environmental problems. Violette received an M.A. in economics from the University of Colorado, where he is presently pursuing a Ph.D. in economics.

Linda Kirschner joined the staff of Princeton University's Center for Energy and Environmental Studies in 1977. Her research projects at the center have included alternative energy technologies; corporate attitudes toward energy facility siting; the decisionmaking process of the oil companies in relation to climate forecasts and energy use; and the integration of university research with state government energy planning and policy development. Before coming to Princeton, Kirschner was Executive Assistant in the New Jersey State Energy Office and Energy Specialist for the New Jersey Department of Labor and Industry.

Barry Merchant received an M.A. in urban planning from Princeton University's School of Architecture and Urban Planning in 1978. Earlier, he spent a year at the University of Edinburgh (Scotland) as a graduate student in sociology and economic history. After serving with the Office of City Planning of Portsmouth, Virginia, Merchant became Housing Program Supervisor with the Virginia Department of Housing and Community Development in Richmond.

Research and Planning Consultants, Inc., a professional research and planning firm, is based in Austin, Texas. Since the firm was formed in 1972, it has helped public and private concerns cope with the complicated guidelines and regulations in America's interdependent system of social, political, financial, and environmental concerns. RPC has specialized in solving policy and management problems.

Ronald T. Luke, who received a Ph.D. in public policy from Harvard and a J.D. from the University of Texas at Austin, is the president of RPC. He was principal-in-charge for the research that appears as Chapters 6, 7, and 8 in this book. He has significant experience in the fields of public policy and legal and institutional aspects of policy planning. Leah Pagan, who is finishing a Ph.D. in anthropology at the University of Texas at Austin, was project manager for the studies. Gail McDonald, who received a J.D. from the University of Texas at Austin, was responsible for the legal aspects, and Barbara Haefeli, who has an M.A. in community and regional planning from the University of Texas at Austin, contributed substantially to the research.